*Babies,
Breastfeeding,
and
Bonding*

♦

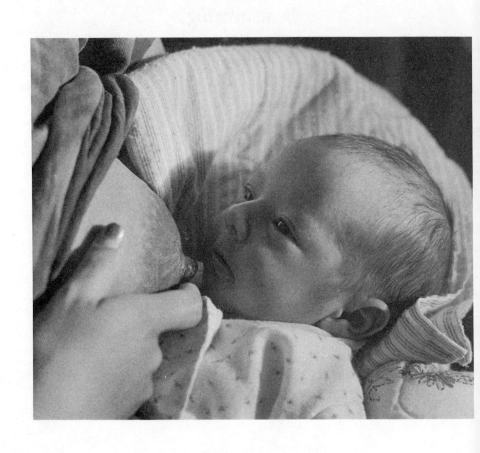

Babies, Breastfeeding, and *Bonding*

♦

Ina May Gaskin

BERGIN & GARVEY PUBLISHERS, INC.
MASSACHUSETTS

First published in 1987 by
Bergin & Garvey Publishers, Inc.
670 Amherst Road
South Hadley, Massachusetts 01075

Copyright © 1987 by Bergin & Garvey Publishers, Inc.
All rights reserved. No part of this publication may be reproduced or
transmitted in any form or by any means, electronic or mechanical,
including photocopy, recording or any information storage or retrieval
system, without permission in writing from the publisher.

789   987654321

Printed in the United States of America

Library of Congress Cataloging-in-Publication Data
Gaskin, Ina May.
  Babies, breastfeeding, and bonding.

  Includes bibliographies and index.
  1. Breast feeding. 2. Breast feeding—Psychological
aspects. 3. Attachment behavior. I. Title.
[DNLM: 1. Breast Feeding—popular works. 2. Infant,
Newborn—popular works. WS 125 G248b]
RJ216.G27   1987   649'.33   87-15108
ISBN 0-89789-135-X (alk. paper)
ISBN 0-89789-134-1 (pbk.: alk. paper)

Contents

Acknowledgments vii
INTRODUCTION *The Return to Breastfeeding* 1
CHAPTER ONE *The Benefits of Breastfeeding* 6
CHAPTER TWO *Preparing for Breastfeeding* 26
CHAPTER THREE *Getting Off to a Good Start* 43
CHAPTER FOUR *Problems in the First Week* 65
CHAPTER FIVE *Special Situations* 81
CHAPTER SIX *The First Two Months* 103
CHAPTER SEVEN *Problems in the First Two Months* 112
CHAPTER EIGHT *Combining Nursing and Your Busy Life* 130
CHAPTER NINE *Nursing Your Older Baby* 140
CHAPTER TEN *Drugs, Chemicals, and Breast Milk* 153
CHAPTER ELEVEN *Shared Nursing* 161
CHAPTER TWELVE *Breastfeeding and the Nonindustrialized World* 169
CHAPTER THIRTEEN *Peoples' Attitudes Towards Breasts* 182
CHAPTER FOURTEEN *Fear of Fluids* 200
CHAPTER FIFTEEN *Reviving the Mother Instinct* 205
APPENDIX A *Resources* 211
APPENDIX B *Additional Reading* 216
APPENDIX C *Composition of Milk* 218
INDEX 221

Acknowledgments

I have a lot of people to thank for making this book possible. Thanks first go to my husband, Stephen, and to my children, Sydney, Eva, Sam, and Paul for love and inspiration. Eva gets additional thanks for production help with this book. I am especially grateful to Dr. John O. Williams, Jr., for his good help.

Many people deserve my thanks for their help in the early years of assembling material for this book: Margaret Dotzler, Melanie Splendora, Louise Hagler, Joyce McMahon, Joanne McMahon, Sheila Schoenbrun, Cornelia Mandelstein, Edine Frohman, Melissa Weidman, Barbara Elliott, Lani Lichtman, Jeanne Kahan, Myra Traugot, and Pamela Hunt. I am grateful to Barbara Wallace for writing the chapter on chemical pollutants in breastmilk.

I am grateful to Kim Maly, Pamela Hunt, Jeanne Kahan, Gregory Lowry, and Nancy Jones for their beautiful artwork.

I owe thanks to the many people who participated in my survey on breastfeeding. Since I don't have all of their names, I cannot thank them individually. Thanks also to those who have consented to have photographs of themselves and their children published in this book.

INA MAY GASKIN
Summertown, Tennessee

*Babies,
Breastfeeding,
and
Bonding*

Introduction

The Return to Breastfeeding

♦

*I*n this technological age, there is a tendency for people to forget that just like zebras, three-toed sloths, and gorillas, we are mammals. This means that we have hair or fur on our bodies, we give birth to live babies after an internal gestational period, and we suckle our young. It is interesting to note that mammals are named for having mammary glands to feed their young. We could have been called "furrals" for our fur, or "wombiles" for having wombs, but we can see which was the most noteworthy characteristic when it came to naming us.

We humans are the only mammals who have devised an alternative to the glandular method of feeding our newborn young. In certain cases, this bottle technology can be helpful, but we are to be commended for this invention only if we as a species do not forget the skill of breastfeeding, which has kept us surviving for millions of years.

This is a "pro-breastfeeding" book. I strongly believe that our world needs millions more mothers to breastfeed their babies, both in the industrialized and nonindustrialized nations. Breastfeeding is a survival skill. It must be carried on by a high enough proportion of mothers in all levels of society so that the knowledge of how to do it is not lost or forgotten to our cultures, as so nearly happened during this last century in many parts of the world.

At the same time, I do not think that every mother will find it appropriate or easy to nurse her baby. I am a midwife, and I must consider these mothers also. I have met many women, who, for one reason or another, were unable or unwilling to breastfeed their babies and who were, nevertheless, very good mothers. Bottlefeeding is sometimes necessary and appropriate. In writing a book promoting breastfeeding, there is a danger of causing mothers to feel guilty or criticized for having made the choice to bottlefeed. Some mothers even feel guilty about bottlefeeding when the choice was not theirs, when breastfeeding just did not work out. It is not my purpose to make individual mothers feel bad if they are not breastfeeding. My feeling is that our value as individual mothers has more to do with the quality of attention and the wisdom that we put into the raising of our children than the way in which we feed them while they are babies.

But when I consider mothers in large groups, I notice that if breastfeeding becomes a weird aberration of maternal behavior instead of the norm and if it is regarded as an embarrassing reminder of our Stone Age past, then all members of society, not just mothers and babies, suffer. Breastfeeding is a special relationship between two people, one of whom is totally dependent upon the generosity and good will of the other. The suckling relationship is one of the sources of real sweetness that we have in human existence. Shakespeare, when he wrote the phrase, "the milk of human kindness," was expressing the truth that compassion is very often first learned at our mother's breast. At the same time, the suckling baby can teach adults about the expression of sweet love and gratitude in a way that no words can. When millions of mothers are made to feel that breastfeeding is low-class, improper, disgusting, old-fashioned, sinful, or physically impossible, as tens of millions of women were taught during the period between the 1930s and the 1970s in North America, the whole society begins to lose some of the stickiest glue that holds people together.

This book is meant to be as much for men as it is for women. Men do seem to be at least as interested in breasts as women are. A man whose attitude is relaxed enough to permit women to breastfeed in comfort respects the powers of women, understands the nature of babies, and encourages the natural inclination of mothers and babies to be close to one another. Our society needs more men to be like this.

The Return to Breastfeeding

When Breastfeeding Became "Impolite"

Breastfeeding is an ancient female skill which is undergoing a remarkable revival in the last third of the twentieth century. This resurgence in breastfeeding has come only after several decades when bottlefeeding was so much the preferred and socially acceptable way of infant feeding that women who felt moved to breastfeed often found themselves faced with impossible obstacles when they tried to do so. If you were born between the years 1930 and 1975 in North America, chances are quite small that you were breastfed by your mother. Around 1900, nearly all American and Canadian mothers breastfed their babies. By the 1940s, the intrepid few mothers who did manage to breastfeed their babies had become invisible members of society. No one wanted to know what they thought or how they had managed to overcome the obstacles to breastfeeding that were unwittingly set up during that period by physicians, hospital policies, nurses, and the social attitudes of the time.

During these years, most North American babies subsisted for the first few months on the milk of cattle. This custom has been practiced in many parts of the world when a mother was unable to provide food for her baby in any other way, but only during the twentieth century in the industrialized countries did the practice of feeding human babies the milk of another species become the preferred way for most mothers.

The middle third of the twentieth century was the period when childbirth came to be seen primarily as a medical, rather than a biological and social, event in North America and most industrialized countries. Knowledge which used to be shared by small communities of women and passed on to each succeeding generation was interrupted and replaced by that which originated from a male-dominated professional medical community. Women were repeatedly told by their doctors and by articles in women's magazines which dispensed advice on childbirth and child-raising not to listen to advice from anyone who was not a professional. Grandmothers quit passing on the knowledge they gained by the experience of giving birth and raising children and deferred to the "experts" in the raising of the modern generation.

Not surprisingly, a vast fund of common sense which had been widespread before that time was lost during this period of drastic social change. As large numbers of people moved from rural or small towns to urban or suburban environments, what used to be known as "horse sense" became a rarer and rarer commodity. Millions of women became mothers without ever holding their newborn babies next to their bare skin. Many held their babies and participated in their care for only three or four hours during the first few days of life, the babies instead being cared for in nurseries by medical professionals. Parents decided what and when to feed their babies according to what the latest child-raising expert advised, and only a small percentage of people knew that it was natural for a breastfed newborn to be hungry every hour or two. Many people thought that human milk was too "weak" to be nourishing to a newborn baby. Countless numbers of people went through their lives never having witnessed the act of breastfeeding until, to many, the thought of a baby suckling from her mother became an idea that was strange and unacceptable.

The Trend Back to Breastfeeding

By the middle 1970s, there began to be a reversal of this seemingly inexorable trend towards increased use of technology in childbirth and child feeding. As more and more women chose natural childbirth instead of medicated birth, most of them also decided that breastfeeding was not only an acceptable but a desirable alternative to the expected bottlefeeding routine. Jaws dropped and eyes bugged all over North America as young mothers, not content to stay confined in their homes, nursed their babies in public places such as airports, beaches, and restaurants. But not all of the women of this new wave of would-be breastfeeders were able to nurse their babies for as long as they wished, partly because, when the knowledge of any physical skill is interrupted, there may be gaps in the recovery of this knowledge for a time.

This book represents an attempt to set down the essential lore which I consider to be vital to the practice and transmission of the skill of breastfeeding, the knowledge which was lost to the general public during the period of almost total bottlefeeding. My purpose is to empower women so that they have a real choice about whether or not to breastfeed. You may choose to breastfeed without knowing enough to have a good chance at succeeding, and that, to my mind, seems only a very limited "choice." Too many women try breastfeeding without enough knowledge of how their bodies are affected by hospital policies, or the attitudes of mates, families, and medical professionals, with the result that they give up breastfeeding without ever having had a fair chance of success. Too many others never attempt to begin breastfeeding because their ideas regarding this natural process are so shaped by a mainstream culture which places very little value on any human process which does not generate money for some category of people.

My hope is that we will become more mature as a culture and learn to value those practices and skills which contribute to the survival of ourselves and our earth.

SUGGESTED SUPPLEMENTAL READING
Pryor, Karen. *Nursing Your Baby.* New York: Pocket Books, 1973.
Raphael, Dana. *The Tender gift: Breast Feeding.* New York: Schocken, 1976.
Wertz, Richard, and Dorothy Wertz. *Lying-In: A History of Childbirth in America.* New York: Schocken, 1977.

1

The Benefits of Breastfeeding

♦

There are several very good reasons for choosing to breastfeed your baby, even if you are not able to continue for a long time. One very practical consideration is that, in choosing to breastfeed, you can always change your mind and begin bottlefeeding with comparative ease. If you first begin to bottlefeed and, after a few days or weeks, decide that breastfeeding might have been a better choice, you will already have several strikes against you in making the change back: your baby will have become used to drinking from a plastic nipple, and your milk supply will have drastically diminished from the amount you had when it first came in. I want to emphasize that it still may be possible to make such a switch, but it isn't likely to be easy. Starting out with breastfeeding is a good way to keep your options open.

The Perfect Food

Human breast milk is so complete in supplying the nutritional needs of human babies that in general we can say that no other food source is needed until the baby is about six months of age. Even at six months, a well-nourished mother's milk is an excellent source of vitamins for babies.

Breast milk is the only kind of milk which was designed by nature for human babies. Formulas made from cows' milk must be changed and added to in order to be suitable for human babies. Because formula milks must be packaged and preserved, they contain various additions which breast milk does not have. Such additives may include emulsifiers, thickening agents, acid-alkaline adjusters, and antioxidants.

Cows' milk contains proportionally three times as much protein as human milk. Unless it is diluted, as formula is, a human baby cannot digest and absorb its nutrients. Even with dilution, the protein in cows' milk forms curds in the baby's stomach which are relatively large and hard when compared to the protein curds from breast milk. The large curds from formula are digested by the baby with only 50 percent efficiency, which means that half the protein must be excreted. The protein in human breast milk, on the other hand, is used by the baby with almost 100 percent efficiency. The formula-fed baby, then, must drink a greater volume of milk than the breastfed baby in order to obtain the same nourishment. Inexperienced mothers need to know about this difference in efficiency of digestion of human milk and cows' milk, because one of the common worries is that the baby is not taking in enough milk to be properly nourished. The mother has a visual image of an eight-ounce baby bottle full of milk and cannot believe that her baby is getting that much volume from her breast. She can relax only when she realizes that her baby doesn't need breast milk in the same quantity that the bottlefed baby needs cows' milk and that her baby and her body will most likely arrive at the right amount for her baby.

Iron and zinc are both more efficiently absorbed from breast milk than from formula, which must have iron added to fill a human baby's requirements. It is unusual for a breastfed baby to be anemic.

Because several minerals and ash come in higher concentrations in cows' milk and formula than in breast milk and because of the 50 percent absorption of the protein in cows' milk, formula-fed babies' excretory systems, primarily their kidneys, have to work harder to get rid of the excess. In a normal, healthy baby, this added work may be of no consequence, but a sick or premature baby may not be able to tolerate the extra strain on his excretory system.

Protection Against Disease

Human milk and colostrum, the yellowish-white "early milk" which is in the breasts during the latter half of pregnancy and the first couple of days after birth, are both rich in antibodies which protect newborn babies against many diseases. Breastfed babies are less susceptible to

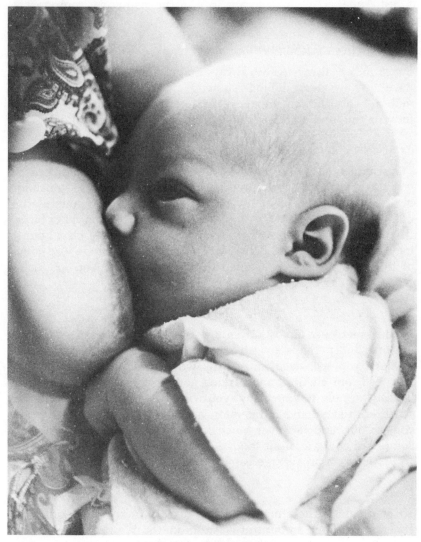

Newborn singlemindedness

respiratory and gastrointestinal infections. Breast milk also provides good protection against staph infections in babies.

The protein in cows' milk is one of the more common causes of allergy in babies. Some babies develop rashes with such allergies; others just can't keep the formula milk down, and their mothers have to search for another formula milk which will be tolerated. Human milk proteins, on the other hand, are virtually nonallergenic to babies.

See Appendix C for a comparison of the nutritional components of breast milk, cows' milk, and formula.

Convenience and Safety

Breast milk is always ready, always the right temperature. You don't have to worry about the milk spoiling, and there is no waste. Breast milk may also be safer because it cannot be inaccurately mixed, as formula can, and it is free from contamination by external debris.

Your Physiology

The stimulation of your nipples by the sucking of your baby causes your uterus to contract rhythmically during the first days after childbirth. These uterine contractions are needed to bring your uterus back to its nonpregnant size and to restore its muscle tone after birth. If you choose to bottlefeed, the same process will take place, but it may take a little longer. Breastfeeding may also help you lose some of the extra weight you gained during pregnancy. You gradually convert your flesh into the baby's.

Economy

Most women need almost no equipment in order to breastfeed. Nursing bras and perhaps a set of nipple shields may be the only possessions you will need, and many women will not need these. I breastfed four children and needed nothing extra. If you are going to feed formula to your baby, you will need bottles and nipples, a sterilizer, a stove and refrigerator, a carrying bag for bottles when you go out, and however much formula your baby will consume before switching to adult food. A year's worth of formula, bottles, and nipples for an average baby will cost about $400.

Ecology

To feed babies safely on formula, it takes a tremendous industry, generating a large amount of waste products. We need to examine carefully the motives of those who advocate the spread of formula feeding to all countries of the world. We would also do well to examine the ecological consequences in the industrialized countries where formula is the main food for babies. If we add up the number of cows needed to produce the milk; the amount of land, food, and water required to sustain them; the fuel, equipment, and energy used to collect, transport, process, package, and distribute the formula; the metal in the cans, (used, then thrown away); the trees needed to produce the paper and cardboard for packaging and promoting infant formula; the amount of glass and plastic needed for bottles and nipples; the energy needed to sterilize the bottles, equipment, and water and to heat the formula mixture to the right temperature for the baby; the soaps and detergents needed to wash the nipples and bottles, we begin to get some idea of the magnitude of waste involved in mass feeding of cows' milk to anyone but calves.

Many nonindustrialized countries have come to count mothers' milk as one of their natural resources. We should not be surprised at this when we consider that the import of unnecessary powdered milk takes about one billion dollars a year from the nonindustrialized nations. Some countries, such as Papua New Guinea, Costa Rica, Sri Lanka, and Egypt, have passed legislation which bans the advertisement of powdered infant formula. In some countries legislation permits the sale of infant formula and bottles only by physician's prescription.

Tooth and Jaw Development

Some parents decide against bottlefeeding because they wish to avoid dental problems in their children. The bottlefed baby does not have to work as hard as the breastfed baby to get the milk to flow. He also learns to thrust his tongue forward, in order to keep the milk from flowing into his mouth too fast. Some dentists believe this tongue action can contribute to malposition of the baby's teeth, although this doesn't happen with every child who is bottlefed.

Beauty

This is perhaps a personal matter, but to me, a mother breastfeeding her baby is a beautiful sight, something we need to see in our daily lives, whether or not we have young babies in our families. I am not saying that it is not beautiful to see a mother feeding her baby with a bottle. If that is what she needs to do, this is pretty, too. But a culture which has begun to feel that the nursing mother needs to be hidden from view has something seriously wrong with its values. I know that young breastfed babies love the sight of breasts. Their eyes brighten when they see breasts, and they are apt to dive for any nipple they get close to, male or female, full of milk or not. We do not completely get over our attraction to breasts as we grow older, nor should we. But if we are made to feel that appreciating the beauty of breasts and nipples is shameful, we may find strange ways of satisfying our unconscious needs. We may also get stuck in a very narrow ideal of beauty when it comes to breasts.

Humor

Not too many people talk about breastfeeding and its humorous aspects, maybe because as a culture, we are pretty inhibited about this natural process. The fact is that breastfeeding can be very funny at times, for grownups as well as babies, for men as well as women. Read on and see why.

Empowerment

I believe that it is empowering for women to know that their bodies are capable of producing food. In our society, we tend to shrug at the powers we naturally have while we look for technologies to deal with more and more aspects of our lives. The woman who wrote the following lines describes a typical new mother's reaction to her newly discovered ability:

> What a surprise it was for me when my milk came in three days after my first daughter's birth. Nobody had ever told me that a sense of power came along with breasts full of milk. I was amazed that my body knew how to do that so well.

Disadvantages

You have probably already thought of the main disadvantage (if you can call it that) of breastfeeding: you will be the person with the responsibility of feeding your baby until you wean. Bottlefeeding, of course, can be done by anyone you choose, so if you are tired, you can rest while someone else feeds your baby. If you are looking for shared responsibility when it comes to feeding, you should know that it is possible for a breastfeeding mother to express some of her milk into a bottle, which can then be given to her baby. Fathers who wish to take part in the feeding of their babies can just as well give expressed milk in a bottle as expressed cows' milk, which is what formula is. Once a woman learns how to express her milk, the process is quick and easy.

It Feels Good

I have to qualify, a little bit, my claim that breastfeeding feels good, to make exceptions for times when nipples are sore. Soreness is not uncommon during the first week or so of breastfeeding, but a mother who has prepared well for breastfeeding and who knows how to get her baby latched on to the nipple rarely experiences nipple soreness after the first few days. When everything is going well, as it does for most women, breastfeeding is a sensual and very enjoyable experience for mother and baby.

Bonding

The word "bonding" was first used by anthropologists to describe the formation of close, specialized human relationships, such as those which link parents and children. I had given birth to all of my children and had been a midwife for several years before I heard the word "bonding" used by mothers or by midwives, doctors or nurses. With the publication of the book, *Maternal-Infant Bonding*, by two pediatricians, Marshall Klaus and John Kennell, both the word and the concept suddenly gained great currency among professionals who worked in the field of childbirth and among parents who prepared for childbirth by reading about it or by attending childbirth education classes. Reading *Maternal-Infant Bonding* was an exciting experience for me, because at last we had scientists who had gathered data which validated the intuitions that mothers and midwives often felt but tended to discuss only privately among themselves.

Klaus and Kennell's book, which has since been updated and retitled *Parent-Infant Bonding*, put forth the idea that there is an especially sensitive period in the hours just after childbirth which makes this time optimum for the formation of strong emotional bonds between mothers and their infants. Farmers, veterinarians, zookeepers, and those who raise animals have long understood that such a sensitive period exists in other mammals, but virtually no one responsible for decisionmaking in the kind of care received by human mothers during and after childbirth recognized that there was any similarity between humans and other mammals in this respect. Klaus and Kennell's work provided a powerful argument for those mothers and caregivers who thought that routine separation of mothers and babies after birth in hospitals was a great mistake with possibly long-reaching consequences for the human relationships involved.

The Scientific Evidence

Klaus and Kennell's studies of the process of how the primary attachment between mother and infant is formed arose from their experiences managing nurseries for normal and sick babies. Perceptive nurses who worked in their neonatal intensive care unit brought to their attention the significant number of babies they had cared for as extremely premature and sick infants, who were admitted to the emergency room as battered babies in the months following their release from the hospital. They noticed that, in many instances, mothers who had been separated from their babies at the time of birth because of illness or prematurity had problems later in relating to or caring for their babies. Such behavior was particularly noticeable in the experienced mother who had already raised a couple of children, but who felt uncertain and anxious when it came to caring for a premature baby.[1]

Klaus and Kennell began working with the idea that there might really be important similarities in the behavior of human mothers and mothers of other species when it came to the development of mothering skills. They cited studies of ewes and rats which documented what happened to mothering behavior when mothers and infants were separated for varying lengths of time beginning at various points after birth. In one study involving sheep it was found that if separation begins at birth and lasts for four hours, half of the ewes are still willing to accept lambs. But when a separation beginning at birth lasts for twelve to twenty-four hours, only a quarter of the ewes will accept their lambs. Similar studies have been carried out involving rats, dogs, goats, and monkeys. All of this work indicates that separation of a newborn or young animal from its mother during the formation of the maternal bond makes a significant change in maternal behavior. The sooner after birth the separation takes place, the stronger the effects. For each species there seems to be a specific length of separation that can be endured.

Other studies of animal mothers and their young attempted to answer the question of whether maternal behavior was set off by characteristics of the young or was primarily triggered by hormonal changes within the mother's body. These studies demonstrated that both factors seem to play an important part in strengthening maternal behavior.

Klaus and Kennell made the human connection by citing studies involving comparison of groups of mothers who had early contact with their babies with mothers who had little contact with theirs. A Swedish study showed that mothers randomly assigned to rooming-in arrangements (babies in their rooms instead of in nurseries) were more confident, felt more competent in caregiving, and appeared more sensitive to the crying of their own infants than mothers who did not have rooming-in.[2]

Klaus and others studied poor, primarily single, first-time mothers from the inner city. The group who had sixteen hours of extra contact with their babies in the first three days of life fed their babies with more affection prior to discharge and at one month were more supportive and affectionate when the baby cried during a stressful office

visit than the control mothers who were with their babies for only twenty minutes every four hours.[3]

Still another study showed that extra-contact mothers talked to their babies differently than control group mothers. Follow-up studies after five years showed very close correlation in the extra-contact group between the mother's speech to the baby at 2 years and the child's level of speech ability at 5 years.

Klaus and Kennell did allow for the existence of some differences between human mothers and mothers of other mammalian species, noting that the ability of humans to rationalize often did make it possible for mothers to develop appropriate mothering behavior in spite of the possible insults caused by early separation. Still, the evidence that they did present was striking enough to the scientific community that many hospitals in North America began revising their policies of routinely allowing mothers only a brief glimpse of their babies before whisking them off to nurseries, to be brought back only for short visits every four hours for feedings. Rooming-in, which meant that babies slept in the same hospital rooms with their mothers, began to be viewed as a safe and desirable practice, rather than the radical concept it had seemed before the publication of Klaus and Kennell's books.

Not everyone in the scientific community had the same appreciation for the work of Klaus and Kennell. It has been suggested by some people that their conclusions were potentially more damaging than beneficial, in that mothers who were not given the chance to bond with their babies, for whatever reason, would feel guilty for the rest of their lives for not having given their children the very best start in life. While it is true that human beings are highly adaptable and that millions of mothers have been able to function as loving and effective parents despite having been separated from their babies after birth, I believe that the tremendous importance of Klaus and Kennell's central idea should not be minimized.

How I Learned About Bonding

Besides having collected observations from attending several hundred women in childbirth and caring for them during the hours, weeks and often months after birth, I have had the experience of giving birth to five children. I know in more than an intellectual way that, just as falling in love with an adult can be interfered with and inhibited by outside influences and distractions, the falling in love that nature intends to happen during the first meeting of mother and baby after birth can be rendered painful and embarrassing to a new mother, sometimes disrupting the relationship for years to come.

My first lesson in what happens to the feelings of mother and baby during labor and after birth came from the birth of my first child in a typical North American hospital in 1966. Although I was not breastfed myself, I assumed that I would breastfeed this first child, partly because I was curious to see if my body really could produce milk where none had been before. Along with that basic curiosity, I remember having had a sense of confidence that I would know what to do when the time came. Although I had studied what was available in the local university library to prepare myself for childbirth (Grantly Dick-Read's *Childbirth Without Fear* and one other not very memorable book written by a man), I did no reading to prepare myself for breastfeeding.

As I approached childbirth, I found that what really scared me about it was not the anticipation of pain. I had had my wisdom teeth extracted, and I knew that I could endure some pain. Besides, my mother had given me a kind of offhand confidence about childbirth, when she told me at sixteen that while some women had a hard time at it and screamed and yelled, she hadn't thought it was so bad. She had had four of us, so I figured she must know. I don't remember finding out if she had had anesthesia during her labors, but she did give me the feeling that whatever pain there was would be bearable. I was aware that some women wanted anesthesia during labor, but I wasn't one of them. My chief fear was of being unconscious or incapacitated while giving birth.

A week before I was due, I made a special visit to my obstetrician to let him know that I had decided against having any anesthesia during labor. I found out how unusual a request this was in the Midwest during that time when, to my very great amazement, he reacted very strongly against the idea of my having what he called an "uncontrolled delivery." I had gone to this visit expecting a pat on the back for being brave enough to do without anesthesia, so I was dumbfounded at being treated as if my desires were totally uninformed and irresponsible.

My obstetrician said that because I was a first-time mother, my baby's head would inevitably act as a "battering ram" against my perineum, very likely causing brain damage to my child. At the time, I didn't know how potentially harmful anesthesia might be to my child, so I wasn't able to counter his argument that way. The "battering ram" idea didn't particularly make sense to me, as I came from a semirural background. My father had grown up on a farm in Iowa, and although I hadn't been raised on a farm, I had spent a few summers with my grandmother and my aunts on their farm. My common sense rejected the idea that brain damage could be the result of normal birth, but I had no language or conceptual structure I could use to argue with this obstetrician-specialist (the first I had ever met), who had studied his discipline for many years. Besides, I had been raised with the idea that a doctor was not somebody you argued with. Malpractice suits were unheard of in those days in the Midwest. Still, when I realized that this doctor liked delivering all first babies with forceps, as a way of protecting their heads, I was sure I wanted to be an exception. My perineum didn't feel like steel to me, and I didn't really believe that brain damage was any more likely to result from perineum pounding than it was from anesthesia or forceps. By the end of the visit, I believed that I had persuaded my obstetrician to consider the idea of my giving birth without such interventions.

Three days later in the hospital, in labor, I decided to enhance my chances of escaping anesthesia by being perfectly quiet and uncomplaining during labor. I was the only mother in the ward that night, so everything was as peaceful as it could be. My method of relaxation, which was an idea that occurred spontaneously to me, was to imagine that I was a mountain lion, and I lay on my side and breathed deeply as my labor became more and more intense. As my cervix dilated, I gazed at the colors and patterns I began to see on the plain wall. Doing so seemed to help me concentrate on relaxing. Despite my composure, the obstetrician and a couple of nurses made it clear, after a few hours, that their minds were made up about my need for Demerol to help me relax. I saw that I would have to argue with three people, not just one, and my opinion wasn't considered to be relevant. Feeling that there was nothing else I could do, I quit fighting the injection.

The Demerol made me groggy and nauseous at the same time, and I noticed no pain relief. The medication changed my perceptions so the colors and patterns weren't so visible to me, and my ability to concentrate was swept away by waves of nausea and drowsiness. I was still quiet and kept minding my own business, helped only by my husband, who rubbed my lower back throughout the time he was allowed to be with me. When the obstetrician and nurses approached me again (they were only with me when they wanted to do something to me), this time to give me the spinal anesthesia I thought I wasn't going to have, I had no fight left in me. I lay there where they put me and did what they said, hating the way they made me feel. I never experienced the feeling of my uterus pushing during this birth. Everything below my waist was numb, and I wasn't sure that I would ever walk again. I did take very seriously their warnings that lifting my head even a little bit during the next twelve hours would leave me with a splitting headache for weeks.

Somehow they got me onto the gurney to wheel me into the delivery room, I was strapped down and my daughter was pulled from me like a giant wisdom tooth, more of an extraction than what I thought a birth would be. Instead of feeling exhilarated and relieved as I thought I would, I felt somehow violated and empty. A part of me was observing my behavior and noted particularly my lack of honest delight at the birth of my daughter. They said that she was all right, which was a relief, but I didn't get a look at her to see for myself for many hours. I could not figure exactly what feeling was missing in me, but I knew that something was wrong about the way I had given birth.

I was stitched up and taken to the recovery room, where I remember comforting my husband (who was sent to the visitors' lounge when they gave me the spinal) and telling him that I was all right and that I thought our daughter was okay. The nurse who had told of our child's birth had given him the impression that there was something wrong with her. When she was brought to me sixteen hours later, in the middle of the night, I was expected to hold her and somehow behave like a mother. I was excited about holding her, but I was very confused about my feelings. Why did I wonder whether they had brought me the right baby? She didn't look like anybody I could recognize in either my family or in my husband's. I certainly didn't expect her to be able to recognize me. My predominant emotion was embarrassment. I thought I was supposed to gush and act thrilled, but I couldn't come up with it. Instead, I felt something like the way a teenager would feel when her first date had arrived and her entire family was scrutinizing her meeting with her boyfriend. I had waited seven years before having a child and had made a conscious decision to get pregnant, so I expected that I would be thrilled and in love with my baby in a more spontaneous way than I was feeling. Instead, I felt inhibited, ridiculous, and suddenly old. My roommate, who was also planning to breastfeed her baby, her second, seemed not to be inhibited in her interaction with her baby, but watching her didn't especially help me in relating to my baby. I felt that I didn't have a natural sense of how to deal with my job of being a mother. I sat in my bed for two days, my daughter in the nursery with all the other babies, bored and wondering why I felt so strange. I had read about "postbaby blues" in women's magazines and had felt that I wouldn't be depressed after childbirth. I wasn't weepy and depressed like the women I had read about, but I certainly felt that something important was missing. At the same time, I was too intimidated by the whole situation even to consider complaining about anything.

The third night after Sydney's birth, I slept well and had my first dream as a mother. I dreamed that I was inside a pyramid with some people in long robes. They were showing me an ancient, beaten gold plate or shield. There was something wonderful and exciting about the dream, as if important secrets were being revealed to me.

Just at that moment, I was awakened by the door to my room being opened and the room lights turned on. The floor nurse was carrying my baby casually in one arm in a way that made me afraid she would drop her, but I was not questioning authority at this time. I was astonished to find that my once small breasts had tripled in size overnight. They were grand now: globular, heavy, even spectacular. I was sure that my daughter would like them, and I felt a self-confidence that I hadn't experienced since before I had the anesthesia. Fortunately, I was left alone, and my daughter and I were able to figure out how to begin breastfeeding, perhaps because of the good presence of my roommate and her nursing baby. I held my daughter close, and she did her part.

From then on, I was a little more like I had thought I would be as a mother, although, after the births of my other children, all of whom were born at home, I realized how deeply I had been affected in my self-concept as a mother by the early separation from my baby and by the gross treatment I was given during labor and birth. With my last three, there was never any separation, and I began caring for them immediately. I loved looking at them and recognizing various facial features and expressions. I loved their smell, their fresh wetness, and I recall a very powerful feeling of protectiveness towards my babies, an emotion I wasn't able to feel after my first birth. In retrospect, I see that I could not have felt able to protect anyone, lying there on the delivery table with my legs strapped in the air, watching a masked nurse leaving the room with my baby. I emphasize my almost total lack of self-confidence following this birth, because it was to haunt me periodically during the first two or three years of my daughter's life. I remember having fantasies of being in dangerous situations with her, unable to protect her. I would be riding in the car holding her, with the window two or three inches down, and have a powerful, though irrational fear that somehow she would kick her way out of my arms and fall out the window.

It was not just my self-concept that was affected by our early separation—it was also my perception of my daughter. During the 1960s, few people knew about the intelligence and awareness of newborn babies. I remember reading during my pregnancy that my baby wouldn't be able to see me clearly at birth because a newborn baby's eyes weren't fully developed yet. I accepted this widespread belief as truth, and, since I did not have the experience of looking into her eyes and having her look back at me during the period of wide-awake alertness that most babies have just after birth, I had no evidence of my own to the contrary. I had babysat toddlers during my teenage years, but had little contact with newborn babies.

Besides this ignorance of my daughter's ability to communicate visually, I assumed that she was not intelligent yet. I had read several authorities who claimed that babies' nervous systems were far from developed at birth, and I took this to mean that they lacked intelligence.

It wasn't that I thought my daughter was mentally slow; I actually thought that all babies were incapable of real communication until some time later in life. I don't know how I thought babies made the transition from being unable to communicate to able to communicate—that process was extremely mysterious to me. In a way, I regarded my daughter as a kind of animated doll, or as an extension of myself, instead of as a person in her own right. I was very con-

The Benefits of Breastfeeding

Sydney and her brother

scientious about attending to all her physical needs, but I wasn't really conscious that she had been fully intelligent and aware and able to communicate all of her life. The realization that she was already Somebody came as a shock. I found that I hadn't been accustomed to giving her my unfragmented attention, and this was precisely what she needed and later demanded from me. I even had to learn to kiss her, something I had been too inhibited to do during her first two years. For a while, I was afraid that I had ruined her by having been such an unskilled mother during her first two years. Finally, I realized that she was learning so fast that what really mattered at that point was how I treated her from then on.

One incident that occurred when she was a toddler stands out clearly in my mind. We were at the beach. Sydney was standing shin deep in the surf about twenty feet from me, playing with some kids who were two or three years older than she. A wave came in and knocked her down. For what seemed several seconds, I stood there horrified but paralyzed, and then watched one of the six year olds help her to her feet. I felt terrible about not having had the presence of the mind to rescue her myself, and I remember feeling bad about the incident for weeks. I wondered why my protective maternal instincts didn't seem to function. I knew I loved her, but I wasn't very good at protecting her.

Later on, I had a chance to redeem myself in her eyes as well as in my own. We were riding down the highway in our schoolbus-camper. Sydney was playing in a loft at the back of the bus. Suddenly I heard a scream and looked back to see her hanging onto the loft by her fingers, her feet dangling about four feet from the floor. I sprang up and dashed back to catch her before she fell. This all sounds simple enough in retrospect, but it was one of the most memorable moments for me in our life together up to that point. I had actually been there for her when she needed me.

The completion of our connection came when Sydney was nineteen and in an intensive care unit following emergency surgery for what turned out to be a malignant brain tumor. Two very sensitive nurses who were caring for her understood that it would be healing for her if I were to be with her continuously while she was in their unit. They allowed me to sleep in her room on a gurney so I could be there for her whenever she woke. To Sydney and me both, this time after the first surgery was a full-value rebirth. Before going in for that first surgery, she had been told that the neurological problems she was experiencing might be caused by an aneurysm. The only person she had ever known who had one of these had not survived. When she woke from the anesthesia, she was totally elated to find herself alive. At the same time, she was as vulnerable as she had been when she was newly born; I knew she needed me as much as she had as a baby. We both faced the greatest challenge of our lives, but we were able to be together this time, and that gave us a strength we could not have had if we had been kept apart. We were together day and night, just as if she had been a new baby.

A few weeks later, we went through a crisis in which our new strength was really put to the test. Sydney was again in an intensive care unit, in a different hospital this time, with much stricter rules. The nurses, although competent technically, were emotionally aloof from these patients who were very ill. The night nurses, especially, were loud and rough with her, and since she had had such beautiful treatment in the previous hospital, this came as a rude shock. Sydney was in a lot of pain, had trouble sleeping, and dreaded the contact she had with the nurses. Instead of showing off to them how fast she could get well, she was withdrawn and listless, and I began to feel that she might give up her will to live. At that point I knew I had to fight to stay by her side even if the nurses were afraid to let me. From the moment I told her that was what I was going to do, her sense of humor returned, and she began to improve. Although the supervisor in charge of the floor didn't want me there and would not allow me to be comfortable, I spent the night at Sydney's side. In the morning, to my great surprise, her doctor thought she was so much improved she could leave the intensive care unit.

Most of the medical care Sydney received was excellent. Even so, I know that she would have died on at least two occasions had I not been able to become the fierce mother appropriate for the situation. By "fierce," I just mean that I refused to be separated from her by medical personnel who thought I should be in a waiting room. I threw no tantrums; I just stayed. One instance was when Sydney began hemorrhaging from the tumor after her release from the hospital following the first surgery. We were visiting her father, who lived a few miles from the hospital where her original emergency surgery had been done. Her medical coverage, though, was from another hospital many miles away. It was obvious to me that she would die if I tried to get her to the hospital where her coverage was, so I directed the ambulance to the nearby hospital. During the ride she slipped from consciousness into a deep coma. I knew there was no time to mess around. To my great relief, just as we entered the hospital, in came the surgeon who had done the original surgery. I rushed over to him and told him he would need to operate right away. He went into the emergency room, took a look at her, and said, "She's almost dead." I told him I knew that. At that point, he said he would need to call the hospital covered by her insurance, and I knew that he was worried about his hospital getting paid for the surgery bill. I butted in and told him that he should prepare for surgery and that I would fight the hospital about getting the payment to happen. At that point, he knew he should do what I said. I went to Sydney, held her by the head and told her to hold on. I believe that she heard me. The paramedic, who was understandably nervous, thought that I should leave the emergency room, but I refused to go, saying that I had to be with her as long as possible, since I was the person who had the most complete information concerning her case. Just then the emergency room physician came in and ordered a CT-scan to be done. I knew how long this procedure would take, and I also knew that the surgeon didn't really need one, since he knew the location of the tumor quite well. On my word, the emergency room doctor rescinded the order. The next two hours were the longest two hours of my life. About one hour into the surgery, I felt my spirits lift, and minutes later, a nurse stuck her head out of the operating room and said that a blood clot the size of an orange had been removed and that things looked good. An hour and a half later,

Sydney was in the recovery room, "sharp as a tack," the nurses said, and rattling off telephone numbers of friends who should be called.

I know that my fighting for her gave us a year together we would not have had otherwise. I doubt if I could have found the courage to order doctors around and create disruptions in hospitals if I had not had the chance to form the really strong bonds between us that were not formed just after her birth. Nearly one year after Sydney's diagnosis was made and several months after our trip to London and Wales (where we visited the graves of our ancestors), it became clear that she would not live much longer. Our family gathered together in California, two thousand miles from our home in Tennessee, where we celebrated Sydney's twentieth birthday with her. During the following three weeks, as she grew progressively weaker, Sydney's father and I took turns staying by her side at his home. She never went into a coma, as her doctors had predicted. She would nap between the doses of morphine I was giving her. She was always aware of what was going on. She even had a sense of humor, my tough kid. As her time approached, she arranged us the way she wanted: she pulled her father to her side, not physically, but psychically, and I came close, too. We were all holding each other, and her breathing, which had been rapid for a couple of hours, began to slow. The *Earth Mass* (*Missa Gaia*) by Paul Winter's group was playing on the tape deck in her room. She asked with her eyes if there was anything to be afraid of. I told her it was all right and that she might see a light. Just then, as the chorus sang "Blessed are they that mourn, for they shall be comforted," she took her last breath.

Her stepmother and I bathed her and dressed her. I rubbed a little cinnamon in her hair and loved her body for the last time. A couple of hours after death a little smile appeared on her lips, a nice gift.

At the time I am writing this, only six weeks have passed since my daughter's death, and I'm still healing. I am sure that the closeness we experienced together for the last year has eased my heart in a way that no sedative could. I do not have to feel guilty for the years when I didn't really know how to be her mother. My family and I have the satisfaction of knowing we did things the right way.

REFERENCES
1. Marshall Klaus, M.D., and John Kennell, M.D., *Bonding: The Beginnings of Parent-Infant Attachment*, (St. Louis: C.V. Mosby, 1983), p. 3.
2. Marshall and Klaus, M.D., and John Kennell, M.D., *Parent-Infant Bonding*, (St. Louis: C.V. Mosby, 1982), p. 44.
3. Ibid., p. 42.

SUGGESTED SUPPLEMENTAL READING

Dick-Read, Grantly, M. D. *Children Without Fear.* Fourth Edition. New York: Perennial Library, 1979.

Eiger, M. S., M.D., and Sally Olds. *The Complete Book of Breastfeeding.* New York: Bantam Books, 1972.

Kitzinger, Sheila. *The Experience of Breastfeeding.* London: Penguin, 1979.

Klaus, Marshall, M.D., and John Kennell, M.D. *Bonding: The Beginning of Parent-Infant Attachment.* St. Louis: C.V. Mosby, 1983.

———. *Parent-Infant Bonding,* 2nd Ed. St. Louis: C.V. Mosby, 1982.

Klaus, Marshall, M.D., and Phyllis Klaus. *The Amazing Newborn.* Andover, Mass.: Addison-Wesley, 1985.

2

Preparing for Breastfeeding

♦

*I*t may seem strange that breastfeeding may require some preparation when it is supposedly such a natural thing to do. Breastfeeding is natural, but it is a skill that requires some learning and preparation for women who live in a society which does not provide social support for natural skills.

Any woman needs self-confidence in order to be successful at nursing. Learning as much as possible about breastfeeding before you give birth will help you develop your confidence.

Learning about Breastfeeding

Women used to pass on knowledge about breastfeeding from generation to generation. This process still happens in those parts of the world where most mothers still breastfeed. In the industrialized world this area of womenly knowledge has been interrupted by a dependence upon technology which has made mothers acquire information about feeding their children from medical professionals and multinational corporations. This learned dependence has developed with its own price. With the absence of shared knowledge about breastfeeding in mainstream society, mothers who want to breastfeed are too often forced to go it alone, to learn by trial and error. Unfortunately, it is possible for mothers to make errors in breastfeeding which force them to quit nursing before they are ready to do so.

By far the best way to learn about breastfeeding is to spend time around women who are nursing their babies. If you have seen women breastfeed, the process will not seem strange to you.

My work as a midwife has mostly been within a community of women who gave birth at home and who provided a strong network of support for each other during pregnancy, childbearing, and the nursing period. My book, *Spiritual Midwifery*, provides a look at the birth experiences of many of these women. What is noteworthy about their breastfeeding experience is that very nearly all of them were successful at it. Only a few women out of more than a thousand had to cut off nursing before they were ready, and two of these mothers were able to successfully breastfeed subsequent babies. One of these mothers weaned her baby at four months, anxious about her milk supply, and another needed to give her babies supplemental formula while she continued breastfeeding. Few of the mothers I have attended in childbirth were themselves breastfed as babies, so their success at breastfeeding did not stem from knowledge that they already had.

Chances are that you do not live in a neighborhood in which there are several nursing mothers. If this is the case, it will be well worth your while to make some contacts with other pregnant women who intend to breastfeed or with women who have already breastfed babies. There may be classes in breastfeeding offered in your community. La Leche League is an organization of nursing mothers whose purpose is to support breastfeeding internationally. Monthly La Leche League meetings are held in most areas. In others, there are similar groups which provide classes and telephone counseling for pregnant and nursing women (See Appendix A for a list of these groups).

Breast Changes During Pregnancy

The endocrine hormones that cause changes in your body during pregnancy are the same ones that are present in your bloodstream during the different phases of your menstrual cycle. Your pituitary gland and your ovaries take turns stimulating each other to produce a cycle of hormones that develops and releases an egg during the first part of your menstrual cycle and prepares your uterus for a pregnancy if that egg gets fertilized and needs a nesting place.

If pregnancy does occur, one of its first symptoms is often tingliness, soreness, or an increase in the size of the breasts. If your breasts usually swell a little before your period, you will probably feel similar,

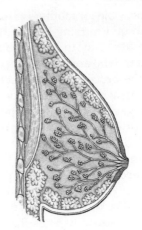

Pre-pregnant

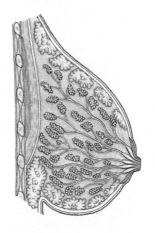

Pregnant

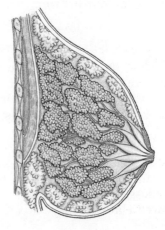

Nursing

Preparing for Breastfeeding

but stronger, sensations when you are first pregnant. Many women notice the difference even before they miss their first period.

When pregnancy occurs, the fertilized egg produces progesterone. As the placenta develops, it begins producing high levels of estrogen and some progesterone. These hormones stimulate the growth of the milk-producing glands.

Breast size and shape vary considerably, according to the character and distribution of supporting connective tissue and to the amount of protective fatty tissue surrounding the connective tissue. The other kind of tissue in breasts, the glandular tissue (milk-producing cells and duct system) does not vary much among different women. This is why size and shape of breasts have nothing to do with the amount of milk a woman produces.

The little ring of bumps around the outer areola (the circle of darker skin around the nipple) becomes more prominent and noticeable, usually within two or three weeks after conception. These bumps secrete an oily lubrication which makes the areola stretchy and supple.

If you are light-skinned, your nipples will darken. If you have large, soft nipples that don't easily become erect, you will probably find them to be more erectile than before pregnancy.

Colostrum, a creamy, yellowish-white liquid containing important antibodies for your baby, is produced by the second month of pregnancy. In some women, colostrum will flow out of their breasts during the latter part of the pregnancy. Others will know that it is there only by "milking" out a little. This difference in women has nothing to do with comparative ability to produce milk.

During the second half of pregnancy, the placenta begins producing prolactin (the Latin word means "for milk-production"), a hormone that causes further growth of the milk-producing sacs and causes them to secrete milk. By the time you are five months pregnant, your milk-making gear is fully developed.

Some stretch marks may appear during the last three months of pregnancy, particularly if you were not fully developed previously. Squeezing and massaging the breasts, with or without cream or oil, and wearing a good bra may help to prevent stretch marks.

How the Breasts Make Milk

Glands are cells, or groups of cells, which selectively remove materials from the blood, concentrate or change them, and then secrete them for further use in or outside the body, or for elimination. Breasts are actually glands of the skin. The breasts are the only glands of the body which directly produce food. They convert substances from your blood into the perfect food for your baby.

During pregnancy, estrogen causes growth of the duct systems of the breasts and of the connective tissue between the duct systems. The hormones, progesterone and prolactin, affect the growth and function of the breasts during pregnancy. During the period of milk-making, the breasts are affected by the hormones prolactin and oxytocin.

Each breast contains an interconnecting system of passageways and reservoirs. Your milk is synthesized and stored and then pushed out through these passageways. There are fifteen or twenty milk glands, or alveoli, in each breast, and milk is produced within each of these glands. Attached to each is its own duct system of tiny canals called ductules, which lead to larger canals and then to the nipple.

Stimulation of the nipple by the baby's sucking (or sometimes by the mother's thinking about the baby) sends messages to the hypothalamus. The pituitary gland responds by releasing prolactin and oxytocin into the bloodstream. The prolactin then stimulates the milk glands to produce the milk from the blood that flows through the especially rich system of blood vessels which develop during pregnancy. The oxytocin travels through the bloodstream to the breast and stimulates the muscle cells lining the milk glands to contract, much as a man's ejaculatory duct does during orgasm. Like ejaculation, this process feels good.

At first, milk is made whether or not your baby sucks at your breasts. Continued milk production depends upon your baby's frequent and regular stimulation of your breasts. During the early months of life, your baby should nurse at least eight times in twenty-four hours and be allowed enough time to finish each feeding. The more your breasts are stimulated by the baby's sucking, the more milk you will make.

Contraction of the milk-producing cells squeezes milk into the ducts, which then contract and squirt the milk into the pools beneath the areola and out the openings in the nipples. The pumping action can be so quick and strong that milk suddenly sprays or drips from the nipples.

One new mother noted: "What surprised me the most about nursing was my milk. One day, when my babe was a week or two old, I was changing shirts and turned around suddenly to check something. As I turned. a spray of milk flew four feet across the room from my full breasts! I couldn't believe it! Not only that, but it sprayed in three streams from each one, which taught me I had more than one hole in each nipple. This experience was a revelation to me. It

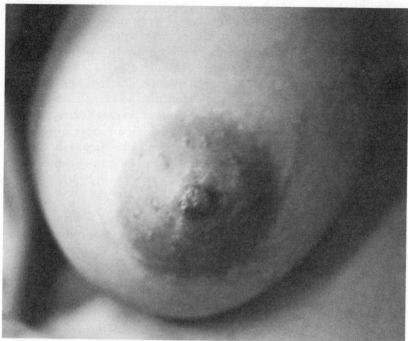
Organic form

gave me new respect for my body to know it was capable of such a thing."

An amusing incident took place when one of the midwives I work with took an anatomy and physiology course from a nearby college. The instructor of the course (who had a Ph.D. in his field), while lecturing on the structure of the female breast, mentioned in passing that milk came out of a hole in the nipple.

"A hole?" my friend, who had breastfed five children, asked incredulously.

"Yes," he said.

My partner was too polite to pursue the matter until after the class was over, not wanting to embarrass him in front of the class. Then she confronted him.

"I believe there are several holes in a woman's nipples," she said. "Our textbook even says so."

"Does it? Well, that's not the reference book I use," he said. "Come down to my office, and I'll show you."

Once in his office, he got out his favorite anatomy text, looked up the breast, and, to his deep chagrin, found that he had been teaching something wrong for several years. Like many academics, he hadn't been able to accept information from a person who had had the opportunity to find out from personal experience how breasts are made. He was totally ignorant about a fact of life that people in more traditional cultures accept as common knowledge.

Just as uninformed was the young mother who told her midwife, an acquaintance of mine, that she didn't plan to breastfeed because she didn't think she could handle the pain of preparation. As a child she had seen her mother enlarging the hole of a rubber nipple and had assumed that the same procedure would be necessary for her own nipples. She was able to breastfeed when the time came.

Caring For The Breasts

It is best to avoid using soap on your nipples during the last third of your pregnancy and while you are nursing. Soap has a drying, irritating effect because it washes off the protective oils secreted by the skin of the nipples and areola. These oils toughen and soften your skin, as well as provide an antibacterial covering for these entrances to your body.

Nipple creams are unnecessary, although you may find that dryness and itchiness of the breasts themselves may be relieved by a cream or lotion.

Some pregnant women, particularly those with big breasts, find the support of a good bra essential, while many others are just as comfortable without one. The signs of needing a good fitting bra during pregnancy are upper back aches, aching breasts, congested nipples, and an extreme sensation of heaviness.

Big Breasts

Some women will change only one or two bra sizes during a pregnancy. Others astound themselves by growing four or five bra sizes during a pregnancy. If you are like this, take special care of your breasts during pregnancy so they will work well for you while you are nursing.

If you have big breasts, it may be wise to get a couple of nursing bras before you deliver. These bras are made so that the cup can be unhooked and lowered to expose each of your nipples for the baby. Your breasts will be given some support while you nurse. Don't be surprised if you have to spend twice as much for a bra that really fits you as the women with smaller breasts.

If your breasts are large and uncomfortable during pregnancy, make a practice of lying on your back for five or ten minutes a couple

Preparing for Breastfeeding

of times a day. Cup them between your hands and squeeze them, gently at first, then increasing pressure until you lessen the congestion within your breast tissue. The difference after this squeezing can be dramatic.

Nipple Preparation

The most important step you can take to prepare your nipples for breastfeeding is to make sure that they can protrude outward enough for your baby to grasp with her mouth. Try squeezing your breast between your thumb and forefinger just behind the nipple. If your nipples are flat or dimpled inward (inverted) and remain so, try pulling on them to see if you can pull your nipple outward without pulling the inner tissue of your breast with it. Some women's nipples are adhered to the tissue underneath, which can make nursing very difficult unless corrective steps are taken.

If your nipples flatten or invert when you squeeze behind the nipple as just described, you have a couple of choices about what steps to take. Many women with inverted or adhered nipples are helped by wearing plastic breast shields inside the bra during pregnancy. Such shields put a steady but gentle pressure on the areola and push the nipple outward through the hole in the center of the shield. This action tends to break up the adhesions under the nipple. Ideally this shield would be worn from mid-pregnancy until the baby is born. See Appendix B for information on obtaining these shields and an interesting historical tidbit.

Many women with moderately flat or inverted nipples are able to correct the problem by pulling gently on their nipples and rolling them between their fingers.

Breastfeeding counselors argue about whether it makes sense to toughen nipples during pregnancy in preparation for nursing. My

Nipples: Protruding, Flat, Dimpled, and Inverted

feeling is that pulling or twisting nipples or rubbing them with a towel causes no harm and very often helps a lot, according to mothers I have counseled. Some mothers use anhydrous lanolin as a toughening agent during pregnancy, with good results. Don't be discouraged if your nipples don't seem to be tough and calloused. The important thing is that they protrude well when pinched or stimulated. If your nipples are extra sensitive, get in the habit of pulling on your nipples ten times each night before you go to bed. Grasp your nipple with all five fingers right at the areola and tug gently.

Mothers who don't wear a bra usually find that the friction of clothing against the nipples helps to reduce the extreme tenderness that comes with the early weeks of pregnancy. So does exposure to sunlight for a few minutes each day. You may use a sunlamp instead, if you limit yourself to less than three minutes' exposure a day.

Big-breasted mothers who must wear a bra all during pregnancy should try to keep their nipples dry, as nipples that are constantly damp tend to be extremely sensitive, making problems during the first few days or weeks of nursing. If there is no problem with constant wetness, it's a good idea to cut a circle of material from the ends of the bra cups so that the breast is supported but the nipples do get rubbed by your clothing. If you leak so much that cutting circles in the ends of your bra keeps you too wet, you may want to put paper nursing pads in the cups to soak up the colostrum. Change these pads frequently and try to leave your breasts out at night so that your nipples are relatively dry some of the time. Remember—constantly wet nipples are sensitive nipples.

Nursing Bras and Pads

Many women appreciate the support of a nursing bra during the early weeks of breastfeeding. The best nursing bras have front flaps which can be unfastened with one hand, nonelastic straps, and cotton cups without plastic linings. Plastic-lined bras keep the nipples wet, which is not good.

If you wish to buy a bra for nursing so that you won't have to shop for one after the baby is born, you'll have to do a bit of guesswork, since there's no way of knowing exactly what size and shape your breasts will be while you are nursing. Your best bet is to go by the size you are two or three weeks before your estimated due date. Pick a cup size that supports the under part of your breast comfortably while being somewhat loose above. You will perhaps need some room to wear a breast pad, and your breasts will be swollen when your milk first comes in. Remember that your rib cage will probably be somewhat smaller after you have your baby. Stay away from bras

Preparing for Breastfeeding

with wires or heavy plastic supports, as these contraptions can cause plugged milk ducts and breast infections when they interfere with the circulation of milk through your breasts. Many women find that stretchy nylon bras work better for them than movable flap nursing bras. They just pull the bra out of the way when they wish to nurse.

There are two kinds of breast pads: disposable and reusable. Some of the reusable breast pads are plastic-lined and should be avoided since they can lead to nipple soreness.

Choosing Maternity Caregivers

Because the kind of maternity care you get can have such a great influence on how breastfeeding will go for you, it is important to choose midwives, obstetricians, and pediatricians carefully. Almost all midwives understand the basic principles that underlie successful breastfeeding, but not all physicians do. If you are looking for an obstetrician or pediatrician, try to find someone who is known to have a positive attitude towards breastfeeding. A local childbirth educator, midwife, or breastfeeding counselor is apt to have such information. Nurse practitioners are often valuable resource people when it comes to breastfeeding support and well baby care.

It is quite fair to inquire about cesarean section rates of physicians while you are shopping. At the time of this writing, cesarean rates

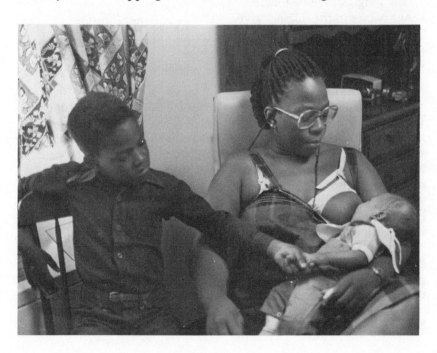

in the United States are scandalously high, compared with those in most industrialized countries. In 1970 the U.S. cesarean rate of 5.5 percent was close to that of England and Wales (4.9 percent). By 1983 the U.S. cesarean rate had quadrupled to 20.3 percent while that of England and Wales had doubled to 10.1 percent. Despite the work of a National Institutes of Health Consensus group (the Task Force, begun in 1980 to make recommendations to halt the steady rise in the cesarean rate in the U.S.), provisional figures for 1985 are over 24 percent, almost one woman in four. No industrialized European country has a cesarean rate over 13 percent, and their infant mortality rates are consistently lower than ours.

Find out what percentage of other patients breastfeed, and be sure to discuss your preferences with both physicians and office nurses. If you pick a hospital that doesn't routinely allow rooming-in, ask for written special permission that will allow for early nursing and rooming-in.

Here is a list of questions you should have answered before giving birth:

- Will I be allowed to nurse my baby immediately after birth? What if I have a cesarean? By the way, what is the cesarean rate here?
- Can my baby stay in my room with me? If not, how often and for how long can we be together?
- Are babies in the nursery given feedings of either formula or sugar water?
- How often are feedings encouraged?
- What kind of help is provided by the nursing staff to breastfeeding mothers?

You should know that the best policies include the chance for early breastfeeding (minutes after birth, preferably, but certainly within the first two hours), rooming-in, and no water or formula supplements. Keep in mind, too, that it will be much easier for you to breastfeed if you are surrounded by people who admire you for making this choice.

If you choose a midwife, find out whether her service includes breastfeeding counselling and postpartum home visits. Most midwives do provide this service, but it's wise to ask.

Be sure to ask enough questions so that you know how you will be treated once you have entrusted yourself and your baby into someone's hands. It is not unreasonable to expect caregivers to explain themselves in this way; you are paying for your care.

Remember that most kinds of anesthesia will leave you and your baby groggy, so do without them during labor if you can. Many babies will begin nursing within minutes after birth, and this early nursing will help to bring on your milk more quickly. The faster your milk comes in, the less will be your baby's weight loss in her early days. Early sucking also promotes the formation of your emotional ties with your baby.

Setting Up a Support System

Taking care of a new baby is one of the most rewarding things you can do, but it is time- and energy-consuming. You can count on being tired during the first weeks after birth, perhaps more tired than you have ever been. Sometimes you will feel joyful and exhilarated; other times, you may wonder how you can keep up with it all. Your chances for a satisfactory experience of breastfeeding will depend to a large extent on the system of support you are able to develop, especially for the first few weeks. Keep in mind that about half of American women who start out breastfeeding have given up and turned to bottlefeeding by the time two months have passed.

The reasons for this high rate of discouragement are imbedded in the kind of society most of us live in. In North America individual achievement is valued above social cooperation; the nuclear family has replaced the extended family, which predominated in the last century. The education of health care providers often emphasizes ways of inhibiting milk production and how to use breastmilk substitutes; and social attitudes, instead of encouraging breastfeeding, very often work against it by regarding nursing mothers as messy and not fit to be seen in public.

The ideal situation for the nursing mother includes encouragement and approval from family and from everyone she meets, an undemanding schedule, and, very important, household help for a couple of weeks. How to arrange all this, you wonder?

Your partner's cooperation is essential. Some employers in North America will give new fathers time off from work around the time of birth. If possible, you'll want your partner to stay home for a week or so, to help you with household chores, food preparation, child care, and to get to know the new baby. Besides, it's nice not to be the only grownup in the house when you are learning to breastfeed. A loved one who tells you how beautiful you are during these first days can make a big difference in your morale and self-confidence. However, the reality for too many North American mothers is that their partners will be unable to take time off work to help that first week.

If this is the case for you, maybe other family members can step in and help you for a few days. It is wise to accept this kind of help only when you are sure that criticism or impractical advice will not be part of the package. Let your family know of your intention to breastfeed as early as you can, so you can provide them with the information necessary for them to be able to encourage and help you.

Accept whatever help is offered by friends and neighbors: meal preparation, errand running, shopping or care of your older children. If you lived in the Netherlands, for example, a home helper would come and assist you for the first ten days of your new baby's life, to increase your chances of establishing a good pattern of breastfeeding. The Dutch are practical people, who consider that giving babies a good start in life is worth the expenditure of tax revenues. Since our society does not allow for such family-centered benefits, you will be well advised to plan ahead to make up for a situation that is less than ideal. Stock up on easy-to-prepare food and do some menu planning in advance, if possible. Diaper service is wonderful for the first few weeks and is usually more economical than disposable diapers.

Breastfeeding and Fathers

Find out early in your pregnancy how your partner feels about breastfeeding. Some men are put off by the idea at first but change their minds when they see the new baby's obvious enjoyment.

Such a change is not unusual when a father has participated in the birth of the baby. Few of our own fathers were present at our births to look after our mothers, to see what it took to get us born, and to see our original face. Now many more men than a generation ago are insisting on being present for the birth of their children. The more this happens, the more we will see men being tuned into the real needs of babies and mothers. One father wrote:

> Nursing has always looked like a normal biological function to me. When our first child was born (at home), I was very impressed with the miracle of life. I was amazed at the beauty and scope of the process, that my daughter had just spent nine months growing from a couple of cells inside my wife. Breastfeeding struck me as a similar kind of miracle: here was this perfect food being produced with no effort at all.
>
> I remember the first time my wife stroked my daughter's cheek with her nipple. My daughter's head turned immediately, and she began to nurse. They were very intimate with each other, and I felt privileged to be part of it.

Not surprisingly, since so many men in our culture old enough to be fathers were not breastfed themselves, many men have mixed

Preparing for Breastfeeding

feelings about breasts and breastfeeding. Some appreciate the increase in size and the more erectile nipples of pregnancy but are not ready to share their partner's breasts with the coming baby. It is not uncommon for a man to feel that his partner's body will be "ruined" by pregnancy and breastfeeding. The truth is that it is pregnancy that causes the major changes in breast shape and firmness, not breastfeeding. In many women, the nipples may darken slightly and protrude more after childbirth and breastfeeding, but there is little or no change in the appearance of the breasts. Some women's breasts are larger after breastfeeding. Mine were, so I know this is true. I also know some women who swear that their breasts are firmer and "better organized" since breastfeeding than they were before pregnancy.

If your partner makes you feel bad about your wish to breastfeed, remember that sometimes men change attitudes and grow emotionally during their mate's pregnancy. It is certainly possible that your partner will grow closer to you during this sensitive time. You may find that emotional growth of this kind is more possible in a relationship which is sexually generous. One woman comments:

> My husband never seemed to mind how small my breasts were before pregnancy, but we both noticed with interest the amount of swell I attained during each of my pregnancies. My breasts would actually fill his hands. Not only that, but they were much more sensitive. Just a light brush of the nipple was erotic where before I might have tolerated only a little touching before I would feel uncomfortable enough to move on to something else.

It may help to remember that one of the best things about being pregnant is that you don't have to worry about getting pregnant. A good touch relationship between you and partner will be very good preparation for both childbirth and nursing. This is a time of your life when you will especially want to be in tune with your body and to appreciate its workings. If you already have a close touch relationship, it will seem very natural to you to be close with your baby. If you and your mate have been physicially close all during pregnancy, he will be much more likely to be compassionate with you and the baby's needs. Fathers who feel left out of the essential relationship are the ones who are more apt to be uncompassionate with mothers' and babies' needs. The same man, once he feels included, may seem a different person.

Pregnancy and Your Emotions

Many women are not prepared for the intensity of emotions they feel during pregnancy. Even if you are the type who usually functions

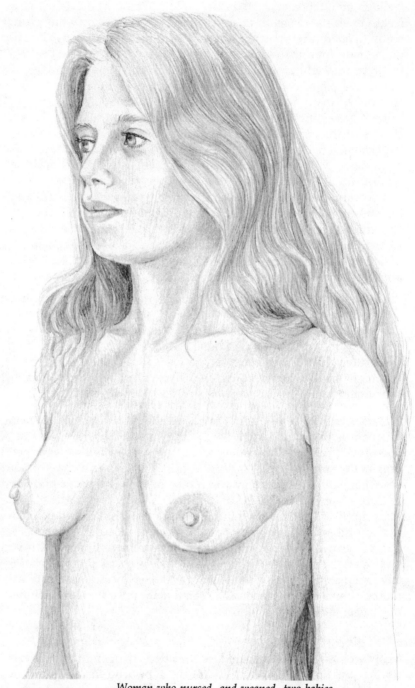

Woman who nursed, and weaned, two babies

on an even keel, you may find yourself sliding into troughs of sadness or peaks of giddiness that do not seem justified by external circumstances. This heightening of emotional awareness is caused not only by the change in hormone levels in pregnancy (and nursing) but also by the sense of increased responsibility that comes with adding a helpless new member to the family.

These intense emotions you feel during pregnancy and nursing are also felt by your unborn baby who, surrounded by your mass, has no choice but to feel what you are feeling. Unborn babies have no information with which to reason their way through the emotions they feel along with their mothers. Your efforts to keep your emotions from swinging wildly will benefit your baby in a couple of ways, first, because the general emotional background becomes calmer, and second, because your baby learns from your efforts how to relax.

It is helpful to remember that the word "emotion" is related to the word "move." Emotions come and go; they may be expressed or suppressed. The important thing is that we can move our emotions as well as be moved by them, and it is possible to learn the skill of moving from a negative emotion, such as fear or anger, to a more positive emotion.

Part of the nature of emotions is that they have a psychological inertia, just as material objects have physical inertia. Once an emotion is "moving" or being felt, it may not be so easy to change it with a thought or two. To be pregnant or nursing a baby is to be more emotionally massive than usual, so it may seem harder to rein in a runaway emotion than it was when you were more emotionally "on your own." Despite the general inertia of your emotions, you may still find that subtle adjustments are possible and effective. This is another way of saying that emotions are fluid; the different emotions do not exist in distinct compartments, separate from each other. It may be easier to slide from one emotion into another, than to stop an unpleasant emotion.

It is easier to deal with heavy emotion if you can learn to identify the bodily sensation that goes with it. For instance, if you feel a tightness in the pit of your stomach when you are afraid, you may find that you can get through the fear better by taking some slow, deep, relaxing breaths than by running over and over the mental content of the fear.

It is good to develop your skill of knowing what emotion you are feeling at any given time. If you can name your emotion, you have more emotional mobility than if you lose an awareness of your center while feeling strong emotions. For me, it is an article of faith that love, expressed with intelligence and appropriateness, is the antidote for any of the more negative emotions.

SUGGESTED SUPPLEMENTAL READING

Baldwin, Rahima and Terra Palmarini. *Pregnant Feelings*. Berkeley, Cal.: Celestial Arts, 1986.

Brewster, Dorothy. *You Can Breastfeed Your Baby*. Emmaus, Pa.: Rodale, 1979.

Gaskin, Ina May, ed. *The Birth Gazette*. 42, The Farm, Summertown, Tenn. 38483. $20 per year.

Gaskin, Ina May. *Spiritual Midwifery*. Summertown, Tenn.: Book Publishing Co., 1978.

Harrison, Michelle, M.D. *A Woman In Residence*. New York: Random House, 1982.

3

Getting Off to a Good Start

♦

Many mothers find labor an excellent preparation for nursing and childrearing. Such a positive thought may not occur to you while you are busy with labor, but labor does tend to teach patience, the value of a sense of humor, and the need to rest every possible moment you can—all lessons which will be valuable to you during your first few months of mothering.

Don't worry about a local anesthesia such as Xylocaine, which is frequently given if stitches need to be done. Such a local anesthetic will not act on your baby's or your central nervous system, so you needn't be concerned about avoiding this type of pain relief.

The First Minutes After Birth

A mother writes:

> My son was born in a great shower of brilliant strength, STRENGTH, and everything was silvery and sparkly. They said, "It's a boy," and put him right next to me. He could see me. He had such big hands. His birth was the most incredible, orgasmic thing in creation. I knew things at the moment of his birth, and he knew them, too, things about God and every birth that had ever taken place, all the laughter and all the tears and just everything. I heard the song of the Mother.

The moments just after childbirth can be one of the most exhilarating times of your life. Again and again at births, I have witnessed the surprised delight of a mother when she sees that her baby does indeed recognize her, even when only a few minutes old, and when she realizes that her baby prefers her company to that of anyone else. It seems only right to her after working so hard for so many months to grow the baby inside of her, and then to give birth.

It is likely that you will experience in the moments just after birth the most overwhelming sense of relief and gratitude which you have ever felt. Whatever you feel immediately following an unmedicated childbirth is likely never to be forgotten, for your memory will be recording impressions and events with unusual clarity at this time.

These first few moments are a very important time for mother, baby, and father. You recognize each other and claim each other. Someone has been added to the universe, someone who breathes, touches, sees, smells, hears, and communicates.

A new mother expressed her feelings this way:

We were just meeting each other for the first time, but it felt like we had known his presence from before, too. He was so obviously happy to be born, and we sat there like that for quite a while, undisturbed. He just kept looking from me to my husband, and the love between us was thick and strong.

New fathers, especially those who get to see their children born, may feel emotions of equal intensity during the first moments after birth. One first-time father wrote this:

The second he was out, he looked so familiar to me that it was as if I'd already known him; he looked just like himself. I really loved seeing him; he was beautiful. It felt like there was no space or time barrier to anything, and we were in Holy times in Holy land.

The best place for your baby right after birth is as close to you as possible. Your instincts, as well as your baby's, will tend to make you want intimate contact with one another. Don't worry, though, if you do not immediately feel this instinctual attraction for your baby—some mothers require more time with their babies and privacy than do others to feel the loving emotions which will deeply link them to their babies. Factors such as your relationship with your mate, the state of your finances, your readiness for the pregnancy, your relationships with your other children, deaths or illnesses within your family circle, and the way you were treated during labor and

Getting Off to a Good Start

delivery may temporarily affect your ability to feel your mothering instincts. Being with your baby is the best cure for any early coolness of maternal feelings. Don't bother feeling guilty about anything; it's a waste of time and energy.

COMMUNICATING WITH YOUR BABY

Don't be embarrassed about talking to your baby. Sometimes new mothers are taught that babies don't understand speech. Actually, your baby knows your voice and your feelings very well, better than anyone (except possibly your own mother) because of having lived inside of you for so many months. He has been hearing you since early embryo-hood and is already accustomed to the sounds and rhythms of your voice. It is interesting to note how a newborn baby, when he is being weighed and dressed, will immediately become alert and turn in his mother's direction when he hears the sound of her voice. Mothers seem to be equally proficient in distinguishing their babies' cries from those of other babies; one study found that mothers could pick their own babies' cry from others, even though they had heard it only once or twice.[1]

You will find eye-to-eye contact with your baby tremendously satisfying and energizing. This contact is another part of the bonding process. Babies usually open their eyes during the first hour or two after birth. If you have received no medication during labor, your baby will most likely be awake, alert, and responsive to the sounds of voices and other stimuli. Babies are beautiful, intelligent, and aware during this time, aware of the newness of being outside of you as well as of the familiarity of your touch and your bodily presence. You will want to have ample opportunity to respond to your baby's efforts to communicate during this special time.

SMELL

Newborn babies have noses as sensitive to their mother's smell as any other newborn mammals, and when they smell their mother's breasts, they usually try nuzzling and licking her nipples. Communication by smell plays an important part in the early bonding process. In other species of mammals, the mother can easily distinguish her own offspring from others, once she has had a chance to spend a

Getting Off to a Good Start

few minutes with her newborn after birth. In humans, too, this sense remains potent. I have heard mothers describe their baby's newborn smell as "heavenly," "intoxicating," or "delicious." One researcher has shown that the baby who is allowed to lick her mother's nipple during the few minutes after birth will be able to distinguish reliably by smell her own mother's breastpad from the breastpads of other mothers.[2]

TOUCHING

Skin-to-skin contact seems to be especially satisfying to our species. With our nearly hairless bodies, we are probably the most touch-sensitive of all the mammals, and so touch is a vital form of communication for us. Since breastfeeding involves more skin-to-skin contact than bottlefeeding, you will have plenty of opportunities to "talk" in touch with your baby during feedings if you breastfeed. I used to like to hold hands with my babies while they nursed. When

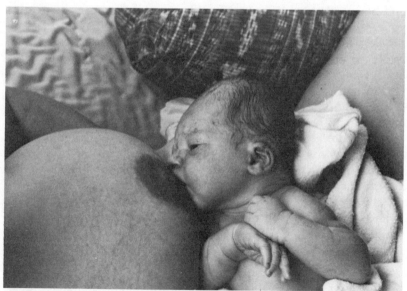

Moments after birth. The breast is bigger than the baby and the nipple is flat, making it hard for him to nurse.

they squeezed my finger, I would respond by squeezing back. The babies' sweet touches and squeezes were pleasureful and relaxing to me, and I'm sure they enjoyed my answering touches. Communication with babies is fun.

If Early Separation is Necessary

While it is true that the time just after birth is one of extreme sensitivity and that contact between mother and baby does contribute to the formation of lasting emotional bonds, you should not feel that your future relationship with your child will be damaged if for some reason you are unable to hold your baby immediately after birth. One of the most erroneous and trouble-causing ideas which has come out of the popular interest in bonding has been that permanent irrevocable damage will be done if these first few minutes aren't spent together. Bonding is not a one-time-only, hit-or-miss kind of process. Opportunities for creating and enhancing the deep ties which are important in mother-baby relationships will occur again and again. The same is true for fathers and their babies.

Early Nursing

Most of the time, the best place for the baby to be is on your chest and belly, skin next to your skin. When you hold your baby close to your breasts, she will often root for, smell, and maybe lick your nipple. This stimulation of your nipple causes oxytocin to be released into your bloodstream, triggering your uterus to contract in a powerful cramp. Such interaction between you and your baby is nature's way of preventing dangerous bleeding from your uterus after birth.

You may find it hard to get your baby sucking right away if you are being stitched, especially if you are lying on your back, or if you are allowed only a short time together. Remember that just touching and holding your baby near your breasts, near your heart, is good for both of you. The baby who needs a few minutes to clear her airway of the fluids which are sometimes in there just after birth will usually begin searching for mother's nipple as soon as her breathing pattern becomes relaxed and she loses her immediate interest in looking around her. One mother wrote:

> When my second child was born, she started right up all right, but was rather lethargic about it, and her color stayed blue. Oxygen helped her, and a few minutes later she obviously wanted to nurse. I thought she should get used to breathing first, enough to pink up, anyway, before adding on something else, but at my midwife's suggestion, I let her go ahead. It really amazed me to see her color

Getting Off to a Good Start

just come on as she nursed, turning nice and pink, lungs clearing—it was obviously exactly what she needed. She kept it up for two hours straight.

Watch for the baby to begin moving his tongue, opening his mouth, and turning his head to the side. All are signals of a baby's readiness

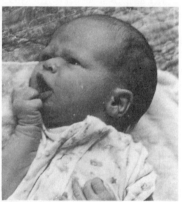

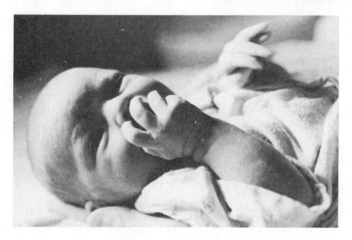

Three hungry babies, ready to nurse

to begin nursing. Some babies are somewhat tense until they latch on to the nipple, while others seem perfectly happy to wait.

BORN HUNGRY
Hunger is, at times, a factor. I can remember quite a few births I have attended, after which the babies seemed quite hungry. Such babies tend to suck immediately with enough satisfaction and intensity that they have their mother's milk in sooner than the average of two to three days because of frequency and intensity of the stimulation of her nipples.

If your baby is one of the born-hungry kind, there's no need to be anxious about him starving while waiting for your milk to come in. Just let him suck often, for the best results in getting your milk in as soon as possible. It's not the length of time that your baby nurses as much as it is the number of different nursing sessions which shortens the period of waiting for milk to come in.

BORN SATISFIED
Other babies don't seem to be hungry at all at birth, sometimes for a couple of days. These babies enjoy sucking for the sake of sucking; they become satisfied after a little while. Then they get tired and go to sleep. The born-hungry babies would rather suck than sleep. They seem to know that if they work hard enough at it, the food will surely arrive.

GETTING YOUR BABY TO LATCH ON
Usually, when your baby lets you know that he wants to suck by smacking his lips, opening his mouth or turning his head, it is possible to get him nursing within a few minutes, provided that you are able to get into a good position and your baby is able to get enough of your areola into his mouth. To get the proper stimulus to begin sucking, your baby needs to get enough nipple in his mouth to reach halfway back onto his hard palate. Early sucking will be good for both your self-confidence and your baby's skill at sucking. Babies are fast learners. Once your baby successfully latches on, the knowledge of how to do it is engraved on his memory, and he will usually go for the nipple quickly each time the breast is offered.

Finding The Best Position
The most important thing to remember is that your baby needs to get as much of your areola in her mouth as possible. You don't want the baby chewing just on the end of your nipple, or you are likely to have trouble with sore or cracked nipples. Besides this, the baby

Getting Off to a Good Start

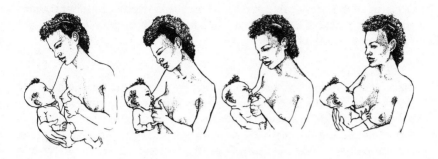

needs to get both nipple and areola in her mouth in order to get milk most efficiently.

BELLY-TO-BELLY HOLD
To begin nursing your baby, you may be comfortable sitting up on a bed with pillows arranged behind you. Get situated before putting the baby to your breast. Sit as erect as you can, while staying comfortable. Hold the baby with her belly facing yours and her arm tucked behind your back. Support your breast with your free hand, keeping your fingers off the areola.

First you want to stimulate the baby to look for your breast. You do this by lightly touching your nipple to the baby's lower lip. The baby will usually respond by opening her mouth or sticking her tongue out. When she does this, lift your breast, pinching your nipple so it sticks straight outward or downward. At the same time, pull the baby gently towards your body. Don't lean toward your baby.

If your baby doesn't latch on the first time, repeat the above steps. Patience is important, because if you are patient about going through these steps, your baby is less likely to get frustrated. Since she isn't likely to keep her mouth open for long, you'll need to pull her toward you fairly quickly. Once she latches on, you'll be able to relax to a more comfortable position.

SIDE POSITION
Many mothers are too tired immediately after birth for the side position to be comfortable. If this is so, try lying on one side, with your baby lying beside you, her head and body facing your breast. Stroke her cheek or her mouth with your nipple and follow the steps given for the belly-to-belly position. It works better to have the baby in a position from which she can reach your nipple easily than to try to push her head towards the breast, since pushing her head will usually cause her to turn towards the pressure of your hand.

The side position is nice for mothers who have had cesareans. You'll probably like this position for night feedings.

FOOTBALL HOLD
The football hold is good for mothers who have had cesareans, or for those with large breasts. This is also a great hold for the baby who can't keep the areola in her mouth and for a tiny baby. You hold the baby's head in your hand, with the baby's body under your arm. You may need a pillow to position the baby correctly.

Your baby will appreciate a firm touch, no matter how small he is. Hold him close to you. He is used to being surrounded by you, so he will appreciate your touch and the sound of your voice. Babies like being kissed and nuzzled by their mothers, so don't be shy.

Trouble Latching On

It is normal to feel awkward about holding your baby the first few times. Don't worry. These feelings will soon pass. Sometimes a baby, when he is put to the breast during the first day or two, will become so frantic that he is not able to begin sucking. This can be as frustrating

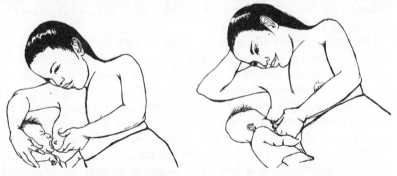

Getting Off to a Good Start

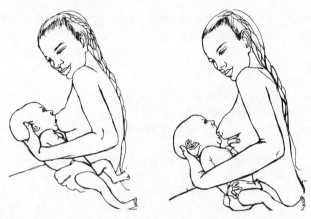

to you as it is to the baby—like pushing two magnets of the same polarity together, causing them to repel each other instead of attracting. The problem is not that the baby doesn't want to suck; he does, but he's impatient, and he doesn't know how to relax so he can get in time with you.

The main help here is not to start thinking that your baby doesn't like you. For one thing, it isn't true, and for another, your being negative will make the situation worse. You are so attuned to your baby's every move that if your baby tightens up his stomach and cries, your stomach will tighten, and you may even feel like crying yourself. In the same way, if you can take charge and relax yourself, your baby will follow suit. Relax your belly by breathing slowly and deeply and try again. Once your baby gets to experience the relaxation and immediate satisfaction that sucking gives, he will become a proficient little sucker very quickly.

Sometimes you can coax your baby to nurse by pursing your lips as if for a kiss. This facial expression seems to get the baby into a sucking mood. Babies not only respond to what they see but appear to feel and imitate your expressions even when their eyes are closed.

A friend of mine was under the impression that her breast had to hang down above the baby's mouth in order for the milk to come out. Gravity is not a necessary element, as the pumping action of the breast will spray the milk into the sucking baby's mouth, even if the mother is lying on her back.

Some babies won't open their mouths wide enough at first, and they just grab the end of the nipple. If your baby sucks on the very end of your nipple, it will soon get very sore and your baby won't get much milk either, as she needs to press her mouth on the milk pools under the areola. One way to get your baby to open her mouth wider is to gently coax her lower lip down with your nipple or finger a few times until her mouth is really wide open. Then just pop the nipple in.

How Long To Nurse

If you can, let your baby be your guide as to how long to nurse during the early days. Since newborns love to suck, and some of them suck hard, don't be surprised if your nipples are a little sore, especially if this is your first try at breastfeeding. In general, the darker the skin color of your nipple, the less trouble you are likely to have with soreness.

You may find at first that it is easier on your nipples if you switch your baby from breast to breast, letting her nurse about ten minutes on each side. You may, at times, find yourself ready to switch from one breast to the other before your baby is ready to let go. You should not try to pull your baby's mouth off the breast, as this can make your nipple very sore. Instead, put the tip of your little finger into the corner of her mouth, breaking the suction between her mouth and your nipple. As your nipples toughen, you can increase the amount of time on each side until the baby is the one who determines how long the sucking period will be. In general, you should nurse your baby until she lets you know she has nursed enough by falling asleep or turning away.

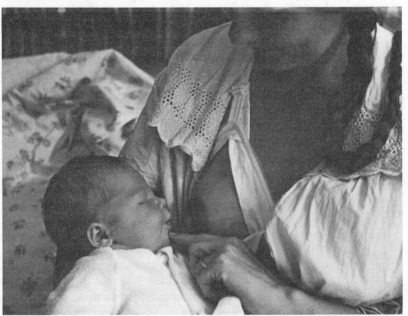

Getting Off to a Good Start 55

I loved the look on my babies' faces when they had nursed their fill. The sheer relief and delight in their eyes and the smile of total satisfaction is language any mother can appreciate. It's proof that what you have to offer is the right stuff!

Care of Your Nipples

Keep your nipples clean for your baby just by washing them daily with clean water. Do not use soap directly on your nipples, even when you use it in bathing the rest of your body. Soap will dry out your nipples by removing the cleansing, lubricating substances which are secreted by the glands on and around your nipples. There is no need for you to apply any creams or ointments to your nipples unless they become very sore or cracked. See p. 72 for information on how to treat this condition.

Dealing With The Hospital

Some hospitals may allow you to have your baby with you during the day, but put all babies in a nursery during the nights. I know many women who could not figure out why their babies wouldn't suck when they were brought to them, until they found out that the babies were being fed formula or sugar water in the nursery. If your baby must sleep in a nursery, insist that he be brought to you to feed as soon as he cries, even if you have to be awakened. Make sure that the night nurses know that your baby is breastfed. Tie a note onto your baby's crib saying, "Take me to my mother when I cry."

Many hospitals give a sample package of formula, rubber nipples, and a pamphlet on breastfeeding as a discharge gift. These materials are provided to the hospitals by the manufacturer as part of their

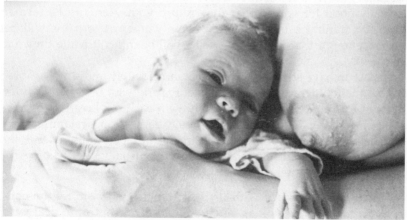

sales promotion. Unfortunately, these kits are not helpful to mothers wishing to breastfeed for two reasons: one, the information given is often misleading, and second, just having the formula during the first few days of nursing your baby may tempt you to use it. You are better off to leave the kit behind.

Educate the nurses if you have to. Tell them that your breasts need to be emptied frequently so they can produce lots of milk and that the more your baby nurses, the sooner your milk will come in. If they aren't convinced, add that your baby needs the essential nutrients and valuable antibodies from your colostrum to protect him from illnesses he might be exposed to from being near so many people.

If the nurses insist on you washing your nipples with soap before putting the baby to breast, ask for a pan of sterile water. Using soap will remove your smell, which is part of the information your baby gets while you are holding him, information that lets him know what he is supposed to do next. Remember, he's your baby.

Afterpains

During your first few sessions of breastfeeding, you will probably notice sensations in your belly very similar to menstrual cramps. What you are feeling is the contractions of your uterus, brought on by the oxytocin released because of the stimulation of your nipples by the baby's sucking. These sensations range from pretty mild to very uncomfortable, usually depending upon how many children you have had. They tend to get more painful with each successive birth. For some women, especially those who have given birth more than twice, afterpains are much more painful than uterine contractions during childbirth. It's comforting to know that these contractions are actually good for you in that they return your uterus to its former size and minimize blood loss. In some women, afterpains will be strong enough that holding the baby will be difficult while they are happening.

If you do have strong afterpains, breathe deeply and slowly, holding your shoulders as low as possible. Expand your belly slowly with each in-breath and collapse it slowly with each out-breath. Concentrate on relaxing. If the contractions really bother you, acetaminophen will help. A hot water bottle or electric heating pad is also useful. By the fourth day, even severe afterpains have usually slacked off.

One woman wrote:

> I was really surprised with my third child at how strong the contractions were. It took as much attention and control to deal with

them as it did with labor. I would have to hand the new baby to my husband in the middle of nursing him those first days because a strong contraction would come on, and I would have to start breathing hard to stay on top of it. I couldn't really deal with the pain and the baby at the same instant.

The First Three Days

It is important that you get plenty of rest during the two or three days just after birth. This is a time to relax and fall in love with your baby.

Before your milk comes in, your breasts will still contain colostrum, a substance which contains valuable antibodies and other goodies for your baby. There isn't a lot of it usually, but don't think that because it comes in small quantities that it isn't needed by your baby. Colostrum contains white blood cells which are there to prevent infection in the newborn by attacking harmful bacteria. Besides this, colostrum is easy to digest with its high protein, low sugar and fat content, so it is an ideal first food. Colostrum prepares the baby's digestive tract for receiving the milk that comes later by stimulating the baby's first bowel movement. Meconium, the black, tarry stuff that passes in the first stool, contains bilirubin, the substance that causes jaundice in newborns.

Don't worry about your baby losing a little weight before your milk comes in. Nearly every newborn will lose some weight after birth, mostly from peeing and passing meconium. A slight weight loss is nothing to worry about, since your baby was born with enough extra fluid to tide him over until your milk is in. This weight loss is usually quickly recovered once your milk supply is well established.

If your baby seems really frantically hungry by the second or third day, keep nursing, resting, and drink a lot. Do not give her a bottle. A newborn who is given a bottle to drink from may quickly develop a preference for it just because it requires less effort on her part to get milk from the bottle than from the breast. If she cries, your breast will comfort her, and she will help bring on your milk.

The more your baby sucks, the sooner you will have large amounts of milk. Remember to make sure that your baby gives equal stimulation to both breasts by switching sides regularly. A full supply of milk will usually be in on the second or third day if your baby has nursed frequently. It comes in on the fourth or fifth day if nursing has been sporadic or infrequent, or if you lost a lot of blood during the delivery. Whenever the milk does come in, your baby's interest in nursing usually increases significantly. You will know when your milk is fully in because your breasts will be very warm and much harder to the touch and much larger than usual.

Human milk is bluish-white and looks like skimmed cows' milk. The first milk that comes from the breasts at each feeding, the foremilk, is comparatively low in fat content. The later milk, the hindmilk, has a higher fat content and has a thicker, creamier appearance.

This time will be one of the most astonishing experiences of your life, comparable only to the thrill of producing a live and healthy baby. To have such an abundance of food so perfectly suited to your baby's needs occurring so naturally and spontaneously from your very own body is amazing and intensely gratifying. When I was nursing my babies, I often remembered the phrase "the joy-permeated mother," because all my cells seemed to enjoy the process.

You need your baby to suck frequently now so that your breasts will not become uncomfortably full. It is all right to wake the baby up if she sleeps for more than two or three hours and you need relief. After a few days, your breasts will become somewhat smaller than they were at the first burst of milk. This decrease in size does not mean that your milk is drying up, so don't panic and think that you won't have enough milk. What has happened is that your supply has come into phase with the demand programmed into your breasts by the baby.

The Let-Down Reflex

Your baby's sucking at your nipple stimulates the release of a hormone which sends the message to your milk-producing glands that it is time to make milk and triggers another hormone to cause these cells to push your milk out to the reservoirs just below your nipples. This ejection reflex is called let-down. Let-down is, for some women, accompanied by a tingling, filling sensation, while for others, there is little or no sensation even while the reflex is working quite well. I'm not sure of this, but I believe that I have observed that women with really large breasts are less likely to have a strong sensation of let-down than are women with rather small breasts. For me, it was a quite delicious feeling, and the tingling was accompanied by salivation and then thirst.

Women who do not experience this tingling sensation when their baby sucks can tell that let-down is working well from listening to the baby's swallowing or by observing milk dripping or spraying from the other breast. Let-down usually takes place simultaneously in both breasts and happens when the baby sucks or is the focus of his mother's attention. Sometimes it happens because there is a longer

Getting Off to a Good Start

interval between nursing sessions than usual and your body decides that it's time for your child to eat.

In some mothers the let-down sensation will come from thirty seconds to a minute after the baby begins sucking, depending upon how comfortable, relaxed, and undistracted they are. In others, full let-down comes a few minutes after the baby begins to suck. This time can vary from day to day, according to the environment and emotional factors. Sometimes just thinking of your baby or hearing any baby cry will cause a let-down.

My boys could get my let-down happening faster than my girls cared to, and the boys were usually finished eating and blissed-out in half the amount of time enjoyed by the girls.

In some women, the let-down reflex has to be described as awesome. I spoke to a woman whose husband had been a campaign manager for a man who went on to be elected governor in Tennessee. The birth of her second child came not long before the governor's reception, and she decided not to miss it. Dressed in a lovely burgundy knit dress with nursing bra and nursing pads for protection, she stood in the receiving line. An acquaintance, on greeting her, noticed her slimmer figure, asked about the baby and then asked if she was breastfeeding. Just then twin white fountains spurted from each breast and shot out four feet in front of her, just missing the woman she was talking to. "Yes," she said, proudly, and kept greeting people.

Because nursing a baby is so much like making love—in that subtle, tender communications in touch are being made back and forth by two people in love—some mothers find it easier to get their let-down reflex working if they are completely alone with their babies during nursing sessions for the first few weeks. It can be hard to relax fully in the presence of other people, especially if any of them are uncomfortable about seeing you or critical about anything you're doing. Worry about milk supply or any kind of emotional distraction will tend to obstruct the functioning of the let-down reflex.

Men can understand better how the let-down reflex works if they think of what it is like to try to relax to pee when there are a lot of people around or when someone is bothering them. My husband tells me that it is a common boyhood prank to startle someone who is peeing, enough to "cut off their water." The flow of milk from breasts works in somewhat the same way: feeling startled or embarrassed can stop the flow even once it has begun, and some conditions can make it impossible for the mother to relax sufficiently to allow the milk to start flowing. Pain from nipple soreness can inhibit the let-down.

Niles Newton carried out a study on herself while she was breastfeeding her own baby. She found that when her toes were pulled painfully, when her feet were put in ice water, and when she had to answer complicated mathematical problems with mistakes punished by electric shocks, her let-down did not function well, and her baby received much less milk than when she was not being hassled.[3]

How Often to Nurse

Let your baby nurse as much as she wants. Schedules were designed by people who did not know very much about babies, especially breastfed ones. Feed your baby if she cries or whenever she wants to eat. You may also decide it is time because of the full feeling in your breasts or even just because you want to.

The three- or four-hour schedule designed for babies born in hospitals was conceived with the cows' milk fed baby in mind. It takes about that long for a bottlefed baby to digest what's in his stomach. The breastfed baby will be hungry much sooner on the average, sometimes as often as every hour or two. If you nurse only every three or four hours, your milk may be slower to come in, and your baby is more apt to cry a lot. Try to nurse at least every two or three hours (three to four during the night) if you are in a hospital just after giving birth.

Sheila Kitzinger has a couple of unforgettable paragraphs in her book, *The Experience of Childbirth*, detailing the obsession her mother's generation had with schedules and the need for regularity in child raising in England in the 1930s.

> My mother aproached the subject of infant feeding from a background in nursing and midwifery and decided that it was more hygienic to bottlefeed and that she would follow what was then the latest system in baby care, the Truby-King method. So she had an all-white nursery decorated, the idea being that any speck of dust could be readily seen and that the baby would not be adversely stimulated by shapes, colours, or other distractions which could interfere with sleep. I was put into these surroundings resembling a scientific laboratory and my parents were confused and troubled when I yelled and yelled! The books said that I should only be picked up every four hours by the clock, and my poor mother waited in anguish, the nursery door firmly closed, until the clock told her that she could at last pick up her screaming baby. Apparently I cried so much that at last, in desperation, my exhausted parents decided to move me back into their bedroom, where life eventually became easier and where I suspect that mother

Getting Off to a Good Start

"cheated" and, because of close proximity and my ear-splitting utterance, was more inclined to follow her own feelings rather than the experts' advice.

A great many women who went through that experience on both sides of the Atlantic in those days believed that they were forging strong characters, assisting the baby's digestion, and that letting a baby cry with rage or hunger was "good for the lungs."

The fact is that you cannot nurse your baby too much. If your baby is full, he will simply refuse to nurse. The usual sign that the baby is full is that he goes to sleep. Full babies usually have blissful, relaxed expressions on their faces, and their hands will be relaxed instead of clenched into a fist. You will quickly learn how to read your baby's body language.

Some babies will fall asleep while nursing and then wake up after fifteen minutes crying for more. If your baby seems to have nursed herself to sleep at one breast, changing her position to the other will often wake her up to feed with a renewed appetite.

Try to make sure that your breasts take turns at being emptied. Stimulation of both breasts will help your milk supply and will tend to minimize nipple soreness in the first few days. Emptying both breasts also serves to prevent breast infection.

Some counselors recommend a system of switching a diaper pin from one side of your shirt to the other. It's a good idea not to always offer the same side first, as this is when the baby sucks the hardest and may make your milk supply uneven.

Weight Gain

Babies vary a good deal as to how fast they recover their birth weight. The baby who is fed whenever he wishes to eat will generally gain much faster than the baby who is held to some sort of schedule. A newborn should eat every three hours at least to gain well, although an occasional baby will choose to sleep longer than this during the night.

Some breastfed babies will recover their birth weight within a week, while others may take as many as three weeks. The latter group are fine if the baby is nursing as often as she wants to, if the weight is gradually increasing, and if the diaper is wet every three hours or so. If you want your baby to gain faster, don't add supplementary bottles of formula. Instead, increase your milk supply by nursing her more. If your baby is obviously not thriving on your milk, consult with the friendly pediatrician, preferably one who has nursed a child or has studied human lactation.

Changing Your Baby

One of your early questions is likely to be when you should change your baby's diapers: before or after nursing. The best decision will depend a lot on your baby. Some seem to wake up ravenously hungry, so much so that they cry and carry on until they are in nursing position. Others are not in such a hurry and seem to nurse better if they are in a clean, dry diaper. Many babies will need to be changed after they have drunk their fill, even if they were changed before beginning to nurse.

Burping

If you have trouble getting your baby to nurse, it may be because she needs to burp. A baby with an air bubble in her stomach will be much more comfortable and may even eat more if she can get off a hearty burp. Some breastfed babies hardly burp at all, while others may need to burp several times during a nursing period. Babies usually swallow a little air while eating, whether they are breastfed or bottlefed. Breastfed babies do seem to need burping less than bottlefed babies.

Some babies routinely spit up a little milk whenever they burp, while others never do. This kind of spitting up is nothing to worry about. If your baby does not burp easily, do not worry about it. Here is one routine that works for many mothers: burp the baby after she has finished with one breast. After burping her, you can change her diaper and feed her from the other breast until she falls asleep from being tired and full. Most babies can then be put down to sleep without a second burping.

There are several ways you can hold the baby so she can burp easily. You can sit her in your lap with one hand supporting her head. Or you can hold her next to your body with her head looking over your shoulder. Or you can lay her on her stomach in your lap. Keep a diaper handy in case some milk comes up along with the air. Don't pound on her back; this is uncomfortable as well as unnecessary.

Gently rub the baby's back, stroke her spine from waist to neck, or simply hold her upright. If no burp has come within three or four minutes, don't worry. Go on with your feeding, and when you lay the baby down, put her on her stomach or her side so that she can easily bring up any air that may still be in her stomach.

All Babies Are Different

There is a great range of behavior among babies, so try no to get too set in your ideas about what is normal. Some babies have voracious

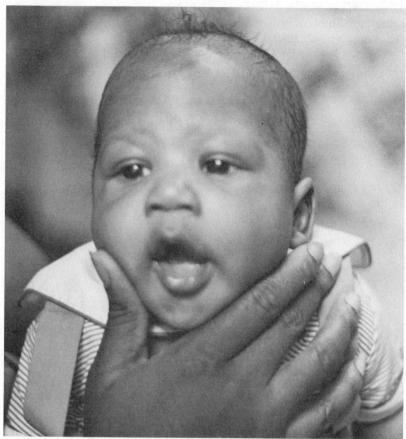
One way to burp: hold baby's chin and pat his back

appetites from the time they are born. I have seen several who nursed for two or three hours straight just after birth. I have also seen many, born by natural childbirth, who did not really become hungry until the fourth or fifth day of their lives.

REFERENCES
1. J. Morsbach and C. Bunting: "Maternal Recognition of their Neonates' Cries," (*Deve. Med. Child Neurol.* 21: 178–85, 1979).
2. J.A. MacFarlane, in *Parent-infant Interaction*, Ciba Foundation Symposium 33, (Amsterdam: Elsevier, 1975).
3. Michael and Niles Newton, "The Let-Down Reflex in Human Lactation," *Journal of Pediatrics*, 33, (1948): 698–704.

SUGGESTED SUPPLEMENTAL READING
Kitzinger, Shiela. *The Complete Book of Pregnancy and Childbirth*. New York: Knopf, 1980.
Odent, Michel, M.D. *Birth Reborn*. New York: Pantheon, 1984.

4

Problems in the First Week

♦

The time just after your baby's birth will be a time of learning for you, especially if this is your first baby. You will learn much about the nature of babies, and of mothers. You will likely begin to understand your own mother more fully than before.

If you have not lived around many babies, yours may seem a mysterious creature at times, and you may feel bewildered when your baby cries. Decisions about what to do are likely to seem momentous. You will probably find that contact with other mothers whose babies are about the same age as yours will help you feel more comfortable during times when your new responsibilities seem awesome.

If you have your baby in a birth center or hospital, you may feel very well on your return home after the birth. Even so, it is important to get plenty of rest and to keep a slow pace while you get used to taking full responsibility for an extremely helpless little person's life. It is your responsibility to spend at least a week, or longer, after childbirth taking care of your baby and resting. You may feel well enough to get up and start working, but if you can, it's good to take it easy anyway. If you have your baby at home or are discharged from a birth center a few hours after delivering, this advice is especially important. It is easy to overwork during this adjustment period.

Lots of new mothers are amazed by how often their babies want to eat and how often their diapers need changing. A newborn who wants to nurse every hour is completely normal. Fortunately for their parents, most babies don't keep up this frequency of feedings for very long.

Keep visitors to a minimum for the first few days after the baby is born. It is important for you to get to know your new baby without having to feel that you must entertain your friends and resume your social life right away. It takes energy to provide food for your baby, so you will need plenty of rest to keep up with your new job. During the first few weeks, yo will be wise to lie down for at least a catnap whenever you can. You can write birth announcements or thank you notes to relatives and friends later, after you have a good routine established.

Lack of Sleep

Waking up every two hours during the night can have a powerful effect on your consciousness. Most new mothers who experience this lack of sustained sleep will have at least a few moments of feeling discouraged and overwhelmed by the needs of the baby. For most babies, this period is mercifully short (although it probably won't seem so at the time), because the baby soon grows to a size where she can take more food at a time so she gets hungry less often and sleeps for longer intervals during the night.

The mother who does wake up five or six times a night will need to compensate for lost sleep by taking naps during the daylight hours. She may need encouragement from her mate, midwife or friends to do this, especially if she is the kind of person who finds it hard to sleep during the day. My fourth child was the first I had who liked to eat every two or three hours during the night. I learned to take naps by pulling a pillow over my eyes to shut out the daylight, and I found that even a very short nap could be very restoring.

To illustrate how seriously lack of sleep can interfere with good sense, I have to tell this story from my friend Carol Leonard. This incident took place when her firstborn son was less than two weeks old. She was bone-tired from feeding him so often. It was the middle of the night, and he woke her up with his crying as he lay right next to her in bed. Too tired to turn on the light, she sat up and picked him up to nurse. Instead of latching on, he cried louder and louder, causing her to burst into tears. Totally frustrated, she turned on the light and noticed that she had him upside down and was trying to nurse his butt instead of his head.

Engorgement

When your milk comes in, it usually does it in a big way. Two or three days after birth, the breasts become hot, swollen, and engorged. In many women the swelling extends well into the armpits. Not every woman will experience the extreme swelling which is common to so many. The treatment for engorgement is frequent nursing. Because engorgement can cause the nipples to flatten, it may be necessary to express a little milk to make it easier for your baby to latch on (see below). The period of extreme swelling has usually passed after a day or two.

Some people recommend the application of heat (hot water bottles, hot showers, etc.), but heat can sometimes aggravate the problem by increasing the amount of circulation in the breasts. Heat can be helpful in easing manual expression to soften up hard nipples.

A Welsh midwife offers the following treatment to ease engorged breasts: keep a large cabbage in the fridge. Peel off two leaves at a time, put them inside your bra and replace them when they are no longer cool. The leaves are cold without being wet and messy, and they curve nicely around the breasts.

HOW TO EASE ENGORGED BREASTS

1. Nurse often, every two or three hours. Nurse from both breasts at each feeding. Don't be afraid to wake your baby if you need relief.
2. Wear a good bra if it makes you more comfortable.
3. If your nipple and areola are hard, making it difficult for your baby to latch on, manually express milk until it is softer. Some women find their milk flows easier in a hot shower. Try wearing plastic breast shields for 15–30 minutes to soften your nipples before nursing if they don't stick out much.
4. Nurse your baby as long as possible at each breast.
5. Gently massage or squeeze your breast as the baby nurses to encourage the milk to flow.
6. Use cold packs (or cabbage leaves) to ease discomfort after nursing.
7. If you can't function without a pain reliever, see if your doctor will prescribe acetaminophen (Tylenol).
8. Don't express milk unless you need to soften your nipple and areola so that baby can get hold. You don't want to increase milk production.

HOW TO EXPRESS YOUR MILK

It's good to learn how to express your milk by hand. Follow these steps:

1. Put some warm towels on your breasts to increase blood circulation. This direct warmth should cover the breasts, not the nipples.
2. With clean hands, stimulate your nipples by rolling them gently between your fingers.
3. Using both hands, massage your breasts starting at the chest wall and stroking down towards the areola. You should be compressing your breast at the same time you are massaging. Rotate your hands so that you compress the milk glands at all points in your breast, moving the milk from the ducts to the reservoirs beneath your nipples.
4. Holding your areola between your thumb and first finger, squeeze rhythmically to empty the milk from the reservoirs under your nipple. For some women, this last step is all that is necessary.

Sore Nipples

Your nipples are most likely to be sore during the first days following birth. Usually the soreness is temporary, and your nipples become tougher from the baby's sucking. Even if the soreness seems minor, you should take precautions so they do not become more sore and eventually crack. If the soreness is felt only before your milk lets down, you need not worry. But if your nipples are sore both during and after nursing and if they look red and chapped, you should do something about them right away. If you wait until the pain becomes unbearable, you will have a much more complicated problem to solve.

In any case, sore nipples do not mean that you will have to give

up breastfeeding. You will need to take special care of your nipples for a while, after which you should be able to go on nursing with no special precautions. Occasionally there will be a little blood in the milk when there is bleeding from the nipple externally. It can be alarming to see your milk with streaks of blood or colored various shades of brown or orange, but this problem poses no risks to the baby if there is no infection.

First, you'll want to determine what is causing your problem.

BLISTERED NIPPLES

One of the more common problems encountered in early nursing is that of blistered nipples. The soreness, blistering or scabs are on the tip. The damage happens when the nipple enters the baby's mouth at an angle and rubs against the roof of her mouth. Take more care in getting your baby to latch on correctly so that the end of your nipple is no longer rubbed (see Chapter 5). Avoid nursing while leaning back, especially if your nipples naturally point upward.

Manually express a little milk to soften the areola before putting the baby on.

GUMMED NIPPLES

Sometimes the damage occurs at the place where the nipple joins the areola. This tenderness or cracking happens when the baby's jaws close on the nipple instead of the areola. Some babies habitually don't open their mouths wide enough or they gum the nipple when the breast is engorged.

HOW TO TREAT GUMMED NIPPLES:

1. Manually express or pump enough milk to soften the areola. Get as much areola in the baby's mouth as possible.
2. Take care in holding the baby correctly. The football hold is a good one. Make sure to get the baby to open his mouth wide before introducing nipple and areola, then pull the baby toward you quickly.
3. Take the baby off your breast if you don't have him on right. You may have to try several times to get it right. Ask for help from your mate, a friend, or a breastfeeding counselor.
4. Follow General Treatment for Sore Nipples on page 72.

SORENESS ON THE UNDERSIDE OF THE NIPPLES

Ideally, the baby nurses with her bottom lip turned out. Sometimes, though, a baby will suck with the bottom lip tucked in, causing friction on the underside of the nipple. This kind of soreness is easy to remedy; you just pull the baby's lip while she is nursing. Follow the suggestions in General Treatment of Sore Nipples on page 72.

THRUSH NIPPLES

Now and then a baby gets a yeast (monilia) infection in his mouth, which then spreads to the mother's nipples. Such an infection can cause tender, red, swollen, sometimes cracked nipples. There can also be a burning sensation.

Thrush infections usually happen after a mother has been nursing for weeks or months. Occasionally, though, a newborn can get thrush while being born, from contacting a yeast infection in the birth canal. Maternal yeast infections are frequent in mothers who have taken antibiotics or are diabetic.

It is easy to find out whether thrush is the problem. Look inside the baby's mouth to see if there are white, milky-looking patches on the tongue, cheeks, or gums. Sometimes babies won't show the mouth patches but will have a diaper rash caused by the yeast. This rash can make the skin look reddened or burned. Sometimes there are patches of red dots.

HOW TO TREAT THRUSH NIPPLES:

1. The most economical way to treat is to use 1 or 2 percent gentian violet solution on your nipples and inside the baby's mouth. Swab the solution on a couple of times a day with a cotton applicator. Both must be treated in order not to keep passing the infection back and forth. The only disadvantage of using this treatment is that gentian violet is very purple, so you'll have to be careful about not staining things you don't want to be purple. Gentian violet can be obtained without a prescription.
2. Another treatment is to use 1 milliliter of nystatin suspension (Mycostatin) by dropper into the baby's mouth four times a day for two weeks. Be sure that you treat each side of the baby's mouth with an equal amount of medicine. Apply ten to fifteen minutes after a feeding, so the medicine will stay in the baby's digestive system longer. Use the same medicine on your nipples, or use nystastin ointment. Treat yourself after each nursing. Nystatin is only available by prescription, and it must be stored in the refrigerator. Treat for the full two weeks. It's a good idea to rinse your nipples with a solution of one tablespoon of vinegar to one cup of water after you nurse, and before applying nystatin.
3. Keep your nipples dry. If you use breast pads, change them whenever they get damp.

4. A little exposure to sunlight each day will help dry and heal thrush nipples.
5. Boil for twenty minutes any rubber or plastic shields, nipples or pacifiers which come into contact with either your nipples or the baby's mouth. The same goes for breast pump parts if you are using one of these.

IRRITATED NIPPLES
There is a kind of nipple irritation which is really dermatitis, an allergy caused by some cream, lotion, or preparation applied to the nipples. Look out for products containing Vitamin E. Creams and lotions with lanolin bother some people, so take note if you have been using a cream on your nipples.

HOW TO TREAT IRRITATED NIPPLES
1. Try using a nonprescription hydrocortisone cream on your nipples after nursing. Do this about five times a day, making sure your nipples are dry first. Use sparingly and make sure that all the cream is absorbed by your nipple skin.
2. Use hydrocortisone cream this way for five days; then discontinue.
3. Follow the suggestions in General Treatment of Sore Nipples on page 72.

CRACKED NIPPLES
Sometimes nipple soreness will worsen until the nipple cracks and bleeds, making nursing too painful to continue. Don't force yourself to nurse if this happens. Take the baby off the affected nipple for 24–48 hours and nurse only from the unaffected nipple, supplementing with a bottle.

In the meantime, you need to manually express your milk every three hours for a couple of days. Use an electric pump if you can and pump your milk at least eight times a day, making sure that you carefully center the shield before beginning to pump.

After two days, gradually resume nursing, with five-minute feedings on the sore breast, beginning with two times a day. Continue expressing your milk at other feeding times until you are back up to a full nursing schedule.

One of the mothers I attended during birth describes the time she had cracked nipples:

> The only time I experienced cracked nipples was with my last child. For some reason, she had the strongest suck of my five babies. Within three days after herbirth, both nipples were cracked and

bleeding. It brought tears to my eyes to nurse her. I was wondering why, after all the other kids, I was getting cracked nipples. I used A & D Ointment, hot compresses, and aired my nipples. I also alternated bottles with nursing on the least sore nipple. By the end of that week, I was healed up and my nipples were tougher than ever. I want women to know that the difficulty isn't always with nursing the first baby.

General Treatment of Sore Nipples

1. Express a little bit of milk just before offering the baby your breast.
2. Take acetaminophen (Tylenol, for instance) half an hour before you think you'll be nursing.
3. Offer the least sore nipple first. Once your milk is flowing well, the baby won't need to suck as hard.
4. Keep your nipples dry as possible. If you use pads, change them often, and never wear anything with a plastic lining.
5. Expose your nipples to sunlight for a few minutes each day or, very carefully, to ultraviolet rays from a sunlamp. If you use a sunlamp, time yourself scrupulously and do not fall asleep. Sit four feet away and expose your breasts for thirty seconds the first two days, one minute the next two, two minutes the next two, and three minutes every day after that. If you sun your breasts, limit exposure to five minutes the first day, ten minutes the second, fifteen minutes the third, and so on, until you have reached half an hour daily.
6. Don't pick at scabs or blisters.
7. Avoid all irritating substances: soaps, alcohol, tincture of benzoin, or witch hazel.
8. Make sure your baby is latched on correctly. Support his weight well so he does not tug or pull at your nipple. You can also vary the baby's position at your breast by nursing part of the time lying down or by using the football hold. The idea is to keep the wear and tear from always being on the same spot on your nipple.
9. Hold ice on your nipple just before the baby latches on.
10. Leave your nipples exposed to the air as much as possible between feedings.
11. If you do need a bra, wear a cotton one for better air circulation.
12. Nurse more frequently and keep feedings relatively short.
13. Nipple shields may or not be a help. I have seen them work for some women, but be cautious in using them, for they can cause a decrease in milk production.
14. If you do use plastic nipple shields, boil them daily.

Problems with Inverted Nipples

If your nipples are flat or inverted, do not despair, because your baby can probably redesign them for you. Sucking on a flat or dimpled nipple will both draw out and lengthen it.

To do this, make sure that the baby gets plenty of areola in his mouth. It is especially important not to give your baby a bottle, as sucking from a bottle encourages the kind of laziness which makes it hard for him to continue working on your nipples.

A nipple shield used at a time like this can be helpful. A mother with flat nipples had a small baby with a comparatively small mouth. She was able to draw out her nipples by having the baby begin sucking with the nipple shield, removing it once her nipple was easier to grasp. After a couple of weeks she was able to leave it off entirely.

MORE SUGGESTIONS FOR FLAT OR INVERTED NIPPLES

1. Offer the baby your breast within two hours after birth for the best chance at success at latching on.
2. Keep rubber nipples away from your baby. There's no good reason to confuse him this early.
3. Experiment with ways to make your nipple stand out. Pinch your breast gently, with your fingers a couple of inches behind your areola. Cradling your baby's head in one hand and pinching your nipple out with the other should give you maximum control.

4. Squeeze a little milk out on your baby's tongue to whet her appetite. This way she'll tend to open her mouth wider.
5. If your baby is too excited to be smooth at latching on, calm him down and wait a moment or two before trying again. Your own abdominal muscles should be relaxed before you try again. Sigh if you have to.
6. When your breasts are engorged, wear breast shields in your bra—the kind that put pressure on the breasts so that your nipples pop out. These should be worn for half an hour or so before anticipated nursing.
7. Try putting ice on your nipple to make it stand out.
8. Express a little milk before giving the baby your breast.
9. Try lying on your side if you have a hard time while sitting. Your partner or midwife may be able to help you with this.
10. Give your baby a day to try nursing on her own before using a shield to help with latching on. If it helps, try using it for a few moments, then slipping it off quickly and going on with the feeding. Remember that your nipples will be better stimulated toward a good milk supply if there is direct contact between your skin and your baby's.
11. If your baby just doesn't latch on after a couple of days, it's time to give a bottle feeding of your expressed milk preferably or formula. Use one of the nipples with a bulbous end (NUK). You can use an electric breast pump or express your own milk. Keep offering your baby your breast. Remember how good your stuff is: your milk, your breast, your attention, your love.

Leaking

You can expect a certain amount of leaking, dripping, or even spraying during the first few weeks of nursing. I have known husbands who were surprised to wake up in a puddle of milk the first time. For some women, leaking goes on for several months, while for others, there are only a couple of weeks of real leaking.

If you leak a lot, you may want to spread a couple of bath towels over your sheets to protect them. The main thing is to keep as dry as possible, changing breast pads often if you use them. Avoid plastic liners so you don't have soggy nipples.

After a few weeks your breasts will learn how much milk you need, and when this happens you will probably quit leaking. However, a few women, especially those whose nipples are located on the lowest part of the breast, may leak throughout the nursing period.

Leaking from one breast while nursing from the other can continue as long as you nurse. Keep a diaper handy. Some women can stop

Problems in the First Week

the flow from the opposite breast by pressing the nipple towards the chest or by sightly twisting the nipple, as if turning off the faucet. It's best not to do this, though, in the first three weeks of nursing, as it could cause a blocked duct.

I remember from my breastfeeding days that milk dripping was invariably accompanied by feelings of love, gratitude, and generosity. I remember thinking that I truly understood the meaning of the expression "my cup runneth over."

How to Know If Your Milk Is Letting Down

Most likely if you are nursing your baby regularly and often, your let-down reflex is working well. The main signs of milk release are:

- Your baby's gulps.
- Uterine cramping while nursing.
- Tingling of the breasts while nursing.
- Dripping or spraying.
- Increased vaginal flow while nursing.
- Lots of wet diapers every day.
- Softer breasts after nursing.

If you experience none of the above signs, your let-down may need help.

HOW TO CAUSE LET-DOWN:

1. Nurse privately, regularly, and often.
2. Make yourself comfortable before putting the baby on the breast.
3. Try getting your let-down going in a warm shower once or twice a day.
4. Apply warm, moist towels to your breasts before nursing. Massage your breasts while you nurse to encourage milk flow.
5. Make sure that you have the baby latched on correctly.
6. Try the other breast if you don't hear swallowing after three or four minutes of sucking. Breathe deeply and slowly while your baby sucks.
7. If you don't hear swallowing after you have given several feedings, consult your physician. Oxytocin is available in a nasal spray by prescription, and this boost may be all you need to get started.

Messy House Blues

New mothers usually have to learn to simplify their lives. Women who have always prided themselves on their neat, organized houses find themselves placing a higher priority on sleep than on straightening up the house.

It is better to have a happy baby and a messy house than a perfectly arranged house and an uptight baby. Sometimes you have to make choices, and the first year of your child's life will present them. It's good to keep up a few parts of your routine that show a lot. Make your bed in the morning, even if you plan to take a later morning nap. You can do a very minimal, quick clean-up in a few minutes. Arrange things symmetrically if you don't have time to put them away. Avoid getting hung up on details.

It is possible that your house will get so messy that it will seem hopeless and begin to upset you. If so, try this: pick one corner of one room where you spend a lot of time. While your baby is taking a nap, give it a thorough cleaning. Remember that someday this child will be old enough to help you clean. Or, hire someone to clean for you.

It is not at all unusual to go through a first pregnancy with the idea that everything will somehow be normal again, that you will soon be back to your usual routine, whatever that is, able to do the things you like to do. Don't be surprised if you do not find this to be the case within the first few months after your baby's birth.

Make sure that you have stocked up on quick-to-prepare food and plenty of snacks. Your partner can be a great help by making sure that you eat regularly and get enough to drink. Pay attention to taking in enough protein, as this will help your milk production. Vegetarian mothers who do not eat dairy products or eggs will need to supplement vitamin B_{12}. Although it is a good idea not to eat so much that you gain extra weight while nursing, you should not diet during the nursing period. What usually happens is that the extra weight gained during pregnancy gradually melts off and turns into milk and baby, so there is a slow and steady process of losing weight while nursing. You need a little extra weight on you until you wean.

Problems With Your Baby

SLEEPY BABIES

New babies like to sleep a lot. Some will fall asleep soon after beginning to nurse. This sleepiness will be exaggerated in the baby whose mother had anesthesia during labor. Jaundiced babies will be sleepier than those without jaundice. Extremely sleepy babies should be wakened so that they will receive feedings as often as needed. Three hours is about the right interval between feedings, though four to five hours is all right during the night. If the baby is so sleepy that she falls to sleep at your breast, change her diaper as a way of rousing her.

JAUNDICE

Jaundice is the yellowness that comes to the skin, and sometimes the whites of the eyes, when there is a higher than normal amount of bilirubin in the bloodstream. Bilirubin is a by-product of the breakdown of old red blood cells as they are processed by the liver. After birth, the baby's liver suddenly has to kick in and do this work. Sometimes it takes a few days for the liver to catch up on its load of red blood cells to process. The type of jaundice that results from this situation affects about half of all babies. It is called physiological jaundice, and it appears three or four days after birth. Usually it is gone after a week. Most cases of physiological jaundice are mild and involve no danger to the baby. A little exposure to indirect sunlight and plenty of breastmilk to drink will clear up the problem.

It is the baby who is so lethargic that he doesn't want to nurse very much who needs to be watched. If your baby is like this, rouse him often to feed. Frequent and numerous feedings of colostrum and then milk will help the jaundice pass and will prevent dehydration. Check with a physician if there is yellowness, lethargy, and failure to nurse.

Bilirubin tests can be done if caregivers feel that bilirubin levels are high or climbing. Levels below 14 or 15 need no treatment beyond frequent breastfeeding.

Some physicians will prescribe treatment under a bilirubin light. Exposure to this light or to sunlight will burn off excess bilirubin. The baby's eyes have to be covered while he is under the light. If your baby receives this treatment, be sure to nurse him frequently.

Physiological jaundice also can be caused or aggravated by bruising of the baby at birth. Premature, sick or small babies are more susceptible.

Jaundice can also result from incompatability of the mother's blood with the babies, when the mother's blood type is O and the baby's blood type is A, B, or AB. This kind of jaundice appears on the first day or two after birth. Babies with blood incompatability jaundice sometimes need blood transfusions to reduce the bilirubin level.

A very small percentage of babies will develop something called breastmilk jaundice. This kind usually develops from the fourth to the seventh day of life and peaks during the second or third week. It may continue for eight to ten weeks.

You need not stop breastfeeding because your baby has breastmilk jaundice. As he gets older, the problem will disappear. If the baby's bilirubin level is quite high, it may be necessary to discontinue breastfeeding for a couple of days to hurry up the drop in the bilirubin level. Express your mik during this time to keep your supply up, and begin nursing again once the bilirubin has come to an acceptable level.

A friend, whose three babies all had this type of jaundice, learned that she could keep nursing and keep her physician satisfied if she gave the babies water as well as her breast milk. Her milk was so rich and her babies gained weight so fast that I felt quite safe about her diluting their food a little. Her comments:

> My first was a small but healthy baby when the midwife came to check on her eighth day of life. She was a sweet baby, hardly cried and slept a lot. She always seemed to have a smile on her face. The only problem was that she was bright orange.
>
> When her bilirubin level was checked, it was 26, and she was admitted to the hospital. They examined her for infection, found none, and let me continue to nurse for a while, until they began suspecting breastmilk jaundice. Then they advised me to discontinue nursing.
>
> I did not want to stop. After a week I was advised it would be all right, if I really wanted, to give her one feeding a day. I kept my milk in by pumping and by feeding friends' babies (who did not become jaundiced).
>
> After a month, I went on to nursing her on a regular schedule, and I discontinued all formula. She nursed until she was twelve months old.
>
> My second baby was born at five pounds, eleven ounces, one month early. To prevent breastmilk jaundice, I tried to supplement her with water and let her sit in the sun, but the day my milk came in, she started to turn yellow. She spent two days in the hospital under the bilirubin light. I continued nursing as soon as her bilirubin count was down. She got a lot of sun and a lot of water, and never got jaundiced again.

Quite often mothers are told to stop breastfeeding. For physiologic jaundice this is certainly not necessary. For breastmilk jaundice, you may want to discontinue for a day or two, but you should be able to resume breastfeeding after the level goes down. Except in the case of breastmilk jaundice, there should be no reason to give water supplements to your baby. If your baby is full of water, he won't be so motivated to drink breastmilk, which is what he really needs.

HOW TO TREAT JAUNDICE:

1. Continue breastfeeding during other treatment, such as phototherapy.

2. Nurse often.
3. Wake up your baby if she is too sleepy to eat at three-hour intervals. A cool wash cloth touched to her forehead may rouse her if nothing else does.
4. If you can't be with your baby fulltime, express your milk into a bottle and leave it with the nurses to give your baby.
5. If you must stop nursing temporarily, keep pumping your breasts so you can keep up your milk supply.

PROBLEMS LATCHING ON
Sometimes babies who have been given some feedings by bottle during the first week become confused about how to nurse from the breast. They push their tongues forward while trying to suck, which pushes the nipple out of their mouth. Sometimes the baby learns or relearns quickly how to nurse, and other times, teaching your baby takes some patience. You may find that lying on your side makes the process easier.

A very few babies are unable to latch on because they are tongue-tied. The membranelike tissue under the tongue is either short or attached close to the tip of the tongue. This membrane or frenum can be easily clipped in your doctor's office.

Occasionally a baby gets confused about what he is supposed to suck and sucks his tongue more than the nipple. These babies often make clicking or smacking sounds while they nurse. Make sure that you get the baby to open his mouth wide before you introduce the nipple. Hold the baby close against you, and touch the baby's lower lip.

Even a baby who has needed to be bottlefed may later be able to latch on to her mother's nipple. It is not a waste of time to keep trying.

AWAKE ALL NIGHT
Some babies get into a schedule where they seem to sleep most of the day and be awake most of the night. Fortunately, most babies get swung around to a schedule more compatible with their parents' after some time passes.

HOW TO DEAL WITH THE NIGHT WAKER
1. Nurse your baby as often as possible during the day, waking her if necessary to get in feedings at two-to-three-hour intervals.
2. Be sure your baby is well burped before you put him down to sleep.

3. Your baby may sleep more soundly if he is in contact with your body. Some babies don't relax to sleep well the first week or two unless they are very close to their mothers.
4. Some babies sleep better if they are snugly wrapped.

WEIGHT LOSS

Most mothers wonder if their babies are getting enough to eat. Babies who want to eat all the time can easily give their mothers the impression that the previous meal wasn't satisfying. I have known mothers who were convinced that their milk was drying up during the first week when their milk production was abundant, but their breasts were a little softer than when their milk had just come in.

Don't be surprised if your baby wants to nurse as many as twelve times in a day. Here are the indications that your baby is getting eough to eat:

- There are at least eight nursing sessions in a day.
- You can hear the gulping sounds of the baby.
- Your baby gives you eight wet diapers a day by the fifth day.
- Your breasts are softer after nursing than before.
- You are no longer seeing the dark-colored, tarry meconium in the baby's diapers by the fourth day and instead there are several poopy diapers a day or one or two with yellow poop.

EXCESSIVE WEIGHT LOSS

Usually the problems I have mentioned above can be overcome. Occasionally, though, all the techniques you try won't be enough. To keep the baby from losing too much weight, it becomes necessary to switch to formula feeding. If this happens, you may feel mixed emotions: relief that your baby will begin gaining weight and disappointment that breastfeeding didn't work out. It's wise to focus on the positive aspects of the change and to enjoy cuddling with your baby while you feed her.

SUGGESTED SUPPLEMENTAL READING

Huggins, Kathleen. *The Nursing Mother's Companion*. Boston: The Harvard Common Press, 1986.

Jones, Sandy. *Crying Babies, Sleepless Night*. New York: Warner, 1983.

Kitzinger, Sheila. *The Expierence of Childbirth*. Middlesex, England and New York: Penguin, 1962.

Presser, Janice, Gail Brewer, and Julianna FreeHand. *Breastfeeding*. New York: Knopf, 1983.

5

Special Situations

♦

*P*ossibly you are one of those mothers who in deciding whether or not to breastfeed has to consider other factors than those which automatically present themselves to all mothers. This chapter is meant to answer some of the questions of this nature which may come up.

Premature Babies

Giving birth prematurely is an overwhelming experience. Suddenly you find yourself facing a whole series of decisions you weren't expecting to have to make so soon.

You should know how valuable your colostrum and milk can be for your little baby. All babies receive protection against infection and many diseases through the antibodies contained in colostrum and milk. Because a premature baby is even more at risk in becoming ill than the full-term baby, it is especially important that premies receive all the protection they can get.

Premature babies who weigh less than two or three pounds are usually too weak to be able to suck well. Often they are born young enough that the sucking reflex is not fully developed. If this is the case, the baby will usually need to be fed by a tube. A long, fine tube will be passed through the baby's nose, down into the stomach and left in place. These babies can and should be fed their mothers' expressed colostrum and milk just after delivery.

Expressing milk for your premature baby

Let the nursing staff know of your intention to give your colostrum and milk to your baby. Most hospitals will have a breast pump that you can use to collect your milk. Hand pumps can be hard to use, so try for an electric pump if you can.

If your baby must be transferred to a different hospital for intensive care, find out how your milk can be collected and transported also.

Remember that the best way to build up a good milk supply is to empty your breasts as often as a full term baby would. This means that you should pump or express your milk at the minimum eight times a day. You can do this at even three-hour intervals or more often during the daylight hours so that you can get a longer segment of unbroken sleep at night.

Before your milk comes in, you will probably get only a few drops of colostrum from each breast. Once your milk is in, you can pump from each breast about five minutes and then do each breast again for a few minutes as an added stimulus.

When your milk is in, pump from each breast as long as you get some milk. Gently massage your breast from chest wall outward to your areola to help the milk let down. Return to each breast for a few minutes.

Make sure that your hands and all the equipment and parts that you use in collecting and storing milk are clean. Hot soapy water is adequate for your hands, while pump parts that come in contact with your milk or breasts will need sterilization once a day besides cleaning in hot, soapy water after each use. Your breasts will be sufficiently cleansed by your daily bath or shower.

Once you collect your milk in a sterile container, you should check with the nursing staff about the amount to put in a container. If you have plenty of milk and time to spare, this will be no worry, since you may not mind any of your milk being thrown away. But since your milk, once thawed and warmed, must be used or thrown away, you need to know how much your baby can take at a time.

Freshly expressed or refrigerated milk is really preferable to frozen, if this can be managed. Milk can be kept for up to two days in the refrigerator and up to two weeks in a really cold freezer. Milk that is being transported to refrigerator or freezer needs to be carefully packed on ice during transport.

Don't be surprised if you start out with a lot of milk and end up with less. When your baby gets old and strong enough to suck, this stimulation will increase the amount of milk you produce. Meanwhile you can use pumps, or perhaps your partner will help in keeping your milk going.

In the early years of my practice, there were a few premature babies requiring hospitalization, and the fathers of these babies were a significant factor in keeping up a good milk supply. Our local hospital did not have a good electric breast pump, so a spirit of inventiveness, practicality and a sense of humor had to come into play. Here is one mother's story of her experience:

> Moses was born in the hospital four weeks prematurely and stayed there for a week after his birth. I could only visit him a couple of times a day, and because he was jaundiced, I wasn't allowed to nurse him. I wondered if I could do anything to bring on my milk. I had heard about babies who started on the bottle and were hard to switch to the breast because they could get the milk more easily from a bottle. I figured if I could get a good flow happening, there would be a better chance he'd enjoy changing from bottle feeding to breastfeeding.
>
> The thought of a pump didn't appeal to me much, so I asked my husband if he liked milk. He did. We were faithful to the cause, waking up every three hours to nurse. He was so sweet about it. Sometimes I thought he looked kind of blue around the gills, but he always insisted he liked doing it.
>
> The day came when I could nurse Moses. I never knew exactly what time I would get to see him, so David and I had a plan. When the nurse told me I could visit the baby, I said, "Excuse me, I have to go to the bathroom first." I met David in the bathroom, and he sucked long enough to get the milk going. Then I went in to see Moses. It was great. I remember how Moses watched me as I gave him my breast for the first time. He was obviously delighted that something juicier than the bottle was coming his way, and he sucked for a long time perfectly content. I never could get him to drink from a bottle after that.

If you have to express milk for a long period of time, waiting for your baby to be strong enough to nurse, you need to take good care of yourself. Eat well and regularly, get enough sleep, and drink a lot of fluids. Be ready to feel weepy and emotional at times, or at least to understand that you are not failing at anything if you sometimes feel like crying over your situation.

Keep up the frequency of pumping, even if that means that you must rent a breast pump. Sometimes a local La Leche League or breastfeeding counselor will have one available.

Your efforts to keep up milk production will be greatly helped if there is someone letting you know that keeping your milk going is worth the time and trouble it takes, as well as giving you affirmation that your milk is yummy, that you are attractive, and all those other things that are so nice to know when you have little opportunity to get affirmed by your baby. If you know that you are delicious to someone (your partner or a friend's baby, for instance), you will probably find it easier to believe in your attractiveness to your baby. Having this sort of confidence gives you an advantage in terms of milk production and in getting your baby to latch on to your nipple for the first time after having become used to rubber nipples.

Here is the story of one mother who breastfed her premature baby successfully because she was given the proper support and encouragement. She wrote her story about one year after her child's birth.

As I look as my son today, I find it hard to believe he was ever premature. He is strong and healthy, and is a clever and busy little being whose energy level should be bottled and shared with everybody. His eyes shine just as they did when he was born. Back then he was a little mouse of a person. Today he is healthy because of breastmilk and all the work we did as a team to keep my breastmilk flowing.

I was a forty-one-year-old single mother, who was determined to have a natural birth. I have another son who was born twenty years ago in a hospital and bottlefed, like most babies born then. However, this new baby was going to be "all natural." Well, it turned out to be a most unnatural birth instead.

I arrived two months early at The Farm, wanting to give myself time to settle in and prepare. I arrived on a Sunday morning after driving all night from Washington, D.C. On Tuesday I was examined by the midwives. There seemed to be no apparent problems or infections. However, I had been a regular smoker and after just having stopped smoking, I developed a severe cough. My stomach muscles became sore from the coughing. By the end of my first week at The Farm, I was kept awake by the pain. I checked in with a midwife, who advised absolute bed rest. By the next night the pain started again. I noticed it was coming in waves, but I still did not suspect birth pangs. I was convinced I was only having stomach cramps. Finally I knew I was in trouble when I had to throw up and shit at the same time during the night. I called one of the midwives. Within minutes a doctor, midwives, and ambulance squad were checking me out. Before I knew it, I was stretched out

Special Situations

in the ambulance holding on to Ina May. I was taken to the emergency room of a Nashville hospital and quickly strapped to a machine which could register the fetal heartbeat. . . . the baby was doing fine. Doctors tried to stop the contractions with injections of ritodrine, but that only made me clench my jaw and made my heart beat faster. That evening I was told I needed a cesarean because the baby was in breech position. They could not stop the contractions, and I had not dilated enough.

It is said that "Ignorance" is the best protection against the harsh realities of life. I was ignorant enough that I never worried for a minute. All I knew about premature babies was that they were a lot smaller. What I didn't know was that prematurity meant undeveloped organs that are still unable to breathe, digest, and filter waste on their own. I did not know this as I was wheeled into the operating room. I just asked to be kept awake long enough to see the baby.

I got to see his tiny little round face crying loudly. He weighed 1440 grams (3 lbs. 3 oz.). I was finally put to sleep, and when I woke up four hours later, Ina May was in the bed next to me in the recovery room, asleep. I was reassured. I did not get to see Michael again for twelve hours. When I finally did, all I saw was pure love. So tiny and frail, he seemed able to make eye contact. Once you see this love and intelligence streaming from a baby's eyes, you are hooked forever. This is Life looking at you.

Michael was not in an incubator. Instead he was on an elevated open platform with very bright lights overhead. He was completely naked, except for eye patches to protect his eyes from the bilirubin lights he was under because of jaundice. He was also getting oxygen from a cap that was like a canopy over his head. He was pretty much breathing on his own. He looked so small and helpless all wired up to heart monitors as well as heat monitors. He had wires attached to his arms, belly, back, and legs. He also had an intravenous needle in his arm, feeding him a sodium and potassium solution. From this time on, he was in Hell. Fortunately he did not get hyaline membrane disease.

For Michael, the following seven weeks meant continuous intravenous feedings, punctures in the heels every two hours, the drawing of blood from his inner thighs (necessitating blood transfusions because so much of his own was taken), X rays, and sonograms.

From my very first day at the hospital, I had been encouraged by Ina May to keep my milk flowing even though the baby could not use it. The La Leche League had a representative at the hospital, and she brought me an electric pump which I could use any time

I wanted. The milk would be frozen and stored for later use by Michael. I was very proud of my first few days' pumping. I was filling up three little 40cc bottles every two hours. I was also encouraged by my growing support group to make sure I was eating and resting properly.

However, I really had to work hard to keep my milk flowing, and I was not doing all the right things: I would not drink enough water, I was not pumping regularly, I didn't pump at night. When my milk supply began to dwindle, the Farm midwives sent me a nursing baby to remind my body of what it was supposed to be doing.

By the time Michael was four weeks old, I had become quite a fixture in the neonatal intensive care unit. I was amazed that there were no other parents around. Only two or three mothers spent more than two hours a day with their babies. The care of these infants was turned over completely to the hospital staff, as if there was nothing a mother or father could do. I was lucky, however, in that the hospital staff knew about the important work the midwives were doing, and they allowed me to stay by Michael's side as long as I wanted. I only had to leave when the doctors were doing their rounds and when the nurses' shift was over.

I was not always dealt with kindly by the nurses, however, since they were not used to having a "concerned mother" asking questions about everything. I always asked why certain shots had to be administered, or were all those X rays necessary, and whether his blanket or diaper had been changed, etc. They were not always sympathetic. I remember one young nurse in particular, who coldly cut me off from holding the baby. When she came on duty, I asked her if I could hold Michael (I was allowed a few minutes each shift). She took his temperature to make sure his body temperature was okay, but she told me his temperature was "borderline" . . . not too high, not too low, but that I best leave him alone. So I sat and waited for another two hours until she had to check him again. I sat stroking his head through a little door on the incubator. She came back and said the same thing , "Borderline." I could not believe my ears. She was not going to allow me to hold my own child before I went home for the night. I started to cry. When she saw how upset I was, she offered to wrap him up in "three blankets" and let me hold him. It was too late. I didn't want to hold him while I was so upset. I went home angry and still crying. I was more upset at her lack of understanding about my needs. Didn't she know how important it was for a mother to hold her baby even if it was just for a minute? I had been by his side all day

Special Situations

(which the medical chart showed), and had not been allowed to hold him. My emotions were on a short fuse, and so her slightest rejection set me off.

The next morning I was confronted by the head pediatrician, a nurse, and a social worker. They thought I was upset because I needed to talk to someone. Could they help? Did I want to talk to someone? What they didn't know was that I had a daily support person who was there just so that I could have someone to talk to. The hospital staff thought I was all alone and so had no outlet for my feelings. They were assuming incorrectly about my emotional well-being. This was my chance to discuss my observations as someone who was at the hospital everyday, so I told them why I thought there was so much tension with me around. First, I told them, I had to deal with over twenty nurses who were assigned to Michael, but were never with him long enough to get close to him or me. Then I pointed out the several times Michael's condition had been diagnosed incorrectly to me, so that I was never sure of his condition from shift to shift. I was once told by an intern that Michael was having "congenital heart failure," which kept me fearing the worst for an entire weekend, until I could get back and check with a different doctor. This doctor told me that the intern had used incorrect terminology, and that it did not mean his heart was going to "give out any minute." I finished what I had to say by telling the doctor to put a note on the medical chart which read that "this mother is difficult and should be handled with kid gloves," and that I was going to continue to be there every day and continue to ask questions when they needed to be asked. He laughed and said that I was not that bad and that now he could see why I was so upset. He suggested to the head that she assign three primary nurses to Michael. They would get to know me, as well as the baby. He also suggested that I consult only with him about Michael's condition. He agreed that the nurses would have to learn to become sensitive toward a mother's needs. He knew that most nurses never had to deal with a mother who was at the hospital every day. He encouraged me to speak up about anything that was on my mind and not to be afraid of making any suggestions about Michael's care.

Michael had a heart problem that affected his ability to tolerate feedings. For a while, it seemed that he would need surgery to close his heart valve, but this was cancelled at the last minute. They were going to give him one more chance to tolerate his feedings by bypassing his stomach and inserting a feeding tube directly into the upper intestine. This seemed to do the trick. With his little feeding tube attached to his upper lip by tape, he began to tolerate his feedings. He began to gain weight daily, a few grams per day at a time. Each day the amount of breast milk was being increased until the "dreaded" IV was no longer necessary. They had begun with 1 cc of my milk every four hours, and within a week, he went to 30cc every two hours. I could not keep up with what he needed. I was lucky if I could give him one small feeding a day. The doctors began using bottle formula as a matter of course, and had switched to my milk later. When Michael was finally up to 40cc every two hours and maintaining his weight, it was time to start thinking about going home. One day, I was encouraged to take him into a private room and nurse him. I was ecstatic. At last, I could hold him to nourish him.

I floated out of the nursery with him wrapped snugly in my arms. It was important to be alone for my first try at breastfeeding. I was nervous, and I wondered if he could nurse. I fumbled for a few minutes until I could put the nipple to his mouth. He snapped like a fish. He just knew what to do. He had never forgotten to suck, even after spending all those weeks in such an unnatural environment with nothing warmer than the bright lights to warm him and a rubber nipple to suck on. He was a survivor. He was now at peace in the world.

After ten minutes (which was all the time I was allowed), I went back to the nursery and gave a glowing report on his success. I reported that he had latched on like a "pro." It was duly noted on his medical chart.

The next day I was told I could take him home! I was floored. I could have taken him home right that minute. I had waited to take him home for what seemed an interminable time. It had been over fifty days, and at last, I could walk out of the door with him. I now needed to make preparations at home, but how was I ever going to feed him when my own milk supply had almost run dry? Not to worry, the "helpful" hospital staff quickly loaded me up with all the free formula I needed to take home. I was given dozens of bottles of formula with iron, each one containing about one feeding. I left the hospital quite secure about having plenty of formula. We were going home at last! In Nashville, I had been staying with a family who had grown quite attached to Michael, and so it was a happy homecoming for us.

I did not sleep the first night home because I kept waking to see that he was still breathing. By the second night I was sleeping a lot better between the every two hour feedings. I was a lot more relaxed. But now I was wrestling with the added work of washing, sterilizing and preparing dozens of bottles—not to mention the expense of buying more and driving to the store to buy it.

I arrived at The Farm one week later, and by that time I was giving Michael all formula feedings with maybe one breastfeeding per day. When Ina May came to visit us, she saw all my little bottles, and she just scooped them up and took them away. I protested that I could not possibly give Michael all he needed. She just smiled and said, "The more you feed him, the more milk you will have." I thought he would starve.

At first he was nursing all the time, so I began to limit him to five minute feedings, so that he would not tire himself out on an empty breast and thus waste calories. At night I would sneak some formula with us to bed, still convinced he was not getting enough breastmilk. But then I began to notice that when I gave him formula, he would wake up with mucus sounds in his chest. I gradually stopped giving him any formula at all. I also enjoyed not having to prepare those bottles.

When Michael was three months old, he came down with a virus. He developed a bad cough, with diarrhea and a high fever. I grew worried when his fever went up after the third day. The doctor gave him an electrolyte fluid and cough syrup, and this helped him a lot. His flu had lasted exactly five days. Although he suffered the full effect of the flu symptoms, his own immunological processes were able to handle it. I was convinced that this was a result of my breastmilk. It is known that mother's milk provides a child with protection against infection. The clinician was amazed at his quick recovery. This bout with the flu showed me that his body was producing its own antibodies. I was glad to know that he was healthy enough to resist infections, and although he had been born premature, I did not have to worry about having a sickly child. I knew he was strong.

Michael and I were one of the few lucky ones. Lucky to have people around to encourage and support me in my desire to breastfeed my baby. It took a lot of patience and perserverance to keep my milk going, and there were many times when I thought it would be easier to quit, but I had people around me who understood the importance of mother's milk. I was reminded to drink plenty of water, eat properly and get plenty of rest. I would not have trusted my own body to produce what was needed for the baby to grow, but I was reminded of the healing value of mother's milk. I could not have done it without such help. I know that the work we have done will ultimately affect the rest of Michael's life, as well as mine, and will shape his very personality. He was worth all the effort. Thank you!

THE FIRST FEEDING

Naturally it will be easier to give a first feeding if your baby is wide awake and alert. It is a good idea to have the room warm enough so that you can take blankets and clothes off the baby so you have skin-to-skin contact. Keep track of the temperature of your baby's feet and hands to see if she is maintaining her body temperature well.

Some babies will latch on well from the cuddled-to-your-chest hold, but many will do better if you use the underarm hold, cradling the baby's head in one of your hands. This position is good for small, possibly reluctant nursers, since you have good visibility and mobility. Holding your baby just in front of your nipple, with your thumb above and your fingers below your breast, lightly stroke your nipple over your baby's lips. Once she opens her mouth wide, pull her head towards your nipple so that your nipple rests on her tongue.

If you can cause this much to happen, you should be able to get her nursing with time and patience. Once your baby latches on, you'll know that he is getting milk when you hear him swallowing. If you hear swallowing with no clicking or smacking sounds, you can be pretty sure that he is well latched on.

You can dispense with supplemental bottle feedings when your baby is strong enough to nurse for ten to fifteen minutes at a time and does so every two to three hours. You should be getting at least six wet diapers a day for full breastfeeding.

Twins

The idea of feeding two babies instead of one may seem overwhelming at first, but the important thing to remember is that your body is perfectly equipped to do it. I know a woman who successfully breastfed her triplets for a year. Breastfeeding twins is actually easier than preparing sixteen bottles of formula every day. The stimulation provided by the sucking of two babies will produce two babies' supply of milk in a well-nourished mother. You may need a little more rest, and you will certainly require more food than if you were feeding only one, so don't think it strange if you find yourself eating four or five full meals a day. Make sure that you have plenty of snacks around the house, and never turn down an offer of help. Try to make contact with mothers who have breastfed twins. Your local breastfeeding counselor may be able to put you in contact with one or more.

You may feed twins simultaneously or separately. If you are able

Special Situations

to feed them together, you'll probably find that you have more time to eat and rest. You may need some help at first in getting them positioned right. If you find it too difficult to feed them simultaneously when they are very young, you may find it easier when they are old enough to hold their heads up.

If you want to feed the twins together, try using pillows to get them in a good position. You may put these under your elbows to support the babies. Get everything you need before you sit down: a container of liquid within easy reach, a protein-rich snack if you are able to eat while they are nursing, and a few diapers to mop up drips. Use one pillow under each elbow to support the babies' backs and one more for your lap. Lay one baby aside while you get the other in nursing position. If you need your hands to be free, you can elevate the pillow in your lap so the babies are held in the right position. Prop the babies up so they will not drag on your nipples and make them sore. Each baby can then be burped by turning her over onto her belly on the lap pillow, or you can gently lift one up and put her over your shoulder to burp while the other goes on nursing.

Even if you usually feed the twins simultaneously, you may want to feed them separately at times in order to relate with each one individually. If you do this, wake the other to eat right afterwards so you can keep their feeding and sleeping times together.

There are three basic positions which work for twins:

1. Babies criss-crossed on your lap.
2. One baby in the traditional cuddle hold and the other in the underarm hold.
3. Both babies in the underarm hold.

Some mothers like to reserve one breast for each baby so each regulates his own milk supply. This is entirely up to you and the babies. If you do find that your milk supply in one breast is down, you can put the stronger sucking twin on that breast to boost its milk production.

A mother of twin boys writes:

> In my experience, all the positioning with pillows proved to be too much hassle, and I soon started nursing them separately. I enjoyed this because it gave me a chance to spend time with each one as an individual and get to know their differences.

Another woman remarks about breastfeeding twins:

> The position I actually used the most was to place the twins so that one was facing with her legs and bottom behind me. The other

twin was positioned in the usual nursing position. They were both held up with pillows. This position leaves a free hand for drinking and burping.

Drinking lots of liquids is very important. I soon learned to sleep when the babies were sleeping. Plenty of rest is important to avoid breast infections. It's definitely good to feed both of them at the same time as much as possible, especially at night. This allows you some sleep, too. My husband also got up sometimes in the night and fed one a bottle of juice while I took care of the other one. Once they get older it's easier to feed one at a time.

PREMATURE TWINS AND PARTNER MOTHERS

RACHEL: Our twins were born ten weeks early and weighed three pounds, five ounces each. They had to stay in the hospital four and five weeks. Stella didn't have any major problems, but Althea had respiratory distress syndrome and then pneumonia and needed to be on a respirator for almost a week. They were both in a special care nursery—Althea in the intensive care for a while. My husband and I were lucky to have the use of a house near the hospital to live in while they were there, and we spent a lot of time every day with them in the hospital. It was a time of very intense feeling and learning for us, with our babies small and precariously alive, and seeing all the other tiny beautiful babies struggling to make it.

I was sure I wanted to breastfeed my babies, and as soon as my milk came in, I started expressing it with a breast pump and bringing it to the hospital. We were lucky that the doctors and nurses were very supportive and encouraging about using breast milk, although I was one of very few mothers who did it. They gave me bottles of sterile water which I emptied at home and refilled with my milk. I pumped regularly at least nine times a day, including once in the middle of the night. It took a long time to do and was not very comfortable. I was always sterilizing and using the pumps so much that they wore out soon and I had to keep getting new ones (the nonelectric kind). But it was well worth it to keep bringing in enough milk to feed two babies!

At first the babies were too small to be able to suck at all. The nurses fed them my milk through a tube directly into their stomachs. As they got stronger, they could drink it from a bottle, and then they let me try nursing them, at first, once a day. There were ups and downs. They had to be coaxed a lot to get them to suck from a bottle or a breast. We watched how the nurses did it; some of them were very good at bottlefeeding.

Daniel or I would feed them their bottles when we were there. Sucking was such effort for these small babies that they could use up all their calories doing it, so if they stopped gaining weight, they would be put back to some tube feeding or no nursing, with breast milk along with an additive for extra calories. They gained weight steadily although slower than some of the formula-fed babies, but the doctors still preferred the breast milk, because it is the natural food for babies and because of the immunities it gives. At one point a young resident was explaining to me how one of the twins had jaundice again or still (they both had it off and on), and he was going to switch her to formula for a while because breast milk could be a cause of it. He went on to say how he was doing this even though it was better in general to use breast milk. As I listened quietly, he talked himself out of it and erased the order!

When we took the twins home from the hospital, they were still well under five pounds and were pretty much bottle babies, used to getting breastfed only once or twice a day. After we had both of them home, I stopped pumping out my milk and started nursing them a lot. They still got some bottles, but they quickly got to like breastfeeding best.

Friends were coming in to help me day and night (some nursing mothers at night so I could get some sleep), but I was still pretty worn out from taking care of the two babies. Then the midwives called and told me about Mary. She had just had her baby, and he'd died while being born. They said that she could help me nurse the twins, and that having the twins to relate with would help her through the heartbreak of losing her baby. It sounded like a good idea to us, and Daniel helped her move into our spare bedroom.

MARY: I was five months pregnant, single, with nowhere else to go. Some friends of Daniel and Rachel's took me in out of the kindness of their hearts. I went into labor five days before my due date and, to my surprise, my water bag broke and the umbilical cord prolapsed just after the contractions began. We lost the baby on the way to the hospital in the ambulance. I had a C-section for the remote chance that he would still be alive.

Ina May, my midwife, was with me the whole way. We felt very close and even figured out that we were distant cousins. She was the first person I saw on opening my eyes in recovery. In the hallway while she was wheeling me to my room, she asked me if I wanted to help nurse Rachel's twins. I said yes. No hesitation. I mostly wanted to be a mother.

The next day I moved to Rachel and Daniel's house. I was handed a hungry baby right away. I remember it being awkward at first because I didn't really know these people nor did I know how to nurse a baby. I learned fast. The girls were always ready to eat. By the time I got them, they were two months old and around six pounds. At first my nipples got very sore, so I used a nipple shield. But the twins didn't like it, and I soon toughened up anyway. The twins would nurse for hours, regardless of my milk supply. I could nurse them both lying on my back, propping them up with pillows. I loved nursing. It is so satisfying and it feels good.

RACHEL: It became apparent that the only way for us to do it together was as a full partnership. We both shared both twins. At night, one baby would sleep in each of our rooms, alternating which baby each night.

MARY: The twins grew fast. Their bony butts filled out, and they were actually fat by five months old. My love for the family grew, too. They gave me the babies I needed, and I gave them the help they needed. Rachel and I naturally had different styles, but we respected each other and kept each other from being too hard or too sentimental, or any of the other various pitfalls of your first mothering experience. I went through changes at first suddenly having a man in my life, but Daniel was very kind and understanding to me and took care of me like a family member.

The twins did not seem to care that one mother was biological and one was not. When they started to talk, we were both "momma." People remarked on how much the twins looked like me, which is understandable, since they spent many hours staring at my face.

The twins are now nine. They are very sweet and kind girls. I think they picked up both Rachel's and my good characteristics. They still call me Mom. They are my daughters. I am very grateful that such an intimate and compassionate arrangement could happen and everyone be the better for it.

Birth Defects

Medical professionals, unfortunately, have not usually been trained to think of breastfeeding as a benefit for babies who are born with congenital anomalies, such as heart defects or cleft lips or palates. Actually these babies may especially need the advantages enjoyed by the breastfed baby.

Depending upon the extent of the problem, it may be possible to begin breastfeeding immediately or you may need to express your milk for a while.

CLEFT LIP OR PALATE
A baby born with a cleft lip should be able to breastfeed. Nursing might be a little difficult if he has trouble making a seal around the nipple and areola. Usually the breast will expand into the crack of his lip to form a seal. If this doesn't happen, you may be able to make the seal by placing your finger or thumb over the cleft. Surgery to repair the cleft lip may be done during the first few days, or at three months.

The baby with a cleft palate will sometimes be able to breastfeed without special measures, depending upon the size and position of the cleft. Sometimes a plastic plate to cover the palate to facilitate nursing until the baby is old enough for surgery. Ask your physician about this. Other babies can be held by their mothers in such a way that they can make a good seal around the nipple. The underarm hold is usually recommended because of the baby will be more vertical, thus making it less likely for milk to spill out of the baby's nose. The mother may need to squeeze her nipple between two fingers to make it possible to get it farther back into the baby's mouth.

Since a baby with a cleft palate tends to get more ear infections than other babies, breastfeeding is good for her. The antibodies in mother's milk help to protect her. Feeding the baby in an upright position will tend to reduce chances of her developing an ear infection.

If breastfeeding just doesn't work out before surgery is done, you can express or pump milk to keep your supply going. Feed the baby with a spoon in the meantime, and go to breastfeeding after surgery.

OTHER PROBLEMS
Babies with cerebral palsy, Down's syndrome, hydrocephalus, or spina bifida will benefit by drinking breast milk. Most of these babies will be able to breastfeed, depending upon the time and patience of their mothers, as well as the support they are given.

Down's syndrome babies tend to be sleepy and laid back about sucking, so their mothers may need to waken and stimulate them to get them sucking. These babies may be helped if a nursing supplementation device is used while at the breast (see Appendix A).

Hydrocephalus and *spina bifida* require surgery soon after birth, so their mothers will need to begin expressing milk right away. After the surgery, there are usually no special problems other than the need to take care in positioning the babies so they are comfortable.

Babies with mild forms of *cerebral palsy* can nurse if they have a strong enough suck and if their tongues and throats are well-coordinated. If your baby can suck but seems to be gaining weight slowly, you may want to use a nursing supplementation device.

ADOPTION

Now that the word has gotten out among women that it is possible to produce milk even if one has never been pregnant, many mothers who adopt babies express the desire to breastfeed the baby as a way of making her more "theirs." As in the mother who has just given birth, it is the regular and frequent stimulation of the nipple that signals the milk producing glands to get to work. Because the adoptive mother does not have the additional hormonal boost that the biological mother would have, it is likely to be necessary to use a

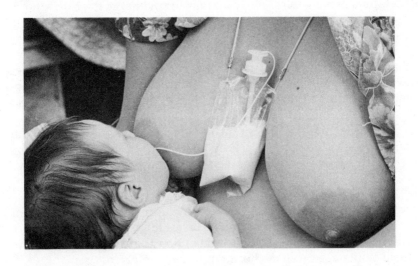

nursing supplementation device which has been designed for situations like these (see Appendix A).

You may be able to locate another woman who has nursed an adopted baby by checking with your local breastfeeding counselor. Read up on the subject and simplify your life in all the ways you can so that you will have a lot of time to sit and hold your baby. If you want to nurse your adopted baby you should eat a healthy diet, adding foods which may help to produce milk, such as those rich in the B vitamins: wheat germ, oatmeal, an occasional beer, and nutritional yeast.

Making milk will take dedication on the part of you and your mate. You may find the rewards of nursing your adopted baby well worth the effort it takes.

One mother's story:

> Even though I'm physically unable to have my own children, I had the pleasure of nursing our adopted daughter for a year. I felt really strong instincts to put her to my breast right away. She was seven days old when I got her and had been nursed by her mother until then. It felt perfectly natural to let her suck at my breasts, and I offered them to her often between bottles that first week.
>
> I used a Lact-Aid device, and when it was time to feed her, I would get her sucking on my nipple tightly, then gently slip the tube into the corner of her mouth and pinch the tube a bit so that the milk wouldn't rush in too fast and make her choke. When she would fall asleep nursing, I would often slip the tube out of her mouth and let her suck on me half-asleep for a while. She loved it. I affectionately called the thing my third breast. I could wear it under a loose shirt and be prepared whenever the baby wanted to nurse.
>
> After three days I was able to squeeze out several drops of clear liquid colostrum and in two weeks, the clear liquid turned to tiny drops of white milk. My supply was pretty much in the "few drops" category for several months, but I noticed a few things that really affected how much milk I made. More protein seemed to make more milk, so I ate a protein-rich diet. The amount of liquid I drank made more difference than anything else I did. Borage tea* helped produce more milk, and I drank it by the half gallon. Adequate rest made a difference. And my frame of mind while nursing really mattered. The more relaxed I was, the more milk I made.

*Borage (*Borago officinalis*) is an easy-to-grow, spreading plant with large leaves and blue flowers. Tea made from its leaves has traditionaly be used for increasing milk flow.

I had to be careful not to get too goal-oriented. If I started to get worried about how much of my milk the baby as getting and would I ever be able to feed her completely on my own, it often had an adverse effect on my milk supply. It worked better to remember my gratitude and joy at being able to nurse this way and to share this feeling with the baby instead of dwelling on how long it was taking and how much I was making.

At one point after I had been nursing for six months, I was almost ready to stop completely and was telling a friend about it. Then she asked how much milk I actually had. I pulled up my shirt right then and there and tried to express some, and lo and behold, a long stream sprayed out about six inches in front of me! Needless to say, I continued nursing for several more months. I never did have enough milk to feed my baby completely on breast milk, but I had enough to squirt every day from then on until I weaned her.

Relactation

Many medical writers in the past have remarked on the ability of women to "relactate" — to produce milk by nursing a child, even when they have not recently given birth. M. Audebert, a well-known French obstetrician of the time, described such a case in 1841:

> Angeline Chauffaille, sixty-two years of age, and who had not had children for twenty-seven years, undertook to nurse her granddaughter artificially. From time to time, in order to amuse it, she presented it with her nipple, but what was her surprise when she suddenly found both her breasts full of an apparently good, healthy, and nutritive milk! She continued to nurse it for a year, and the secretion had not entirely ceased after the child had been weaned two months. At this juncture, her daughter again became a mother; her milk dried up, and the grandmother was able to nurse the second child.

If, for some reason, you want to begin nursing after having been feeding your baby on the bottle, it is possible to relactate. Grandmothers in many areas of the world quite often provide milk to their grandchildren. If less than a week has passed since you weaned or if the baby is one week old and has never nursed, you should be able to get into full milk production by nursing every two hours. Even if you have had hormone shots to dry up your milk, relactation is possible. In fact, drying-up shots don't work very well on many women.

If you find that you need to supplement your milk for a few days with formula or someone else's breast milk, do this after you have nursed the baby. Remember to empty both of your breasts more than once during a feeding session. Keep track of the number of wet diapers your baby produces. You'll want to see six or seven in a day to be sure that your baby is getting enough to eat.

If you are trying to relactate with a baby who is a few weeks old and never been nursed or a baby who has been weaned for more than a week or ten days, you will likely need to give supplementation while you nurse. A nursing supplementation device is ideal for this purpose.

Previous Breast Surgery

Nursing is possible for women who have had breast surgery in those cases where the milk ducts have not been severed. Women who have had minor surgery to remove a lump should have no trouble nursing. Those who have had implants to increase the size of the breasts will usually be able to nurse.

Women who have had breast reduction surgery should try to breastfeed and see what happens. Their ability to produce milk will depend upon the amount of tissue removed and the extent of the surgery.

Those women who have had surgery which relocated their nipples will usually have problems nursing. A nursing supplementation device may be necessary.

Herpes

Mothers with active genital herpes lesions inside the birth canal at the onset of labor will have their babies by cesarean. Breastfeeding is safe as long as hands are thoroughly washed before feedings. Sometimes mothers with herpes have active lesions on the labia or inner thighs, not requiring a cesarean for the baby's safety. The same precautions apply at home whenever there are active lesions.

The other type of herpes virus, the kind that appears as cold sores or fever blisters on the mouth, requires precautions also. Thorough hand washing is necessary, and care should be taken not to bring the baby into contact with the sores. Now and then this type of herpes will appear as an outbreak on the breast, nipple, or areola. If this happens, you should pump or express milk until the lesion is gone and feed the baby only from the other breast.

Diabetes

Diabetic mothers may look forward to breastfeeding unless the disease is very incapacitating. The sugar content of the milk of diabetic mothers will be the same as that of the nondiabetic, and the trace amount of insulin to be found in the milk will not harm the baby.

The blood sugar levels of a diabetic mother's baby will have to be closely monitored for the first couple of days. During pregnancy, the mother's high blood sugar levels are passed through the placenta to the baby, which causes the baby to produce a high amount of insulin in response. Following birth, the baby no longer gets the high blood sugar through the placenta but goes on producing a higher than usual level of insulin. This overabundance of insulin drives the baby's blood sugar levels below the optimum level, leaving the baby hypoglycemic.

Usually this situation stabilizes within a day or two, but it does bear close watching. Babies of diabetic mothers are often given supplements of sugar water or formula to prevent low blood sugar. It is best if minimum levels of such supplements are given so that nursing can get off to a good start. Once the breast milk is in, the baby should get enough sugar from breast milk to maintain normal blood sugar levels.

Weaning will present another time when caloric and insulin levels are likely to need adjustment. Trouble during this period can be avoided by making weaning a very gradual process. Those mothers who have mild diabetes, which they control by diet alone, should have no problems breastfeeding. They will need to increase their caloric intake and to eat a high-quality diet, following a pattern of three meals with midafternoon and evening snack. Each meal and snack ought to contain both carbohydrate (such as bread or rice) and protein (such as tofu, meat, beans, or cheese), to avoid insulin release and to provide for a sustained release of glucose.

During the period of breastfeeding, you and your doctor will need to carefully monitor your blood sugar level, insulin dose, and caloric requirements. As your baby grows bigger and takes more milk, you will need to adjust your insulin dose and intake of calories to keep a balance and to prevent insulin shock. Diabetic nursing mothers need at least 20 grams of protein and 100 grams of carbohydrates a day.

Home testing of blood sugars should be done by using test sticks that measure only glucose (Tes-Tape or Diastix), rather than those which also measure lactose. If acetone is present in your urine, you know that you need more calories and carbohydrate.

Special precautions should be taken to avoid sore nipples and breast infections, since diabetic mothers are more prone to infection. Get plenty of rest, watch for thrush in your baby's mouth and on your nipples, and be sure that your baby is positioned well during feeding sessions. If you do get a plugged duct and experience the beginning symptoms of a breast infection, treat right away. If you can't ward it off quickly, you should take the ten-day course of antibiotics that your physician will prescribe.

Vaginal yeast infections are usually common in diabetic mothers because of the extra sugar in their vaginal secretions.

Epilepsy

Epileptic mothers can and do breastfeed their babies. Most medications which are prescribed for the control of epileptic seizures are considered safe for nursing.

The precautions that an epileptic mother must take for her breastfed baby are the same that she would need to take if the baby were bottlefed: padded arms on chairs, padded guard rails on beds, plenty of playpens around the house for quick deposit of the baby if a seizure is imminent, and tags on stroller for lone outings with your baby, with instructions about what to do and whom to contact if you have a seizure.

Other Problems

Mothers who are blind, deaf, or who have less active than normal or overactive thyroid glands may also breastfeed their babies. Those who are deaf or blind should have an easier time with breastfeeding than with bottlefeeding, provided that they have correct information and good support.

Mothers with thyroid disorders will need to keep in close communication with their physician, to carefully monitor medication levels. Breastfeeding should be stopped whenever there is treatment involving radiation.

SUGGESTED SUPPLEMENTAL READING

Chamberlain, Mary. *Old Wives' Tales*. London: Virago, 1981.
Cohen, Nancy Wainer, and Lois Estner. *Silent Knife: Cesarean Prevention and Vaginal Birth After Cesarean*. South Hadley, Mass.: Bergin and Garvey, 1983.
Joslin, E.P., et al. *The Treatment of Diabetes Mellitus*. Philadelphia: Lea & Febiger, 1959.
Lawrence, Ruth, M.D. *Breast-Feeding: A Guide for the Medical Profession*. St. Louis: C.V. Mosby, 1980.
Nance, Sherri. *Premature Babies*. New York: Arbor House, 1982.
Noble, Elizabeth. *Essential Exercises of the Childbearing Year*. Boston: Houghton-Mifflin, 1982.

Weed, Susun. *Wise Woman Herbal: Childbearing Year*. Woodstock, N.Y.: Ash Tree Publishing, 1985.

Worthington-Roberts, Bonnie, Joyce Vermeersch, and Sue Williams. *Nutrition in Pregnancy and Lactation*. St. Louis: C.V. Mosby, 1981.

6

The First Two Months

♦

Your first two months of parenthood are likely to be challenging, rewarding, and enlightening. The challenging part is that you can't help but feel the weight of the responsibility that you have taken on by having a child. This feeling is going to sink in more every day.

The rewarding part of being a parent comes as you watch your child grow. As a nursing mother, you get to experience the particular satisfaction of knowing that your own body continues to support your baby's growth.

I have talked with several mothers recently whose biggest surprise about motherhood was that there do seem to be behavioral differences between boys and girls that are not related to social conditioning. Realizations such as these are what I mean by the enlightening part of being a parent. Another realization which can be startling is that your child often mirrors your attitudes and even your thoughts.

Taking Care of Yourself

It is easy to spend so much time caring for your baby in the first few weeks that you neglect to care for yourself. Because you and your baby are one system, taking care of yourself is in fact taking care of your baby.

During the weeks after childbirth your body will be going through a process which will reverse many of the changes of pregnancy. Your uterus will shrink in size while it casts off the inner lining, called "lochia," which was there during pregnancy. The flow of lochia should gradually change from red to pink to brown to white over a period of two or three weeks. Mothers who become too active too fast may find their flow of lochia becoming heavier and redder. If so, this should be taken as a signal to slow down.

Mothers who have had cesarean births need to remember that it takes time to recover from major abdominal surgery. Some, but not all, will still be taking pain medication when they have gone home from the hospital. These mothers will need extra rest and support to have the best chance at satisfactory breastfeeding.

Exercise after childbirth is important for restoring your abdominal muscles and your self-confidence. Start with Kegel's exercises, to strengthen the muscles of your pelvic floor. Tightly squeeze the muscles around your anus, your vagina and urethra several times a day. Gradually work up to 100 Kegels a day. You can see how you are doing by trying to stop the flow when you pee.

Another form of exercise which is very good for you during this period is walking. Take your baby with you and spend a quarter to half an hour walking outside. Not only will the exercise be good for you—so will the change of scenery.

Try to find a way to meet other new mothers if you don't already know some. A childbirth educator, midwife or breastfeeding counselor in your area may be able to put you in contact with mothers who can be good companions for you. It's no fun to be totally solitary when you are a new mother, and the people who are the most likely to know how you are feeling are those who are currently going through the same things you are.

Sometimes new mothers are surprised to find that the nursing period can be about as emotional for them as was pregnancy. This is because breastfeeding and postpartum changes also involve differences in hormonal levels. When you add these factors to the sense of increased responsibility and the constant fatigue that can go with being a new parent, it becomes easier to understand why you may weep more easily than you once did.

YOUR DIET
The health of both you and your baby depends upon the adequacy of your diet during pregnancy and breastfeeding. American medical practice in the twentieth century has taken little recognition of the importance of good nutrition for pregnant mothers. Medical men for

many years followed the pronouncement of a German obstetrician, around the turn of the century, that, "Semi-starvation of the mother is really a blessing in disguise because curtailment of food would produce a small, light-weight baby easier to deliver." This dangerous teaching still permeates the thinking of many medical professionals, unfortunately, so you may have to create your own motivation to eat a good diet.

Again, I learned from my own experience how much good nutrition matters during pregnancy. My obstetrician, the one recommended by my friend who went to Radcliffe, required that I, for the good of my baby, should keep my weight gain to twelve to fifteen pounds. Fortunately for Sydney, I had enjoyed the first three months eating everything that appealed to me in Europe, so I starved only the last six months of the pregnancy. By "starve," I mean that I allowed myself only 1200 calories a day (I should have been getting 2500 calories), in order to keep from getting scolded at each prenatal visit. To do that, I ate no sugar, salt, and as little oil or fat as possible. Even so, I gained twenty pounds during the pregnancy. I was constantly hungry, and I know now that I was undernourished. Many women, under such a regimen, have low-birth-weight or premature babies and develop toxemia. I believe that my good diet previous to my pregnancy and during the first three months of pregnancy kept me from developing these more severe problems. I just felt irritable, tired, and weak. Besides requiring that I stay on this strict diet, my doctor wanted me to take diuretics during the pregnancy, to keep me from "holding too much water." I didn't know this at the time, but these drugs are usually used for people sick with kidney or other disease, and, as we have seen, are considered dangerous for pregnant women, who are supposed to contain more fluid than when they are not pregnant. My father saw me when I was seven months pregnant and commented on how unhealthy I was looking. At the time, my feelings were hurt, as I did not realize that he, looking at me as a farmer, knew more about what constituted good health during pregnancy than my doctor did. I knew better how to care for myself during my three last pregnancies and gained thirty-five pounds each time, a more normal weight gain for a pregnant woman, and my father no longer worried about my health.

Your diet while nursing won't be greatly different from the ideal diet during pregnancy, except that you will need to take in about 500 more calories a day. Add another 500 calories if you have twins. You will need to eat plenty of protein each day, preferably some with each meal and again in snacks between meals. You will need about 65 grams of protein a day. Protein-rich foods include soy beans, tofu, cheese, eggs, yogurt, fish, poultry, all legumes, nuts, seeds and meat. If you are the kind of vegetarian who eats no animal products, you will need to supplement your diet with 4 milligrams of Vitamin B_{12} daily. If you do eat beans, you can add to their amino acid content by combining them with grains, such as bread, rice, or noodles.

Your diet should be rich in vitamins and minerals. Calcium is important so that you don't develop osteoporosis (brittle, porous bones) later in life. You need 1600 milligrams of calcium a day while nursing. If you are a milk drinker, one quart a day is about the right amount. If you don't like milk or can't digest it easily, there are many other foods which will provide the calcium you need while breastfeeding. Tofu is a protein-rich food which is very low in calories, high in calcium, and extremely versatile.

There are dark green vegetables besides broccoli which are rich in calcium, but the calcium they provide is not easily absorbed by the body. I recommend that calcium supplements be taken during pregnancy and breastfeeding, especially for mothers who don't want to be bothered with counting the milligrams of calcium they are eating daily.

The vitamins you need to be sure you are getting during pregnancy and nursing are vitamins A, C, and folic acid, which is part of the B complex. When you get enough vitamin A, you are less likely to get infections. Vitamin A is contained in milk, eggs, yellow and orange fruits and vegetables, butter, and margarine. Vitamin C helps the strength of the uterus, and is needed during breastfeeding as it is not stored in the body. You need to eat vitamin C daily, so that your baby can get it in your milk. Vitamin C is found in citrus fruits, potatoes, canteloupes and dark, leafy greens. Folic acid helps to prevent anemia and is found in eggs and dark, leafy green vegetables.

Don't expect to regain your pre-pregnant shape while your baby is a few months old. You will gradually lose weight and your waistline will begin to reappear during the first couple of months, but it's really

FOODS THAT ARE RICH IN CALCIUM

SERVING	MILLIGRAMS CALCIUM
tofu (8 oz.)	290
yogurt (8 oz.)	288
cheese (swiss) (1 oz.)	260
cottage cheese (1/2 cup)	106
broccoli (1/2 cup)	68
salmon (3 oz.)	207

best not to lose all of your extra fat during the early nursing period. Weight loss of a pound every two or three weeks is about right. Dieting at this time is not advisable, as it can interfere with your milk supply, your energy level, and your sense of humor.

Maintaining a nutritious diet while you are a new mother means planning ahead and being a smart shopper. Snacks such as nuts, yogurt, seeds, and nut butters will be a lot better for you than sweets such as cake, ice cream, cookies, and candies. Fresh or dried fruit is both satisfying and nutritious. You will surely notice that you drink larger quantities of liquids as a nursing mother than you ever did before. I didn't bother with glasses less than a quart in size while I was breastfeeding. The easiest way to tell that you are drinking enough is to notice the color of your pee. If it is very light yellow, you are doing all right. If it is medium to dark yellow, you should be drinking more.

DIETARY SUPPLEMENTS

I believe that vitamins, iron, and calcium supplements should be added to the diet during pregnancy and breastfeeding for most women. Instead of going on taking prenatal vitamins, I would recommend taking a multivitamin that has all the components that were in your prenatal vitamins except vitamin B_6 (pyridoxine hydrochloride), since it inhibits the secretion of breast milk in a nursing mother.

Those mothers who take the time and are attentive to their diet have no need for supplements, if they are sure that they are getting their daily requirements of vitamins and minerals in their food. Under certain conditions, it is possible to overdose on vitamin supplements.

FOODS WHICH CAN INTERFERE WITH NURSING

Some mothers can eat from a list of foods without any problem, while others can't eat certain types of food without their nursing babies feeling some negative effects. Chocolate and caffeine have been the two biggest offenders among the women I have counselled. In addition, many women also avoid eating vegetables from the cabbage family, garlic, onions, or (rarely) beans during the nursing period so that their babies do not become gassy or crampy. I have seen chocolate eaten by the mother cause severe cramping for as long as twenty-four hours in a breastfed baby.

Your Routine With Your Baby

You will probably find yourself beginning to settle into a somewhat predictable routine after the first week or two of your child's life.

Depending upon your temperament and the other demands on your time and attention, you will nurse your baby whenever she signals or according to a more or less regular schedule compatible to you both.

Keeping to a schedule can present problems, because most babies aren't that predictable and because they do go through changes in appetite and sleeping/waking habits as they grow. It's best to be flexible, whatever routine you tend to develop.

It is very normal for a breastfed baby to want to nurse from eight to twelve times a day, averaging every two hours. Eating with such frequency does not mean that your milk isn't satisfying; rather, since breastmilk is easily digestible to a baby, he can be ready for another feeding soon after filling his stomach.

Sometimes mothers can't count how many times their babies eat during a day because they may find themselves nursing for three hours or so continuously, feeling their milk let down several different times during the session. Individual babies differ quite a bit in how they like to eat. Some mess around, eating and dozing while keeping the nipple in their mouth, causing their mothers wonder if they'll ever get full or want to really sleep, while others stuff themselves as full as possible as fast as they can and sleep soundly until they are awakened by hunger. I had both kinds.

It may seem uncanny that your baby gets hungry whenever you do. In fact, you may find that you have to eat sometimes while you are nursing if you want to eat at all. I believe that babies are telepathic with their mothers and that it is quite natural for both to feel hunger simultaneously. I even found that with my own baby who didn't have a huge appetite that I could stimulate hers by eating while I was nursing her and, later, spoonfeeding her.

It is a good idea to weigh your baby at the age of two weeks. This is a good time to find out if your baby has regained her birth weight or gained beyond it. If she has, you will be reassured that all is going well with your breastfeeding. If your baby is below her birth weight, it is early enough to take steps to make sure that she begins gaining faster. The longer a pattern of slow weight gain goes on, the more upsetting it will be to you when it is finally discovered.

Keeping Up A Good Milk Supply

Your breasts will be many different sizes during your first two months of breastfeeding. If you are like most mothers, sometimes you will seem full to bursting, making you feel like a goddess of abundance, while at other times your breasts may seem deflated and empty. You are not unusual if you go from wondering what you are going to do with all the milk you have to worrying if there is going to be enough, all within a short space of time. Such a drastic change can be upsetting if you don't know that this amount of variation is normal in mothers who successfully breastfeed and that it does not mean that your milk is "drying up."

I have seen several mothers who went through a short period of fear and loss of confidence when their breasts settled down to being soft between feedings after they had been very full all the time during the first week or ten days. Everything was fine just as soon as the mother understood that you get an oversupply of milk in the beginning (your body doesn't know you didn't have twins), followed an adjustment to the reality of your baby's appetite after the first week or two.

You may be surprised by the depth of your feelings of responsibility for your baby. When you know that your baby's only food comes from your own chest and if that supply comes into doubt, it is easy to panic and go for something that seems more certain.

Most babies do go through some fluctuations in appetite, which will in turn cause changes in your milk supply. The important thing to remember is that your breasts will adjust to your baby's demand for milk. You are not a container with a finite capacity which can be exhausted. You are more like a computer, and your baby programs you to the amount that is appropriate for her at the various stages of her nursing time. If she wants to nurse much more on a certain day than she did the day before, it may be that she is going through a growth period, and she needs to program you to give her more milk from now on. To do this, she needs to nurse for a longer period than usual. If you can sit there and know that this process is natural, you won't have to panic and jump up and give her a bottle of formula from the sample the hospital gave you at discharge that you probably stashed in the cupboard in case of an emergency. Many babies go through growth spurts when they make a jump to needing more food than usual at around two weeks and six weeks of age.

The trouble with giving a supplement at a time like this is that you can quickly find yourself losing confidence that you have enough milk or that your milk is sufficiently nutritious for your baby. When you begin giving supplemental feedings, you will have a strong tendency not to sit and nurse your baby for the amount of time he needs to build up your milk supply. If you take the edge off your baby's hunger, he would rather sleep than nurse. Remember, too, that everything you feed your baby besides breast milk will take longer to digest than breast milk. This also means less nursing time, which means less milk.

Introducing solid foods works the same way. If you take away your baby's appetite by giving solid foods, such as cereals or other manufactured baby foods, at too young an age, you take a chance on your baby's developing an allergy to a food he might be able to handle if it were introduced later. At the same time, you tend to reduce your own milk supply. Under ordinary circumstances, babies less than two months don't need to be given supplemental feedings of formula or baby food.

There are a few things you can check for to know if your milk supply is sufficient for your baby. You should be nursing about seven or eight times within a day and getting about that many wet diapers. You should be offering both breasts and allowing all the nursing time your baby wants. If you are doing all these and are still worried, see the section "Not Enough Milk" in Chapter 7.

Dietary Supplements For Babies

If you are well-nourished, your breast milk is the ideal food for your baby, containing all the right nutrients. Some physicians believe that vitamin levels aren't as good in human breast milk as in cows' milk, but in making this judgment they are not taking into account the greater absorption of the nutrients in human milk by the human baby.

IRON
It is rare that breastfed babies will suffer from iron deficiency anemia. The Committee on Nutrition of the Academy of Pediatrics recommends a source of iron in fortified baby cereal by four to six months of age. Many others agree that no iron supplements are needed in the first six months for the breastfed baby.

VITAMIN D
Only a few babies will suffer from a deficiency of vitamin D during the breastfeeding period. Low-birth-weight babies, premature, or dark-skinned babies who receive little sunlight on their skin are those most at risk. The recommended dose of vitamin D for babies is 400 units per day. Twice that amount is considered toxic.

FLOURIDE
Some pediatricians recommend that fluoride be given in early infancy in order to reduce cavities in childhood. There are others, though, who say that too much fluoride can cause spotting of tooth enamel. Whichever way you decide, fluoride supplements are not necessary before six months of age.

Normal Baby Behavior

There is a wide range of behavior that is normal in babies. The one thing you can definitely expect is that your baby is going to cry sometimes and that your own baby's cry will bother you much more than any other child's cry.

Babies cry for many different reasons: hunger, fatigue, the need to relax, wanting to be held. Babies like to nurse, not only because they are hungry, but because they want the intimate contact and the sucking. Lots of babies get especially frustrated in the evening, and it can be hard to calm them. Very important to getting through this period is to not succumb to the temptation of giving your baby formula at times like these. Evening fussiness and the refusal of your baby to settle down to comfortable nursing does not mean that he dislikes your milk, or you. If you have a baby who is crabby in the evening, try to have your evening meal already prepared earlier in the day so that you will not have to face the additional pressure of cooking at that time of day. See Chapter 7 if your baby is one of those who seems inconsolable. See also "More Serious Crying" in the same chapter.

BABY POOP

Breastfed babies' poop is watery and yellow, often forming curds. It is pretty innocent stuff, since these babies are being fed the purest food there is. It doesn't smell bad, and it rinses off with water. Some babies poop once or twice a day, while others will go for several days without and not be uncomfortably constipated. The baby who really is underfed will have small, infrequent, greenish or brown poop.

SUGGESTED SUPPLEMENTAL READING

Brewer, Gail Sforza, and Tom Brewer, M.D. *What Every Pregnant Woman Should Know.* New York: Random House, 1977.

Dalton, Katharina. *Depression After Childbirth.* Oxford: Oxford University Press, 1980.

Hagler, Louise. *Tofu Cookery.* Summertown, Tenn.: The Book Publishing Co., 1982.

Hagler, Louise. *Tofu: Quick and Easy.* Summertown, Tenn.: The Book Publishing Co. 1986.

7
Problems in the First Two Months

♦

*I*f you find yourself turning to this part of the book more frequently than the rest, don't think that you have ruined your child or that your baby is going to be permanently hard to live with. The time after birth, whether you are breastfeeding or not, is an emotional time for every mother. Because your consciousness, via your hormones, has been altered by pregnancy and childbirth, your ups will seem more intensely joyful than usual, and your downs may seem cosmic. Unless you are one of those very rare and lucky mothers who enjoy such support that you can avoid being overly tired, then you will probably feel sad or depressed about your ability to keep up with some area of your normal responsibilities, new or old.

It helps not to have expectations of a somehow perfect course of events that is impossible to live up to. What is more appropriate is a sense that it is all right to reach out for help when it is needed and that it is normal to need help during the new mothering period.

Not Enough Milk

One of the most desperate feelings a breastfeeding mother can have is that she is losing her milk, that when her baby wakes up, there isn't going to be enough milk in her breasts. If you seem not to have enough milk to satisfy your baby, you should take steps to build up your production. The main action to take is to let your baby nurse as often as possible, since frequency is actually more effective in building up your supply than the length of time of each nursing.

Sometimes the feeling of not having enough milk is caused by the slowness of the let-down reflex, which at times can be inhibited by a lack of privacy. Let-down inhibition in these cases can only be corrected by being alone with your baby, away from any distractions or responsibilities. Other things don't need to get done during this time or they can be done by someone else. You can now pay full attention to the nipple stimulation when your baby nurses, and you can make sure that this happens frequently.

Concentrate on the good feeling of nursing and not on any worry about there not being enough. Not only the frequency of stimulation matters, but also the quality of your attention while you are nursing. Worry creates distraction, interfering with concentration on the physical sensation of the stimulation your baby gives you.

I worried about my milk production with only one of my babies. I found that worry did interfere with my let-down, holding it back, and that when I would transfer my attention to the physical sensations of nursing my baby would feed better and my milk would let down more often during a feeding.

I knew a mother who couldn't at first get her let-down reflex to work well with her baby son. She had nursed a daughter with no problems, but she had been raised in a way that left her with inhibitions about feeling any pleasant sensations in her body while feeding her boy baby. When she was able to relax and let go of this inhibition by talking it over with close friends, her milk production increased so markedly that her baby boy gained a couple of pounds in two weeks.

Make sure that you are getting plenty to eat and to drink. Don't try to lose weight and increase milk production at the same time. Relax in a warm or hot bath a couple of times a day and try to get some extra sleep.

Here's how one mother went about building up her milk production:

> I had to bottle feed my baby for ten days while I was taking some medicine which wouldn't have been a good kind to go through my milk to my baby. It was hard not letting her nurse for ten days. I kept removing the milk from my breasts, but by the end of the ten days, I could hardly get anything out. I was worried, thinking I

wasn't going to be able to nurse her anymore, but my milk did come back.

Warm baths really helped. The milk was slow in coming back because I couldn't just lay with her and nurse her all the time—I had lots to do. But every time she was hungry, I would let her nurse and she would get some. Then she would get frustrated and throw herself around, so I would put her on the other side until she would get frustrated there. Then I would give her a bottle of formula to satisfy her. It took a couple of weeks to get my milk back all the way. During that time I had to give up feeling uptight about the house not being as clean as I would like it. I kept trying to spend more time with my baby.

I also saw that the more formula I gave her, the less nursing she would do. I tried to balance things so she would get enough to eat and still suck on me all she could. It was good to just lay with her while she slept and let her suck; when she was really sleepy, she didn't care if she was getting milk or not and I could feel my milk glands tingling and getting ready to do more work.

Another mother's story:

My youngest child was breastfed, as were her two older sisters. She was different, though, in that at three months she started sucking her thumb. She was the first of my kids to take up this habit. I had also begun giving her supplemental feedings of baby cereal and applesauce. As a result of these feedings (I found out later), my milk supply had decreased, as she was stimulating my nipples less. But she was taking care of her sucking needs by sucking her thumb. I didn't like the direction things were going in.

At this time, one of my friends suggested that I take my baby off the solid foods and let her nurse as often as she liked. The result was all that I hoped for--my milk production increased bountifully, and my daughter stopped sucking her thumb, as all her sucking instincts were being satisfied by nursing. I breastfed her until she turned fourteen months old, and she never started sucking her thumb again.

Blocked Milk Duct

Milk ducts may become blocked from overall engorgement, or from pressure from a badly fitting bra. Blockage causes milk buildup, making a lump which may cause the skin above it to become red. An engorged breast will be lumpy all over. A breast with a blocked milk

Problems in the First Two Months

duct will have one prominent lump. One woman I know could not even sleep on her belly while nursing, as the pressure would cause a blocked duct. A blocked duct can result in flulike symptoms in the mother, including fever and achiness and can at times lead to a full-blown breast infection.

If you ever suspect you might be developing a blocked duct, start right away to take these precautions:

1. Make sure the affected breast gets well emptied. Offer it first so you will have the best possible emptying. Express any milk left after the baby has drunk her fill.
2. Feed the baby at least every two hours so that all your milk ducts will be frequently drained.
3. Massage the affected breast from above the lump, towards the nipple, while nursing and after your baby has finished. This may help to drain out any remaining milk.
4. Apply a moist warm compress on the area above the lump.
5. Take off your bra while you nurse. Some women find that they can't wear the designs of nursing bras that have a band across the top, which becomes very tight just when their milk begins to flow.
6. Vary the baby's position while nursing. Putting the baby's chin close to the plugged duct sometimes helps.
7. Drink plenty of fluids and lay down and rest as much as you can.
8. If the lump doesn't go away within a day or two, you should check with your doctor; you may need to take a course of antibiotics to keep from getting mastitis.

A mother wrote:

About a month ago, I woke up in the night and noticed I had a hard lump under my breast. I realized I had a blocked duct, so I put some hot, wet cloths on it and went to sleep. When I woke up again, the knot was bigger, red, and really sore. The baby nursed on it, and I could tell it was clogged. I called a midwife, and she said to put hot packs on it and let the baby continue nursing. I didn't have a fever yet, so I didn't need an antibiotic. It got worse, and I started feeling faint, and it started hurting just to have her suck on it. I stayed in bed and kept hot packs on it. Then, one time while she was nursing, it opened up. She really healed me, and I started feeling better. It was great to have it leave like that. Within an hour or so, I was feeling much better.

Mastitis

A blocked duct that does not get treated the right way can result in mastitis, or breast infection. Mastitis can make you feel very sick, with flulike symptoms such as fever, achiness, and the infected area will be hot, red, swollen, and tender. It is most likely to occur in the first few months of nursing, although it can happen at any time during the nursing period.

If you get mastitis, there is no reason to stop nursing. In fact, you need to keep nursing your baby in order to empty your breast well. The bacteria which cause mastitis are rarely present in milk and are not harmful when drunk by the baby. Fortunately, mastitis is easily brought under control by a course of antibiotics, bed rest, and lots of fluids.

Follow the steps outlined above for a blocked duct. Your breast may be very sore when the baby first begins to suck, but just remember that nursing your baby is part of the cure for this condition. You need milk to flow through your breasts, not to stand still in them.

I have noticed that mastitis most often occurs at a time of upset in a mother's life, for instance, while taking a long trip before the baby has had a chance to establish a strong rhythm of nursing and sleeping, or after an emotional event such as a fight with a partner or a family tragedy.

The reason for this connection is that emotional factors and stress in general affect the let-down reflex. If you are unable to relax and fully let down your milk, or if your milk lets down and your baby is too distracted to suck well, you are more prone to mastitis. Weaning too suddenly can cause mastitis. It may also be brought on by wearing a bra that is too tight or by sleeping on the belly, which puts pressure on the breasts. A cracked nipple, anemia, and fatigue are other possible causes.

If you have recurrent bouts of mastitis, you may want to have your breast milk cultured to find out if your strain of bacteria is resistant to some drugs.

TREATMENT OF MASTITIS

1. Go to bed.
2. Call your physician. Antibiotics will most likely be prescribed. Sometimes it is possible to clear up infections with frequent nursing and wet, warm compresses, but to go without antibiotics means that you risk having a recurrent infection or developing an abscess. Be sure to take the antibiotics for the entire time they are prescribed, even if your symptoms disappear.
3. Watch for thrush in your baby, especially a thrush diaper rash, after antibiotic treatment. You may also develop a yeast infection.
4. Nurse at least every two hours. There is no harm to your baby in nursing from the infected breast; in fact, you should begin with

Problems in the First Two Months   117

the infected one. Weaning because of a breast infection can lead to a breast abscess.
5. Drink more fluids so that you notice that you are peeing more often than before treatment.
6. Apply moist hot compresses before nursing and between feedings.
7. Check your temperature every four hours. If you need relief from fever and aching, take acetaminophen tablets.
8. Do without a bra if you can. Wearing a bra can restrict the flow of milk through your breasts.
9. Try taking 1,000 milligrams of vitamin C four times a day while treating the infection.

Once treatment for mastitis has begun, there is usually marked improvement within twenty-four hours.

Breast Abscess

An abscess is an accumulation of pus which becomes blocked off within the breast. These can happen when a mother stops nursing while she has a breast infection or when treatment for an infection doesn't begin quickly enough. Fortunately, breast abscesses are rare.

A breast abscess may be the problem when a breast infection does not seem to respond to treatment within forty-eight hours or when a lump persists, one that does not change with nursing. Having an abscess is usually a painful experience, since it must be drained in a doctor's office or hospital. Recovery shouldn't take long after draining.

Still, there is no reason to wean your baby. It is wise to stop breastfeeding on the affected breast for a few days after it has been drained. Use an electric pump, if possible, to keep up your milk flow, or manually express until your baby can nurse from both breasts. Don't worry if you leak milk from around the incision at first. The incision will eventually heal.

Too Much Milk

Many women would not consider it a problem to have too much milk. Mothers who do continue leaking and spraying after the first few weeks may have problems getting their babies to nurse well at first because the milk comes out too fast and makes the baby cough and choke. Probably the most effective solution for this inconvenience is to express a little milk manually before putting your baby to breast.

If you must be separated from your baby for longer than the usual interval between feedings, you'll probably find it necessary to express some milk in order to be comfortable. Remember it's best to continue to nurse your baby from both breasts at each feeding. Doing so will not tend to increase your milk production, and it will help to prevent plugged ducts.

A friend of mine was a nurse in the Peace Corps in Malaysia. In the course of her practice, she had to make a routine visit to a new Malay mother, to see if the new baby and the older children were being well nourished and cared for. The new mother invited my friend into her house and served her the usual sweet coffee and milk. They sipped coffee while the mother held her new baby. My friend noticed how plump the baby was and asked in her barely passable Malay what he was fed.

"Susu kita," the mother answered. My friend wasn't sure what that was but decided to fake it. Then a two year old waddled through. My friend asked the mother what she fed this obviously well-nourished child.

"Rice, vegetables, meat, and susu kita," she replied. My friend was getting curious. Then three more healthy-looking children entered the room. My friend asked what the older children ate and was told, "Rice, vegetables, meat, and susu kita."

"What is this food?" she asked the mother. The mother laughed and pointed to her enormous breasts, and my friend realized that susu kita meant mother's milk. Susu was the Malay word for "milk," and she remembered that kita was the word meaning "our," in the sense of all of us, the speaker and the one spoken to. "Our milk," what an interesting way to say it! she thought. Then she became even more curious.

"What kind of milk is in this coffee?" she asked.

"Susu kita."

Lumpy Breasts

It is normal for a breastfeeding woman to have lumpy breasts. When the breasts are full of milk, they feel lumpy. A tender lump that appears suddenly and doesn't go down after nursing is probably a blocked duct. When you have a lump such as this, accompanied by a red streak on the skin above it, a fever, and flulike symptoms, it signals a breast infection. Sometimes there are small cysts which fill with milk. These ordinarily appear just before nursing and get smaller or disappear after nursing.

Lumps which appear and don't change in size for a week or more should be checked by a doctor. Only very rarely is there anything serious wrong. You can keep on nursing even though your doctor may recommend ultrasound, mammography, breast biopsy, or removal of the lump. Many women have.

Lopsided Breasts

Many women notice that one of their breasts has begun to produce more milk than the other. This situation usually happens when the baby develops a preference for one side more than the other and gives the preferred side more stimulation. The cure is to begin nursing the baby on the smaller side, to even out milk production. Keep offering that breast when your baby is hungry.

Postpartum Depression

It is not unusual for a new mother to feel sad or depressed at this time, even when she greatly looked forward to motherhood. The changes in hormone levels during pregnancy, labor and delivery, and the nursing period can have the effect of intensifying emotional states. Most new mothers will feel moody and anxious at least some of the time while their babies are very young. The more support and rest they are able to get during this time, the less likely it is that they will succumb to depression and need further counselling or intervention.

If you suffer from more than a passing tendency to moodiness at any time during the nursing period, it is wise to look at your entire situation to see how it can be improved.

Some mothers, under the pressure of fatigue, isolation, poor nutrition, worry about their babies, or their own inability to live up to unrealistic expectations for themselves, become truly depressed and bewildered, feeling unable to cope with motherhood. Such sustained depression can be linked to several causes: uncompassionate treatment during labor and delivery or to unwanted separation from the baby afterwards. Mothers of sick or premature babies seem to be more at risk than those whose babies are fully mature and healthy at birth, although women with healthy, thriving babies can become depressed, as well.

I have seen postpartum depression in mothers who had been forced to move their households around the time of birth. Moving at this time doesn't upset everyone, but it certainly can be disruptive to some women.

It is hard to say why some mothers react to the stress of giving birth, breastfeeding, or weaning by becoming depressed, while others seem to be able to adapt to the emotional changes which accompany these physical processes without losing the ability to cope. Some seem to do all right through part of the process, then become overwhelmed when no one is expecting that they will have trouble.

The best way to avoid postpartum depression is to get plenty of sleep and lots of help during the time that you are a vulnerable new mother. If, despite all the precautions you take, you do begin to slide into a depression, it is wise to take the following steps to pull yourself out of it.

HOW TO COPE WITH POSTPARTUM DEPRESSION

1. Try to find someone who can take over at least some of your mothering duties for a little while.
2. Make some kind of schedule for yourself that includes time for you to have a nap every day. See if you can find someone to look after your older children or to help with meal preparation.
3. Spend some time with other grownups, especially people you can talk with about what is bothering you.
4. Take time to eat a nutritious diet. Skipping meals, especially breakfast, will only aggravate your problem. It is a good idea to take a vitamin supplement and a B-complex tablet every day.
5. Try to fix yourself up each day: get dressed, brush your hair and your teeth—in short, spend some time taking care of yourself.
6. Get some exercise each day.
7. Seek further help through your midwife, doctor, or local mental health agency if your symptoms don't improve. If your doctor prescribes a medication, make sure that it is a type which can be tolerated by a nursing baby.

A mother of four wrote down her thoughts on postpartum depression:

> I don't consider that I had true postpartum depression, but I have a very clear memory of one hard night when our first baby was six or seven weeks old. The room looked all black and red, and the baby was crying inconsolably. I felt crazy and thought all kinds of terrible, violent things.
>
> The birthing had been confusing. My husband was with me, and it was a short labor. But the doctor wasn't available when the second stage began (he had fallen back to sleep after the hospital had called him), and I was told to wait until he arrived. He got there after about twenty minutes, and then one of the nurses got mad at him and stamped her foot because he dropped his sterile glove. I pushed the baby out really fast and needed a few stitches. I was pretty sore afterwards and wondered if I ever wanted to give birth again. I felt estranged from my baby, whom I didn't see for ten hours after he was born. My own mother was thousands of miles away, and I didn't know anyone well who had a baby.
>
> I grew to be friends with my son. I know now that this kind of

birth experience can cause later depression. My memories have helped me to understand how serious postpartum depression can occur and to feel compassion for any women who undergoes it.

Another woman described her serious and sustained bouts of depression with each of her two children:

> Looking back on nursing my kids, I find some of the weirdest memories of my life. I experienced almost constant hallucinations and delusions, brought on by a combination of changing hormone levels, my own strong imagination, a marriage that wasn't working, and what I now realize was a mistrust of my body and my mothering instincts.
>
> One night, when I was on the point of harming my baby, I called out for help in utter desperation. I was literally stuck in a mythic world with visions of gods and saviors running through my head. There were also dark forces trying to harm my baby. My midwife cared for my baby for a few days while I received counselling and support from other friends. I was able to resume caring for my child when the hallucinations subsided.

Problems With Your Baby

CRYING

You should assume that you are going to be hearing some crying if you are going to have children. Your baby's cry is designed to be effective at alerting you to his needs, even if you are sound asleep. Researchers have found that parents' blood pressures and breathing rates increase when they hear their baby's cries. Nature intended it this way, since it contributes to the survival of the young. Practice relaxing when you hear your baby cry by taking a deep breath and moving slowly and deliberately.

After a couple of relaxing breaths, go and see if your baby is crying because he needs help. A baby will have a certain kind of cry if he has moved around so there's a blanket over his face, or if his head is up against the side of the crib.

Babies have different styles of crying, according to what they want to say. Many mothers can tell the difference between a hungry cry, a wet cry, a full diaper cry, and an angry cry.

Sometimes babies cry, not because they are hungry, but because they want your attention and your body presence. If your baby cries for this reason, carrying her in a baby carrier while you do housework and care for older children may cut down on the length and ferocity of crying sessions. You may use a commercially made baby carrier or a sturdily woven cloth square (Guatemalans call this a "cargador") to tie the baby against your front or your back.

Babies who get plenty of body contact from their parents during the early months do not become clinging and emotionally dependent children as they grow older; in fact, the reverse is more likely to be true.

You should hold your baby as much as possible during the first months. Your baby needs your presence as well as your milk. You will need support yourself, in proportion to the amount of time you have to spend comforting your baby.

If your baby is crying because he has awakened and is hungry, pick him up if you are ready to feed him. Don't get so upset by the crying that you get in a rush. If you have to go to the bathroom first, do it. He won't starve or go crazy in the meantime. Get yourself set up so you can be comfortable while nursing so that your milk will flow better.

Change your baby's diapers before you feed her during her first few weeks. Sometimes this won't be convenient or comfortable, but generally it's a good practice. It's good for her to be dry and comfortable while she is eating. If she is yelling frantically, tug on her leg gently or lean down and whisper in her ear.

Usually your baby, if crying, will stop when you pick her up. If she doesn't, try to calm her before you put her on your breast. She can't nurse well if she is crying because her stomach muscles are too tight, her breathing will be out of rhythm and she will swallow air, adding to her difficulties. If you make it a practice to try to stuff your breast in the mouth of your crying baby just to stop her crying, you won't accomplish anything worthwhile. If you can calm her first, she'll eat more at a time and be able to digest it better.

If she hasn't stopped crying already, she is likely to when you sit her up into nursing position. If she started to cry before you get your breast in her mouth, draw her back a little, stroke your finger on her cheek to let her know there is still some there. Then give it to her just as soon as she begins to calm down.

Sometimes, in order to calm your baby enough to get her on the breast successfully, you'll need to put her up over your shoulder and give her a few light pats on the back or squeeze her bottom a couple of times. If she is really frantic, you may find it more effective to hold her up to your shoulder and then dance slowly around with a step-dip, step-dip rhythm. It's best to take a dip just as she fills her lungs for a new cry, because your rhythm can then overcome hers, and she can forget what she was crying about. Squeeze her butt and make low, grunting sounds which vibrate your chest. Or sing to your baby. Singing is likely to make both of you feel better.

If your baby is one of those who arches his back stiffly while crying, there is a simple way to get him to relax. To maintain that stiffness, the baby must keep his abdominal muscles rigid. He cannot do this if you hold him over your shoulder so that the tightest part of his middle is right over your shoulder. Walk around and bounce downwards gently when you feel him taking a deep breath to let out another yell. He won't be able to get such a big breath if you take your dip at the right time, and he will usually give up and melt onto your shoulder and enjoy your dance within a few minutes.

MORE SERIOUS CRYING OR "COLIC"
Some babies go through intense crying sessions in their early months of life, no matter how much they are fed and held. Such babies classically sleep for very short periods of time, often wake up crying loudly, and cry whenever they are put down. Sometimes they cry even when they are being held. Some people call this kind of crying colic. It's not an illness, and there's no one cure for it. There are several things you can do, however, to make your mind easier during this phase of your baby's life. The best thing about colic is that it eventually passes, and parents and baby get to catch up on their sleep, usually by the end of the third month.

Colic is sometimes miraculously cured by the elimination of a gas-causing food from the mother's diet. Some of the most frequent culprits are chocolate, cabbage, onions, and green peppers. Too much fruit juice or fruit may have the same effect.

Learn to slow down your movements when you handle your baby. Many babies are set off by too sudden handling, jerky movements, or too delicate a touch. The best way to handle a baby is with a firm grip and deliberate but fluid movements.

It will be easier to slow down your body movements if you take deep, slow breaths when you sit down to breastfeed. Release any tension you feel in your arms as you hold your baby so that he won't feel that you are worried or uptight. Irritable babies react to the tension in their mothers' bodies by tensing up themselves.

Sometimes a baby who is gaining weight well will cry for a while no matter how much you walk him. In a case such as this, you can make sure he's fed and dry, put him in his bed, pat him on the butt and tell him to go to sleep and then leave him alone and let him do it. He'll probably cry for a few minutes and then go to sleep. You might take a warm, soothing bath to relax while you wait for him to go to sleep.

Other possible remedies for the hard-to-soothe baby include turning on your vacuum cleaner or switching on your FM radio so that it puts out "white noise."

When my first baby was very young, I was bewildered because I had thought that I was going to know what caused her every cry. I expected motherhood to be reasonable. I used to wonder if she would injure herself physically or psychologically by crying so hard.

I think that many new mothers, particularly those who have not been around young babies a lot of the time, experience the same bewilderment I did. You can get so that your entire sense of well-being depends upon your ability to stop your baby from crying.

By the time I had my second baby, I had noticed that if I let myself get distracted or driven by the crying so that I became very tense, my baby would cry even harder. On the other hand, if I breathed slowly and deeply, refusing to be driven, I got so I could calm her holding her close. She would begin to cry with less force, winding down until she would relax onto my body.

SPITTING UP AND VOMITING

It's normal for young babies to spit up a little bit after each feeding. Now and then a baby will lose an entire feeding without being really sick. Sometimes this type of vomiting is caused by something the mother ate; at other times it could be an infection, or no cause can be found. The distance between a baby's mouth and stomach, after all, is *very* short. Call your doctor if vomiting persists or your baby runs a fever.

There is a condition called pyloric stenosis which occurs at a rate of about one in every 150 male babies and one in every 450 female babies. These babies can't seem to keep anything in, and when they throw up, they do it with a force that sends the milk in an arc from the mouth. Pyloric stenosis can occur in girls, but first-born boys are the most apt to have it. The condition is easy to diagnose visually and is corrected by a fairly simple operation. You can sometimes see the wave of muscular contraction as it moves through the intestine.

The main danger to the baby is in those cases where the mother doesn't understand the difference between mere spitting up and projectile vomiting. She waits to see if the baby will get better, and he throws up so much and so often that he becomes dehydrated, stops gaining, or loses weight. Because formula is harder to digest than breastmilk, breastfed babies with pyloric stenosis may not be detected as quickly as those who are bottlefed.

Babies who have had this surgery (which consists of cutting part of the affected muscle) can go back to breastfeeding within a few hours. Your milk supply should recover about as quickly as your baby's appetite.

My friend and fellow midwife, Carol Leonard, of New Hampshire, went through an experience with her son, that illustrates the problems that can develop with pyloric stenosis when it is not recognized early. Her son was six weeks old before he began the projectile vomiting. When she took him in to see her local pediatrician, she mentioned that she suspected that the problem was pyloric stenosis. Her brother had had the condition as a baby, and she was familiar with its symptoms. For some reason, her doctor doubted her and began testing the baby for all sorts of other problems. A brain scan was ordered, and because pyloric stenosis can cause dehydration so quickly, he was put on an IV. Carol was one of the few women the pediatrician knew who was breastfeeding, and he began to suspect that her son was a "failure to thrive" baby. Carol remembers the degrading feeling of being watched as the pediatrician and nurses observed her mothering behavior through one-way glass. Meanwhile her baby became so weakened after about six days and looked so much like he was starving to death that Carol became afraid that he wouldn't live through the ordeal. Many blood tests were ordered, and it had become nearly impossible for the lab team to find a vein. Carol came close to the point of announcing that if her son was going to die, she would take him home to do it. Finally, a specialist was called in for a consultation. He went straight to the baby, used his first two fingers to feel the area around that baby's navel and announced, "He has pyloric stenosis." The surgery was performed immediately. Carol was instructed to give her son milk by dropper for twenty-four hours. Several hours into this regimen, she was so exhausted and disheartened that she burst into tears. Just then her son broke into a smile that lit up his whole face, one that said, "I'm going to be okay." She picked him up and began to nurse him immediately and scarcely put him down for a week. Her milk production was soon back to normal and so was his weight.

REFUSAL TO NURSE
Sometimes babies will pull away from the breast, as if they don't want to nurse. There can be several causes for this behavior. Sometimes the baby has a stuffed-up nose and can't breathe while nursing, which is frustrating when he is already hungry and uptight. A few drops of breastmilk in the nose will often dissolve the mucus and make breathing easier. Holding your baby more upright while nursing also tends to help. A cool mist vaporizer can be useful in clearing your baby's nose while he sleeps.

At times a baby pulls away from her mother's breast because the milk is coming too fast. This situation does not usually persist because the baby learns how to deal with it, the mother learns to express a little milk to lessen the force of let-down, or milk production settles down to a more reasonable level. Some mothers slow down the flow of milk with the help of gravity by lying underneath the baby while nursing.

Sometimes reluctance or refusal to nurse comes from an unpleasant tasting milk or body smell because of something the mother ate or applied. Spicy foods, perfumes, and deodorants have turned some babies off. Interestingly enough, no one has ever reported a case of a baby refusing to nurse because of the mother's unadulterated body odor. Maybe that's because nursing mothers just smell good.

Feverish or sick babies often temporarily lose their desire to nurse very much. Ear infections are a fairly common cause of refusal to nurse. Check with your doctor about this, or buy an otoscope and learn what an ear infection looks like.

Babies who cry with frustration and squirm while at the breast are sometimes babies who are showing an allergy to something that is traceable to certain foods which the mother has recently eaten. Gas cramps are typical, as are stuffy noses, a rash, or redness around the anus.

Babies who have thrush will sometimes be frustrated nursers. The overgrowth of yeast that characterizes this condition can exist not only in the baby's mouth but also in the esophagus and stomach. Babies with extensive thrush can be very cranky, and they cry a lot until they are cured. I know of one case in which the mother did not realize what the trouble was for about six months, during which time her daughter cried far more than most babies. After treatment with nystatin, her daughter's personality seemed to go through a complete change, and she became a very placid, easy-going baby.

SLOW GAINERS

It is wise to check your baby's weight about every two weeks during the first couple of months. Now and then there are babies who don't gain weight at a rate which is considered normal. Most likely the problem is not your ability to produce adequate amounts of or rich enough milk. Usually the problem has to do with feedings that are too short or too infrequent. Babies who gain well will be nursing about eight times during the day, ordinarily, and most very young ones will wake up at least once a night. Some babies fill up quickly and don't want to nurse any more and others like to take a long time to fill themselves. In the latter case, a mother who is too impatient to let the baby nurse as long as he wants, can not only decrease her milk production, she is also less likely to be having a full let-down of her rich hindmilk, the kind that puts fat on her baby. Most babies have to nurse a while to get the hindmilk as well as the foremilk, since the hindmilk is released only with a good let-down reflex.

If your baby is slow to gain weight, there are several things you can do before considering that supplemental feedings of formula will be necessary:

1. Make sure your baby only sucks on you—no pacifiers!
2. Take time off from the other things you normally do, and spend your time lying around with your baby. Make sure that you get to fully relax, knowing that your usual duties are being covered by someone else or can wait. It works better if neither of you wears much, so you might like being in your bed, where you can be warm.
3. Nurse your baby every two to two and a half hours during the day and every three hours during the night. Wake your baby up for night feedings if she tends to sleep for long periods during the night.
4. Switch breasts if you don't hear good swallowing sounds after your baby has sucked a little while. You might find yourself changing breasts every four or five minutes, a good way to stimulate your nipples to start up increased milk production.
5. Get plenty to drink. Avoid caffeine in any of your drinks, as it can interfere with good milk production.
6. Burp your baby often during a feeding session. Some babies swallow air, which makes them feel full, and they don't want to nurse anymore, until they get the air out by burping.
7. Get help from a breastfeeding counselor or midwife who will give you good advice and support without making you feel guilty. Guilt is a waste of time and energy and doesn't especially enhance milk production. It will help if you can remember your sense of humor.

After taking these steps for two to three days, you should begin to notice some improvement. A normal weight gain for a young baby is around four to seven ounces a week. When you are trying to put weight on a baby, it's a good practice to weigh him once a week. That is often enough to tell what is going on, and not too often to give a distorted view of the baby's progress.

It is important to know what dehydration in a baby looks like. When a baby doesn't have enough fluid in her system, her skin is wrinkled and dry looking, and in extreme cases, when the skin is pinched, it remains folded for a few seconds, almost like cloth. A dehydrated baby needs medical attention.

Quite often a doctor, in a case like this, will advise that the mother discontinue breastfeeding. Such advice is unnecessarily drastic. It is usually possible to get the baby on a weight-gaining course without weaning. Nurse your baby every two to two and a half hours, switching breasts often during each feeding, using a nursing supplementation device. This way your baby gets supplementation at the same time that your breasts are stimulated to produce more milk. If possible it's good to supplement with breastmilk (perhaps you have a healthy friend who is willing to donate some), since human milk is more easily digestible than formula and will not discourage your baby from eating as often as he needs.

Another course of action suggested by Kathleen Huggins in her excellent manual, *The Nursing Mother's Companion*, is to pump your milk after each feeding and add this to any supplemental formula that your baby will take. Cut down on the amount of formula you give if your baby won't eat as often as every two and a half hours, because it is the frequency of stimulation which will step up your milk production. Cut out the formula when your baby starts to gain and your breasts are fuller.

Sometimes there really will be a problem of a baby who just doesn't get nourished enough to grow well. The "failure to thrive" baby, as he is called by the medical profession, is usually the cause of great emotional anxiety to his parents. No one wants to see her baby grow thinner at this age, and feelings of guilt and despair can be strong. Instead of simply providing the most practical help that can be arranged, medical professionals sometimes complicate the problem by making the mother feel that she is not doing a good job of mothering. The cure can at times be quite simple, especially when the problem is related to parents' attitudes with regard to touching their baby. In these cases a great deal of subtlety and sensitivity to the mother's feelings is necessary to remedy the situation.

My early teacher in midwifery, Dr. J. O. Williams, Jr. of Mount Pleasant, Tenn., once told me about one of the most significant learning experiences he received during his years of medical training. As background I should mention my observation that babies feel immediately uncomfortable if the people looking at them and handling them have any sense of revulsion about the human body. Babies are equipped to sense such feelings or vibrations as they look at the expressions on the faces of their parents and, even more, from their parents' touch. Dr. Williams' pediatrics professor told the story of a young couple, both university graduate students, who brought their firstborn five-month-old son to him for examination because the baby had gained so little weight since birth. This was a classic case of a failure-to-thrive baby.

The pediatrics professor, looking at this skinny, wide-eyed baby, began asking the parents about how often and what they were feeding him. They stressed how clean they kept him, to protect him from disease, and described how they put on rubber gloves before changing his diaper and how they changed to a different set for feedings. The doctor knew that he would have to be both drastic and practical. He told the couple that he would need to take the baby into his care for a little while in order to save his life. They were worried enough to agree. Instead of hospitalizing the baby, he put him into the care of a friend, a cuddly Italian grandmother with some time and love she could spare. The baby was soon cuddled and relaxed into eating well and enjoying it. No medications were required to accomplish this complete turnaround in the baby's condition. He was soon returned, healthy and plump, to his parents, whose worries about the transmission of germs were relieved by knowing that it was better to be conscientious about handwashing than to wear rubber gloves. They had also learned that the amount of cuddling and loving that a baby gets is directly related to his ability to thrive.

SUGGESTED SUPPLEMENTAL READING
Huggins, Kathleen. *The Nursing Mother's Companion.* Boston: Harvard Common Press, 1986.

8

Combining Nursing and Your Busy Life

♦

Most mothers of babies above the age of two months find that they have to combine breastfeeding with a large range of other activities, including jobs outside of the home, traveling, shopping, or just visiting. Sometimes you will want to take your baby along with you; other times you'll feel better leaving your baby at home with a relative or babysitter. Either way, you will want to develop some skills in organizing and planning for your baby's best care.

Taking Your Baby With You

Fortunately, a breastfed baby is easier to take traveling than a bottlefed baby. You have no baggage associated with feeding to carry with you, and you don't have to worry about your baby's milk spoiling while you are en route.

Your greatest difficulty is likely to be the problem of how to be discreet while nursing in public, or where to find a place to do it, in societies that have become unused to the sight of a mother nursing. Lots of mothers have mastered the art of breastfeeding with a shawl or blanket draped over the shoulder and the baby's head. You can also plan your wardrobe to include tops which you can easily pull up from the waist for nursing without a lot of exposure.

The main thing to realize is that other peoples' distaste, when confronted with the sight of a mother nursing her baby, is more their problem than your own. Someone may try to make it your problem, but you don't have to let them. I believe that ultimately, the best cure for such insensitivity to the welfare and comfort of mothers and babies is for the sight of nursing to become very common in restaurants, bus stations, airports, parks, stores—wherever mothers and babies are likely to go. There is no reason why mothers shouldn't enjoy the same comforts of travel, shopping, and leisure that women in other parts of the world enjoy.

The following anecdote was related to me by a man who grew up in Belgium:

> When I was in Antwerp, Belgium, I used to follow crowds to the zoo, and, in my opinion, these people knew how to relax and enjoy themselves. After you had viewed all the animals and marveled at all the beautiful flowers, you would go to the beer garden and order sandwiches and beer and all day long, there would be bands. It seemed like the perfect way to pass the time. Well, one day while I was listening to the music, a baby started to cry, cry, cry. It was disturbing the music, until quite a bunch of people started to clap their hands in time with the music. They all started to yell, "Titah! Titah! Titah." The young mother started to laugh and began to nurse her child. Then she got a big hand for quieting the baby. I noticed that in Europe, no one gets excited when a woman nurses her child.

Contrast this incident with a young mother's experience in De Soto, Mo. While nursing her baby in a department store parking lot, she was warned by a police officer who happened by that she would be cited for indecent exposure if she continued. The outraged mother demanded an apology and, when she got none, took the matter as far as the St. Louis County Counselor. The Counselor agreed with the officer that "if the manner in which the nursing is accomplished exceeds the bounds of decorum as determined by local standards of decency," a nursing mother could be arrested.

It is when we look at social attitudes and mores in countries other than the United States and Canada that we begin to see how needlessly strict attitudes in North America have become since bottle-feeding replaced breastfeeding as the social norm. Latin American women are not bothered, or even particularly noticed, if they pause to nurse a baby in public. In Chile, the mother who needs to nurse her baby during her grocery shopping is able to do so in the nursery provided by many stores. A woman out for a walk with her baby can sit down on a park bench and nurse without attracting any great notice. Although bottlefeeding became as fashionable among urban middle-class women in Chile during the first half of the twientieth century as it did in North America, it seems that the development of psychological barriers to breastfeeding was less pronounced in Chile and other Latin American countries than in North America.

You need not assume that you are going to encounter social difficulty if you choose to breastfeed outside of your home. Many mothers do not have any problems. You may find that you receive only compliments and encouragement when you nurse in public. A friend of mine who lived for a while in the South Bronx in a supposedly "tough" neighborhood tells this story:

> I had a nice experience one time when I was nursing my daughter on the bench in the park across from our house. I didn't know how this was going to work out, since a lot of times guys who had been drinking would sit there, and I thought somebody might say something weird or something. But this guy walked by and very nicely said he thought it was really great that I was nursing the baby and that he had been breastfed. [Many people who now live in the Bronx were born in the South, delivered by midwives.] He was so respectful and sweet that this incident caused me to relax and not

be self-conscious about nursing my baby when I was out of my house.

I have counselled quite a few mothers who have become so intimidated about breastfeeding in public that it takes more than a pep talk to bring out a proper perspective on breastfeeding etiquette. I usually end up suggesting, half-seriously, that they make a practice of carrying with them a supply of paper bags when they go out with the baby. I advise that they announce their intention to nurse the baby and offer paper bags for people to put on their heads if they would like to protect themselves from the sight. I don't know anyone who has gone to these lengths, but mothers have told me that just considering doing this has made them feel more comfortable about nursing in public.

Mothers in at least two countries have found that organized actions can make a difference locally. Sheila Kitzinger has helped to organize groups of breastfeeding mothers to have public picnics in Oxford, England. About fifty breastfeeding mothers in Toronto organized a public breastfeed when one of them was asked to leave a shopping mall after feeding her baby in public view. Such events can make visible, in a way that might not otherwise be possible, the important issues surrounding breastfeeding and the feelings that it arouses in people.

AIR TRAVEL

If you need to take your baby with you when you travel by air, it is wise to arrange a flight on a plane that is lightly booked. You are more apt then to have a place next to you to lay your baby when he is ready to sleep. Breastfed babies do better with changes in pressurized airplane cabins than most passengers, since they can nurse during takeoff and landing, the times when pressure changes are likely to be the most drastic.

Occasional Separations

Every mother will find times when she needs to be apart from her baby for longer than the usual interval between feedings. In order to be comfortable and to keep your milk production to its usual level, you will need to express your milk at such times. You may express your milk manually or use any one of a variety of breast pumps. See the section on Expressing and Storing Your Milk, in this chapter.

Longer Separations

If you must be away from your baby for more than a couple of days, you may be able to freeze enough milk for the time you'll be away.

If not, you can use a commercial formula. Remember to keep pumping or expressing your milk every three to four hours so that your milk production will continue until you are back with your baby.

Even if you or your baby becomes sick and needs hospitalization, you should know that it is rare that weaning is required. It may be that you know more than the medical staff at the hospital about expressing and storage of your milk, so you may find that you are the expert. If your hospital doesn't have an electric breast pump (most will), try to rent one and keep it in your room. Ask the nurses to refrigerate your expressed milk.

Check with the list in chapter ten about the safety of medications you might be given while in the hospital. If you must take a medication which is not considered safe for your baby, keep pumping and throwing the milk away until you are no longer taking the drug.

Here is one mother's experience with major surgery while nursing:

> I had been having problems with my reproductive organs for many years [endometriosis]. When my fourth child was just a couple of months old, the same old problems came back and continued to get worse. I knew the outcome was probably going to mean a hysterectomy.
>
> When my baby was eleven weeks old, I went ahead and had the operation. I did not want to stop nursing. I talked with my doctor about it. He was a very kind gentleman who encouraged me to continue. I pumped my breasts while I was in the hospital, and as soon as I could, I tried nursing again. It worked! It took a couple of days to get my milk production up again, and I only nursed my baby a couple of times a day. I felt like if I nursed her more it might slow down my recovery.

Back to Work or School

The move back to breastfeeding in our society has coincided with a drastic increase in working mothers. During the days when few mothers nursed their babies or worked outside the home, it was almost unheard of for a mother who did have an outside job to breastfeed her baby. These mothers usually weaned their babies when their maternity leave was up.

These days more and more mothers are finding ways to combine breastfeeding with maintaining their careers. Their strong motivation to continue nursing is a necessary ingredient of their success. They feel that the rewards of breastfeeding are worth the trouble it takes to find ways to overcome the obstacles of being away from their babies during their times at work. They know that the breastfed baby is generally healthier than the bottlefed baby. They know that they will be saving a few hundred dollars, as well as a significant amount of time preparing formula and bottles. Most of all, though, they mention that the reunion with their babies at the end of the workday is made sweeter by the close physical connection of nursing. Breastfeeding provides a way of emotionally compensating for the time spent apart, reminding both mother and baby of their special, intimate relationship. I know teachers, nurses, doctors, medical students, midwives, secretaries, judges, and executives who have been able to keep their careers active and continue nursing.

NURSING AND WORKING
Unlike most western European countries and some Latin American countries, the United States does not, as a matter public law or policy, require that maternity leaves be of a specific length or that employers provide any sort of benefits for breastfeeding mothers. In Cuba, Law 1100 of March 27, 1963 granted to every working mother, among other things, one hour a day within the regular working hours for breastfeeding and caring for her baby after the twelve week pre- and postnatal paid leave of absence. Scandinavian countries have laws requiring that employers of more than a certain number of mothers with babies provide a nursery with paid child care attendants at the work site. Breastfeeding mothers are given a designated number of minutes during the working day to nurse their babies.

Until such time that similar laws are enacted in the United States and elsewhere, mothers must be inventive and carefully plan how to continue breastfeeding before going back to work. The more flexibility you can find in determining your work schedule and the length of your maternity leave, the easier it will be for you to continue breastfeeding. You may be one of the mothers who is able to function quite well with the usual six-to-eight-week leave period. If this is not so, try to see if you can get an extension of your leave. Some mothers are able to arrange to work at home, to take fewer classes, to share their job with another person, or to work parttime.

Those mothers who do at least part of their work at home can schedule their work times around their babies' feeding times. Such arrangements can also reduce the amount of time the baby must spend with a paid babysitter or relative.

Some employers realize that agreeing to shorter hours benefits them as well as their nursing mother employees, especially if these employees have skills necessary to the organization. These mothers are less apt to take sick leave or to waste time while on the job.

If you are one of those mothers who cannot afford to reduce your pay by working parttime, it is worthwhile to see if your employer will agree to some more flexible arrangement.

Some employers will allow mothers to bring their babies to work with them, depending, of course, on the type of work and the safety of the workplace. Some mothers are able to arrange with their babysitters to bring the babies to them for feedings at lunch or during coffee breaks. Such arrangements depend upon the willingness of the babysitters to provide this service and the proximity of workplace to the babysitter.

CHOOSING A BABYSITTER

Your peace of mind while at work will depend in large part on your choice of babysitter for your child. You will want to take great care in finding the right person for this important work, someone with a philosophy of child care which coincides with your own. You will need to work out whether the babysitter will come to your home or your baby will go to the babysitter's home.

While you are shopping for a babysitter, find out the names of other families whose children have been cared for by the babysitter so that you find out how satisfied they were with the care given. Because you won't want to have to change your caregiver once you have gone back to work, it will be important to find someone who can promise a long-term commitment to caring for your child.

Be sure to listen to your intuition when you choose someone to care for your child. Your own good sense is a much better guide about who will make you feel at ease than any system of licensure or certification. If you find that you must pay a surprise visit to the caregiver in order to satisfy your mind about her integrity, do so. Before you make a final commitment to go ahead with a certain caregiver, be sure to discuss who will be called in an emergency, how an illness (your baby's or the babysitter's) would be handled, fees, written agreements, and how much advance notice will be necessary for any departure from the usual schedule. Such thoroughness will be well worth the time and effort it takes in the beginning.

Expressing Your Milk

If you are going to need to be away from your baby enough that you miss one or more feedings per day, you will most likely need to express your milk. Most mothers who are separated from their babies this much without expressing will find that their milk production diminishes to the point that there is not enough for the baby during the times of day when they are together. Of course you can be more flexible when your baby is older and is not so dependent upon you as the main source of food.

HAND EXPRESSION

Lots of mothers are quite happy with hand expression. You can learn how to express your milk this way during the early days and weeks of nursing. First, you place your thumb about an inch and a half above the areola on the upward side of your breast and your forefinger about the same distance above the areola on the lower side of your breast. Then push your thumb and finger straight back toward your chest and gently squeeze them together. Keep your fingers in the same position on your breast rather than sliding them down onto the areola. Squeezing in this way pushes the milk out of the sinuses behind the areola. Once you have emptied the sinuses beneath your fingers, you can rotate a few degrees and empty the other sinuses.

Some women find that breast massage before beginning to express the milk helps to facilitate the process. Catch the milk in a clean container. Once you are practiced at hand expression, you will find that it takes around twenty minutes to empty both breasts. Switch back and forth from breast to breast to be sure that you are completely emptying your breasts.

Others find that they must stimulate their nipples lightly by hand, while thinking of the baby, in order to experience a let-down of the milk. Mothers who still have trouble getting their milk to flow may need to use Syntocinon Nasal Spray, a prescription drug which is the same hormone that is naturally secreted during nursing.

Getting Your Baby Used to the Bottle

Your baby will need to be able to drink from a bottle if someone else is to feed her. While some babies will accept milk from a bottle from their mothers, others refuse unless the bottle is offered by someone other than their mother. If you must go back to work, you may wish to get your baby used to having a bottle offered by someone else a couple of times per week during the weeks leading up to the date you return to work.

COLLECTING AND STORING YOUR MILK

You will probably want to collect and freeze some milk for the times you will be away from your baby. It makes sense to begin collecting and storing about ten days before you go back to work. A deep freezer will safely keep your milk for six months. A refrigerator freezer that is working properly will keep it for two weeks.

To freeze your milk in your refrigerator compartment, collect the milk in clean plastic containers. You may use the disposable plastic liners intended for some bottles or small plastic baby bottles. Glass or hard plastic bottles are better for the deep freeze. Collect the milk in amounts of two to three ounces per bag or bottle. Experiment a bit so that you can find the best time or times of day to collect your milk. Never refreeze after you have used any. Leave some room at the top for expansion. Label each container with the date collected and don't worry about frozen milk looking yellow.

Most women want a private place where they can collect their milk. Don't be shy about making your needs clear to your employer or supervisor. If there is no refrigeration where you work, you may want to invest in a thermos bottle or cooler to be kept at your workplace. A wide-mouth thermos works well if you use plastic bags for collection and surround them with ice.

Fresh milk is best for your baby if you can arrange it, since freezing does destroy some of the antibodies contained in the milk. Do not keep fresh milk in the refrigerator for more than two days. To preserve all of the nutrients in the milk, it must be gradually warmed to room temperature in a container of warm water before using.

ESTABLISHING A ROUTINE

Your success at combining nursing and working will depend, in large part, on how well you are able to establish and follow a routine. You are going to want as much predictability in your life as possible while your baby is young. Schedule in naps whenever you can. Sleep will be extremely precious, so let your friends and relatives know when you can and can't be called or visited. You need not feel guilty about being less accessible than you once were or because you go to bed earlier than you did before the baby's arrival.

Nurse your baby as often as possible while you are at home together. Express three times a day if possible during the time you are apart.

Mothers who find it hard to express enough milk to leave with the babysitter may find that it helps to spend weekends at home in bed with the baby. Close proximity and relaxation such as this can stimulate milk production which can then last a few days into the next week.

Getting Your Priorities Right

It should be no surprise that a fulltime work schedule can make it hard to keep breastfeeding a baby. Many women, by scheduling their time carefully and by planning ahead, are able to combine working and nursing. More women would be able to keep up breastfeeding if our society was better informed about the positive benefits breastfeeding can have on the society as a whole, especially when we are thinking, as we always should, about the welfare of coming generations. We need more workplaces with nurseries on site for the benefit of employees who are nursing mothers. We need to get rid of the erroneous idea that promiscuity is encouraged by providing adequate benefits in housing, nutrition, health, and education for low income families with children.

I like to remember these words of Eleanor Roosevelt:

> Where, after all, do universal rights begin? In small places, close to home—so close and so small that they cannot be seen on any maps of the world. Yet they are the world of the individual person; the neighborhood he lives in; the school or college he attends; the factory, farm, or office where he works. Such are the places where every man, woman and child seeks equal justice, equal opportunity, equal dignity without discrimination. Unless these rights have meaning there, they have little meaning anywhere. Without concerned citizen action to uphold them close to home, we shall look in vain for progress in the larger world.

SUGGESTED SUPPLEMENTAL READING

Dalton, Katharina. *Depression after Childbirth*. Oxford: Oxford University Press, 1980.

Stanway, Andrew M.D., and Penny Stanway, M.D. *The Breast*. London: Granada, 1982.

Wheatley, Meg, and Marcie Hirsch. *Managing Your Maternity Leave*. Boston: Houghton-Mifflin, 1983.

9

Nursing Your Older Baby

♦

*B*abies between the ages of two and six months are especially fun. Although they do communicate before this age, they reach farther, become more predictable and active in their attention during this period. They are capable of such utter delight during nursing that it is infectious. You learn that they can lift your spirit even when you are exhausted beyond belief.

Two to Six Months

LOVEMAKING
Most couples resume lovemaking during this time if they have not already done so. Quite a few women find that their vaginal juices are not so plentiful during the nursing period. This dryness is related to the hormone levels associated with milk production. These women are helped by using a lubricant such as K-Y Jelly for lovemaking. You should be the one to determine the pace, position, and degree of penetration according to what feels good to you.

Don't be surprised if you leak or spray milk during orgasm. Most men who are fathers of breastfed babies consider this display a lovely expression of feeling as well as food.

CONTRACEPTION

Many women find that they have little or no desire to make love while they are nursing a young baby. Conscious or not, this lack of interest often is related to unwillingness to become pregnant so soon. A young baby who wakes you up night and day is the most powerful statement there is of one's fertility. Knowing how a baby started gives a healthy respect for the process leading to conception.

Such fears may be well-justified in women who worry about what type of birth control to use during the early nursing period. A woman who used the Pill before becoming pregnant would be wise not to use it while nursing as full-dose birth control pills may decrease milk production. Long-term effects on babies are not known and will not be known for many years. Condoms, IUDs, and diaphragms are used with comparative safety. Those women who prefer to keep track of their fertility cycles in order to abstain during the fertile period are likely to find it hard to determine when ovulation is coming while breastfeeding. If you do choose this method, make sure you find a counselor who can document that she has a good record for her method of determining safe times during your cycle (or lack of one). It is necessary for counselors to keep track of three indicators of fertility: basal body temperature, cervical mucus, and the length of your menstrual cycle. It is important to know that breastfeeding alone is not a reliable contraceptive.

Taking Care of Yourself

All during the time you are nursing you will probably feel how important it is to take good care of yourself, to get nutritious food to eat at specific intervals during the day, and to get enough sleep and relaxation time.

You may have to reorder your priorities somewhat in order to care for yourself adequately. Your house may be messier than before you became a mother; your garden may grow some weeds. The important thing is to remember that your baby will be a baby for only a few months and that this will be an extremely formative time during which your baby as well as you will benefit from your health and well-being.

It is not wise to diet during the nursing period. Many women do gradually lose weight during these months, particularly if they get some form of exercise each day. Because you will need a lot of liquids to drink while you are nursing, you can keep from gaining unnecessary weight by drinking beverages other than soda or other sweet drinks. Good-tasting water is one of the best drinks for a nursing mother.

RECURRENT BREAST INFECTIONS

Some mothers experience one breast infection after another. Breast infections are related to stress, lack of sleep, missed feedings, exhaustion from traveling, restrictive clothing worn while breastfeeding, or incomplete let-down of the milk.

If you are prone to breast infections, try to eliminate as much stress than you can from your life. Get plenty of rest and drink lots of liquid. Avoid sleeping on your belly and, in general, keep anything from pressing against your breasts. It is also a good idea to gently massage your breasts while you are nursing.

Take the entire course of antibiotics if your doctor prescribes them. Usually a ten-day prescription is given. Get your hematocrit checked, as you may have become anemic. If you are anemic, make sure that you take an iron supplement.

You may find vitamin C a good preventive to breast infections. Some mothers find that limiting salt intake during the nursing period decreases their chance of developing a breast infection.

Nursing Patterns

Babies' nursing patterns do change as they grow and develop. Most parents notice that their babies do not grow at a steady, even pace. Instead they seem to go through growth spurts every few months, during which time they nurse voraciously and act as if they are not getting enough to eat. The result of the extended nursing sessions during such periods is an increased milk production from that time on, and your own appetite may increase without your gaining weight, because you are putting out more milk and therefore more calories.

When your baby is about three to four months old, you may notice that he drinks more at a time but less often. If your baby's weight gain is adequate, there is no reason to try to feed your baby more often.

Your baby will probably know how to empty your breasts more quickly than during the first weeks of life. Babies get very efficient at provoking let-down after they have nursed for a few weeks, and by now, even if you at first had difficulty, you will probably know how to aid the process.

About half of all babies will still be waking up at night two to six months after birth. Some others will continue waking at night even past the six-months point. Those who go through a period of sleeping all night and then revert to waking up for night feedings may be having teething pangs. Teething babies are often fussy, drool a lot, show changes in their nursing pattern, and like to bite and suck their fingers. Some babies enjoy biting on a cold washcloth. You may want to apply acetaminophen drops on your baby's gums. You can get these without prescription from a pharmacy.

Biting

Mothers never enjoy being bitten, but, on the other hand, babies can learn to enjoy biting. I know one mother whose response the first time she was bitten by her child was the instinctive one: she let out a sharp yelp and surprised herself by cuffing her baby, much as a mother cat would when bitten. The contact was gentle but definite, and the baby didn't enjoy it. Her baby never bit her again, but the mother felt somewhat guilty about the incident. By the time she had her second baby, she had decided that she would not follow her instinctual response, fearing that she had been too harsh with her baby. When her second baby bit her the first time, she took her off the breast and told her, "No, don't do that."

The baby kept on biting her, and talking to her and taking her from the breast made no difference. She ended up weaning the second baby earlier than the first because the biting became so painful. Looking back on it, she thought that her instinctual response to the first baby had been the correct one.

My son recently asked me what part of the book I was writing, and I told him I was writing about how mothers can keep their babies from biting. I told him that some babies keep on biting their mothers after the first time because the mothers, for a number of reasons, don't teach the baby to stop.

"Why not?" my son asked.

"Because they're probably afraid that baby won't like them anymore," I said.

"Babies always like their mothers," he said. "They know that's where their food comes from. The mothers don't have to worry that their babies won't like them."

Starting Solid Foods

Most babies do not start wanting or needing to eat solid foods until they are between four and six months of age. Usually this is the period when the baby becomes able to sit up with support from behind and not fall to one side or the other. She'll often let you know by watching your food going into your mouth or even reaching for it. Babies around this age have pretty good control of their neck muscles, and they no longer push their tongues out when you put food into their mouth. Their digestive systems are mature enough for certain solid foods, and their bodies are beginning to require some additional iron, since their iron stores, high at birth, have decreased.

The reason why you don't want to introduce solid foods too early is that babies are more likely to form allergies to foods given during the first three months than later. Introducing solids can also cause decreased milk production, leading to early weaning, and potential obesity later in life.

Sometimes mothers feel a pressure from relatives or other mothers to introduce solid foods before the four-to-six month period. If you feel this, remember that your milk is nutritionally complete for your baby during the first four to six months, as long as your baby is growing at a good rate. In addition, many mothers find that if they hold off from giving solids until the age of five or six months, their babies are able to eat most of what they need from the table instead of commercially prepared baby food. There is nothing beneficial to be gained by not giving your baby solids by the age of six months. It is rare for babies to form allergies to foods introduced at this stage.

The best food to start with is an iron-fortified baby cereal mixed with your milk. You do want your baby to get some iron supplement by this age, and the cereal and milk combination supplies the right proportions of protein, carbohydrate, and fat.

Your baby is less likely to develop an allergic reaction to rice or barley cereals than to wheat as the first solid food. The boxed, dry cereals which don't need cooking are more nutritious (in terms of iron) than a cooked variety, so if you prefer to serve cereal that is already cooked, you should add iron. There is no need to serve the protein-fortified cereals to babies this age. They may even be hard to digest.

Nurse your baby before offering the cereal so that you can be sure that your baby gets breastmilk as the priority food until she is eating three meals of solid table food each day.

Start with offering one meal a day. Some mothers prefer to make this meal the one before bedtime, since it has been known to keep some (but not all) babies this age asleep through the night. It's good to mix the cereal and your milk into a thin gruel at first, then, as your baby becomes more adept at eating, you will want to make a thicker mixture and offer more at each feeding. Don't be hurt or worried if your baby thinks the cereal is not worth the effort at first, as he will likely develop an interest before too long.

Information on offering other varieties of solid food is given in Chapter Twelve. It is wise to introduce only one new food at a time so that if your baby does have an allergic reaction, you can pinpoint the food that caused it.

SLOW WEIGHT GAIN

Some babies slow down in their weight gain around the age of three to four months. The baby who gains less than four ounces per week needs some kind of special attention to begin gaining faster.

Any baby who is gaining slowly and who sucks on fingers or a pacifier should be nursing more often. Increasing the number of feedings will also step up milk production. Some babies lose interest in nursing because they are being given solid foods or juices too early or in quantities too large.

Mothers sometimes produce less milk than is needed because of missed feedings or neglected opportunities to express milk. The same directions for increasing milk production given in Chapter Nine apply here.

REFUSAL TO NURSE

Sometimes a baby who has been a reliable nurser for several months will go through a period of refusing the breast when it is offered. If this refusal comes between the ages of two to six months, you can be sure that your baby isn't behaving this way because it is time to wean. Sometimes the cause can be traced to an ear infection, teething, a mouth sore, a cold or a change in the taste of the milk. (My seven-month-old baby weaned himself when I became pregnant with the next.)

PREFERENCE FOR ONE BREAST

Babies sometimes develop a preference to one breast over the other. If you would rather not be lop-sided, you can make a practice of offering the less popular breast first. The baby who continues refuse one breast can be adequately fed from the other.

Feel your breasts to determine if there is any difference in the amount of lumpiness in each. If the refused breast is noticeably lumpier than the other, it's a good idea to have a breast exam from a doctor to rule out the possibility of a tumor.

Between Six and Twelve Months

The baby during the period between six and twelve months of age has begun to eat lots of different foods. Some babies will continue to prefer breastmilk over all other foods during the second half of the first year, while other babies, towards the end of this period, begin to show a preference for three meals of solid food a day. Whichever behavior your baby shows, you will probably find that your baby is more easily distracted while nursing than he was during the early months of his life.

As in the earlier months of nursing, you will notice that you still need to eat regular meals of nutritious food and get plenty of sleep. Once your baby begins eating solid food, you may not realize how much sustenance your baby still takes from you.

If your period returns during the second six months of your baby's life, you may find that your baby becomes fussy or less interested in nursing than usual. Not all babies seem to notice a change in the taste of their mothers' milk during menstruation, but some do.

More about Solid Foods

After your baby has adjusted well to eating cereal a couple of times a day, you may introduce other foods, such as fruits and vegetables. Give your baby one new food at a time and wait a few days to see how she tolerates it. You may wish to offer vegetables before fruit, since babies may develop such a preference to fruit that they refuse vegetables when they are offered later. You can puree fresh or frozen vegetables after they have been cooked. Commercially prepared baby foods are less nutritious and are often too salty for a young baby. You may wish to use the commercial variety when traveling because of their transportability.

You need not feel that your baby must eat a lot of vegetables to stay healthy. A few spoonsful will provide most of the nutritional requirements of the older baby.

Babies will often take more fruit than is good for them. Too much fruit can cause bellyaches and diarrhea. The same goes for fruit juice. A few ounces a day are good for the baby, but too much will reduce the appetite for breastmilk and other foods, causing stomach upset and diarrhea. Fruit juice given from a bottle can cause tooth decay in even a young baby. For this reason, it is best to give fruit juice by cup. The more acidic fruit juices, pineapple, tomato, and citrus, can cause allergic responses in many babies, so be careful when you introduce them. Never store canned fruit juice, once opened, in a metal can.

If your baby wants just a little bit of solid food when she is between six and eight months old, do not worry. Your breastmilk is still the staple of her diet.

Eight to Twelve Months

Most babies develop an active interest in solid foods between the ages of eight and ten months. This is also the period when foods higher in protein may be added without a high risk of stomach upset for the baby. Protein-rich foods include tofu, nut butters, cheese, lentils, pea soup, eggs, poultry, and fish. Keep in mind that any beans offered to your baby must be extremely well-cooked, or they will not be digested.

During months eight to ten, it is still wise to nurse your baby before offering the table foods. From about ten months on, it is usually time to give solid foods first and offer the breast once the baby has eaten his fill of solid foods.

Your baby will probably graduate from eating cereals to eating grains in other forms during this period. She may enjoy oatmeal, bread or zwieback, noodles, rice or crackers. Watch your baby carefully when you first introduce these foods. Plain bread is not as safe to eat as toast for the baby who hasn't learned to gum, "chew," and swallow expertly.

Keep track of your baby's growth chart during these months. If the growth curve falls off and your baby isn't taking very many solids, it is time to offer solid foods before offering the breast. Try to feed your baby at family mealtimes, as she is more likely to want to eat when everyone else does.

If you want your child to be a vegetarian, you must be very careful to see that she has a source of vitamin B_{12}. Your baby will get vitamin B_{12} from your milk, as long as you are nursing a lot. (If you are a vegetarian, you also need a source of vitamin B_{12}, such as dairy products, eggs, or prenatal vitamins.) Once you wean your baby, she will either need a vitamin B_{12} supplement or dairy products or eggs to fill this nutritional requirement.

Nursing During Pregnancy

If you become pregnant while you are still nursing your baby, you have the choice whether or not to wean. Some women seem to be able to keep up with the additional demands on their bodies posed by nursing while pregnant, while others simply do not prosper. Some babies will voluntarily wean themselves when their mothers become pregnant.

Teaching Nursing Manners to Your Baby

If you never feel that you have become a martyr to your baby's needs, skip this section—it isn't for you. But if you notice, when your baby is around the age of seven or eight months, that you have become a plaything for your baby in a way that doesn't feel good to you, read on. You may need to teach your baby some good nursing manners so that breastfeeding will once again be enjoyable for you, as well as your baby.

In my view, nursing should be a physically pleasant experience for both mother and baby. Once the new mother's nipples have toughened so that any initial tenderness is gone, breastfeeding becomes a sensuous and fulfilling experience for the mother, even when she is tired. Newborn babies, once they set up a regular sucking rhythm, melt onto their mothers, continuing to suck and rest until they are full or too tired to drink anymore. However, an older baby often becomes interested enough in other things that he can become distracted and bored even while eating. When this happens, breastfeeding may not be as comfortable and fun as it was when the baby was younger and more innocent. Your baby may learn that it is amusing to pull your hair while nursing. Mother doesn't like it, obviously, because she makes funny faces when it is pulled and tries to pull her head back, but that is part of the fun. Your baby may delight in kicking you with one foot while nursing. It is not really painful, but it is irritating.

You are not obliged to become a punching bag just because you are a mother. Allowing an older baby or toddler to punch, kick, or walk on you only teaches your child bad manners, which he not only will impose on you but perhaps on other people he meets later on in life. A mother who submits to abusive behavior from her own child runs the risk of raising a future adult who is inconsiderate of others.

I have known mothers who adopted such a submissive role in relation to their babies that they weren't able to like them when they were three or four years old. It is easy enough to slip into a submissive role if you are already short on sleep. There is no need to judge yourself or your baby harshly, or for you to think that you have caused permanent damage by letting your baby bully you a little. Your baby will respond to your love and forgiveness.

If your baby handles you in a way that isn't comfortable while nursing (when this happens, it is usually around the age of seven or eight months), hold his hand firmly while he drinks. If he tries to pull away, try holding a little more firmly. Usually he will catch on to what you are saying to him in touch ("Settle down, please") and will relax and continue nursing in a way that is pleasant for you. If your baby keeps struggling, you might find it necessary to remove the baby from your breast and set him a couple of feet away from you. You may get a surprised or even a reproachful look. Remember why you did it. Mothers are not supposed to be abused by their children any more than children are supposed to be abused by their parents. If the look is one of surprise, invite your baby to come back and finish nursing. If your baby doesn't learn what you want after one interaction such as this, repeat it as necessary. Babies learn fast if you are consistent.

You needn't feel guilty if you can't make yourself enjoy your one year old's rough antics. Gradually wean him and you'll probaby enjoy him more.

Weaning

There is no "best" age to wean a baby. Women in different cultures wean their babies at different times, usually according to what is best for the babies in view of the local food supply. In many nonindustrialized countries, where food is more scarce, children are nursed until they are three or four years old, using their mothers' and grandmothers' milk to supplement the solid foods they eat. This long nursing period helps to make an easier transition between the diet available to the really young baby and the diet eaten by the grownups. There is no reason, however, why a mother living in a wealthy, industrialized country with abundant food supplies must feel that she needs to wait this long to wean her baby. On the other hand, if your baby is gaining and developing well, and you and your baby are still enjoying the nursing period, there is no good reason why you should stop.

There are a few signs that it is time to wean. For example, you may feel yearnings to reclaim your breasts from the total access your child has had to them. Once your baby is about a year old and is eating there meals of solid foods per day, there is nothing wrong with weaning if you wish to do so. I believe that it is harder on a child to be nursed because of guilt or peer pressure on the mother and to be resented for it than it is to be weaned.

Mary Breckinridge, founder of the famous Frontier Nursing Service, tells a story about one of her Kentucky mothers in her fascinating autobiography, *Wide Neighborhoods*. When asked about the health of the Appalachian babies the Frontier Nursing Service midwives delivered, she said they would be hard to deal with

> if they become any more mentally and physically abusive than many of them are now. . . . Not so long ago, a woman with an eighteen-month-old boy came to our hospital out-patient clinic at Hyden Hospital and sat down to nurse him. The Medical Director said to her, "Don't you think it is time to wean your baby?"
>
> "Yes, I know, Doc," she replied, "I know, but every time I try to, he throws rocks at me."

Partial weaning begins as soon as your baby starts eating some solid foods along with nursing. Most babies start to show some interest in solid foods by the age of six to eight months. Others show little interest until eight or nine months. Sometimes a baby about the age of ten or eleven months will wean herself completely after she has been partially weaned for a few weeks. There is no reason to fight this tendency by insisting that a baby this old continue to nurse if she clearly doesn't want to.

If your baby does seem to be weaning himself, you have the choice whether to wean him to the bottle or to the cup. One disadvantage of weaning to the bottle is that eventually there will have to be a second weaning, from the bottle to the cup. Another is that a child who depends upon taking a bottle to bed every nap or every night is more likely to develop cavities than the child who gets his drinking done in a faster manner. The slow drip of sweet liquid, including milk, promotes tooth decay.

If you decide to wean your baby to a cup, this is possible, even at the age of seven or eight months. You do have to pay special attention to getting enough liquid into her. This means that you will have to sit down with her and help her to control the flow so that she doesn't pour her milk or juice onto the floor or up her nose. If you notice that your baby tends to get dehydrated (so the fontanel is depressed or the skin is dry-looking), she needs more liquid. You will need to either increase the amount she gets by sitting patiently with her and giving her drinks from a cup, or by switching her to a bottle.

Don't be surprised if your baby acts for a while as if she is going to wean herself, and then goes back to more nursing times a day. In addition, if you are traveling, your baby may want to nurse more than usual.

It is preferable for weaning to take place when both you and your baby are feeling healthy and well-rested. Weaning can happen so gradually that you and your baby are not at all upset by it. It is a natural process that eventually takes place between all mammalian mothers and their babies.

You may find it easiest to eliminate one feeding at a time over a several week period. The mid-morning or mid-afternoon nursing is generally an easy one to start with. As an alternative, offer your baby something good to drink from a cup or bottle and then provide some interesting activity: a walk or a good, long cuddle in some other spot than your usual nursing spot.

If you usually nurse your baby to sleep, try giving him a big hug and kiss and lie him gently down in his bed and pat his back for a while. Your baby is used to having long periods of closeness and cuddling while he nurses, so it's good to give him plenty of physical attention during the weaning process.

By the time you are down to one feeding a day, most of the weaning process has already happened. Some babies might cling to that last feeding for a few weeks after having eliminated the rest, while others seem to be able to take it or leave it.

Some mothers find that they can eliminate daytime feedings with no fuss, but their babies want to be nursed several times during the night. The best way to handle this situation may be to have your partner wake up to break the news to the baby that you are not coming.

I know of one couple who experienced this with their fourteen-month-old girl. For four months, she only wanted to nurse at night. Her mother didn't resent the night wakeups, since the baby was sweet about nursing and always went right back to sleep. At eighteen months, however, she began demanding to sleep in her parents' bed, and she would wake up and scream if her mother so much as turned over. Her father noticed that the situation had to change, so he told the mother, "You have done your job. Now let me take over. If you go in there all full of milk and hormones and mother-scent, there is no way that you two can keep this from being a fight." The next night when the baby woke up, her father went to her. The first night she cried and carried on, and the second night he even had to walk the floor with her. By the third night, she barely whimpered, and after that, she began sleeping all night.

One of my favorite weaning stories comes from a midwife who remembers her grandmother, who lived on a Midwestern farm. The women of the family were exchanging weaning stories, and grandmother began telling how she weaned her youngest son after he had got old enough to be rough with her. Anticipating that he would be wanting a drink soon, she went over to the woodstove, covered her hand with the soot that had accumulated inside the stove top, unbuttoned her dress and rubbed the soot on her breasts. Her son toddled in, and she opened her dress top. Horrified at the sight of her blackened breasts, he cried, "What happened?"

"Pigs got 'em," she replied. He never wanted to nurse again.

The main thing to remember about weaning is that your baby's attitude toward weaning will be largely affected by your own. If you are not ready for weaning, there's a very good chance that your baby will not be ready either. If you think that weaning is going to mean a terrible loss for your baby, you might as well nurse for as long as it takes for you to be able to make a smooth transition.

SUGGESTED SUPPLEMENTAL READING

Breckinridge, Mary. *Wide Neighborhoods: A Story of the Frontier Nursing Service*. Louisville: University Press of Kentucky, 1981.

Korte, Diana, and Roberta Scaer. *A Good Birth, A Safe Birth*. New York: Bantam, 1984.

10

Drugs, Chemicals, and Breast Milk

♦

*B*reast milk in the last half of the twentieth century contains many ingredients that nature did not plan. It is sad but true that many toxic chemicals and even radioactive substances have become part of the environment. Many modern poisons are very stable chemically, that is, they take many years or decades to break down into their most basic and nontoxic constituents. Chemical or radioactive pollution of any portion of the food chain can eventually end up in humans. If you are planning to breastfeed, there are many drugs that you will want to avoid and certain measures that you may want to take to ensure that your baby receives the purest milk possible.*

Modern Poisons in the Environment

One of the first chemical poisons to be found in mothers' milk was DDT, the most widely used pesticide of the last fifty years. Even though its use was banned in the United States in 1973 and it has been restricted or banned in most other countries, in the 1980s every nursing mother on the planet had a measurable quantity of DDT in

---

*I want to thank Barbara Wallace, Ph.D., for researching and writing parts of this chapter.

her breast milk. Cows' and goats' milk also contains DDT. It seems that we are all stuck with a certain amount of DDT in us at present. In most cases, the amount of DDT is, apparently, too low to be directly harmful to babies.

There does seem to be good evidence that the milk of vegetarian mothers is to be less contaminated by DDT and other pollutants than the milk of mothers who eat meat or high-fat animal products. A study by the Environmental Defense Fund in the United States has shown that a vegetarian diet is associated with one-third to one-half of the amount of DDT in breast milk as compared to the DDT level in the milk of women who eat meat regularly.[1]

Other possible environmental chemicals in breast milk are the industrial pollutants PCB and PBB, which remain stable for a very long period of time in the environment. Polychlorinated biphenyl (PCB) is used in the manufacture of electronics, paints, packaging materials, and the fluid used in carbonless copy paper. All of these and many other uses cause some amount of PCB to enter the environment. The Food and Drug Administration (FDA) has established temporary tolerances for PCB in foods, but since exposure to PCB can cause liver tumors, these levels have been challenged as being too high for safety.[2]

The levels of chemical contaminants in breast milk depend on a combination of factors. In 1973, polybrominated biphenyl, or PBB, was accidentally introduced into the food chain in Michigan when 500 to 1000 pounds of PBB was accidentally substituted for a cattle feed supplement.[3] Eventually the contaminated cattle were killed, but not before large amounts of PBB-contaminated milk reached the open market. As a result, when the Michigan Public Health Department tested human milk, they found that 96 percent of the women from the lower peninsula and 41 percent of the women from the upper peninsula had detectable residues of PBB in their milk. Some Michigan women were advised not to breastfeed their babies because they had such high levels of PBB in their milk at the time.

The Farm's Breastmilk Study

In 1979, twelve members of The Farm, the alternative community in middle Tennessee where I live, all of them nursing mothers who were total vegetarians (no animal products at all in the diet), collected their breast milk to be analyzed for seventeen different chemical substances. For the seven substances for which United States average levels were available, comparisons showed that for each, except PCB, the vegetarian mother with the highest level had a smaller amount of the chemical substance than the nonvegetarian mother with the lowest level of chemical pollution. Only for PCB, was there an overlap between the vegetarian and nonvegetarian group. Even in this case, the average vegetarian level was less than the average nonvegetarian level. The other six substances that were significantly lower in the vegetarian group than in the United States average were all chlorinated hydrocarbons used in agriculture (i.e., DDT, its metabolite DDE, beta-benzene hexachloride, dieldrin, oxychlordane, and heptachlor epoxide). Levels in the vegetarian mothers were only 1 percent to 8 percent of the United States average. The only vegetarian woman who had more than trace amounts of these chemicals was the one mother who was nursing her first baby and had observed the vegetarian diet for less than a year. For three of the substances, DDE, heptachlor epoxide, and oxychlordane, the mean vegetarian levels were only 1 to 2 percent as high as the average levels of the United States.[4]

Reducing Risks

Partly as a result of this finding, the Environmental Defense Fund advises that breastfeeding mothers cut down on meat. The fat in meat can be a main source of several of the toxic chlorinated hydrocarbon chemicals such as DDT. These chemicals, as well as industrial pollutants such as PCB and PBB, are usually stored in body fats. Once inside fat cells, the main way they leave the body is in breast milk or, to some slight extent, when weight is lost.[5]

If you reduce the amount of animal fat you eat, you can reduce the intake and body load of chemical pollutants. Skim milk, yogurt, and buttermilk contain lower levels of pollutants than high-fat products.

Testing Your Milk

Mothers who have reason to believe that the levels of contamination in their milk may be high can have their milk tested. If you live in the United States, it is now possible, through your doctor, to test your contamination level of agricultural and industrial chemicals prior to pregnancy. Women with abnormal contamination levels then can look at their diets, at the jobs, and at their homes to see how to cut back on the toxics. Here is the address of a laboratory that can test for heavy metals, and agricultural and industrial chemicals: Enviro-Health Systems, Inc., 990 N. Bowser Road, Suite 800, Richardson, Tex. 75081. You can also inquire of the Environmental Protection Agency, the Public Health Department in your state, your local public health service, local television or radio stations, or your doctor.

One important factor to keep in mind in evaluating the possible level of chemical pollution in milk is what the level of lactation has been. Since cows are continuously lactating and therefore excreting the chemicals, cows' milk may have a lower level of chemicals than human milk. Similarly, a mother who has breastfed many months will also probably have a lower level than a mother who is just beginning to breastfeed her first baby. Problems with infant formulas include the fact that there has been little research by the FDA on pesticide levels in these formulas. They may contain higher levels of phosphates and sodium or contaminants such as antibiotics or hormones, and they are sometimes incorrectly mixed. For example, 500,000 cans of formula were recalled during the first months of 1982 in the United States because of the right amount of vitamin B_6 had not been added. The lack of vitamin B_6 can cause irritability and convulsions in babies.[6]

Because toxic chemicals and metals have such damaging effects on fetuses and newborn infants and because they are present in varying levels in our environment, it does make sense for mothers to make some assessment of probable levels in themselves. Of course, the best course is to reduce the risk of accumulating high levels of toxins by following a lifestyle that reduces exposure to them.

Strontium 90 and Lead

Strontium 90 can be present both in human milk and in cows' milk. Anita Jarvis and co-workers examined Strontium 89 and Strontium 90 levels in cows' milk and breastmilk in 1961 and 1962 when nuclear testing was taking place. Using the most conservative and accurate comparison, they found breastmilk levels to be only one-fifth as large as cows' milk levels.[7]

Lead can be passed from mother to fetus via the placenta and from mother to baby via breastmilk. A recent Canadian study of lead levels in 210 nursing mothers found lead levels considerably lower than the allowable level. It appears that breast milk does not seem to be a major problem. This conclusion is further supported by the fact that, in general, blood-lead levels in children one year or less are lower than they are in slightly older children. However, since an infant is quite sensitive to lead from any source, and since many very young infants depend on breastmilk for their entire food supply, a nursing mother who thinks that she might have had extensive lead exposure, should ask her doctor to have her milk tested for lead.

One of the lead "hot spots" in North America is the Niagara neighborhood on the edge of downtown Toronto. This neighborhood shares its living space with a secondary lead smelter, a major ex-

Drugs, Chemicals, and Breast Milk

pressway, and a number of heavily traveled streets (Canada allows higher levels of lead in gasoline than the United States and most other industrialized countries).[8]

One study found lead in higher levels in cows' milk than in breastmilk.[9]

If you are not a long-term lactating vegetarian mother, there are several steps that can be taken to lower possible chemical pollution levels in your milk. Firstly, eat as low on the food chain as possible. This means that you eat as many plant foods as possible, since toxic levels in fruits and vegetables tend to be lower than those in animal foods. Animals, when they eat other animals or plant food that is contaminated, concentrate these toxins in their own bodies. Secondly, avoid fish, game birds, or animals. Thirdly, grow your own vegetables, avoid organochlorine pesticides, and use other pesticides and herbicides as little and as intelligently as possible (e.g., make your last application should be long before the vegetables are ready to be eaten that chemical breakdown is assured). And finally, if your milk has been tested as quite high in chemical pollutants, consider expressing the milk for some time and discarding it to rid your body of the chemicals and to provide your child with cleaner milk at a later date. This procedure has been followed successfully in at least one documented case in Japan where many months of expressed-discarded milk resulted in milk clean enough to use.

Almost any drug a mother takes will come through her milk to her baby, some drugs in greater concentrations than others. Some are harmless, while other drugs may be harmful even in small amounts. Sensitivities and allergies develop more easily in newborns than in older babies, and those provoked by medications taken by the mother operate in the same way.

Drugs in Your Environment

It is important to remember that very little is known about the effects of many drugs on breastfed babies. Levels of drugs in milk are hard to measure, and no one is ready to overtly experiment on nursing mothers. For this reason, you should take medications only in extreme circumstances, checking very carefully into the possible effects on the baby if you go on nursing. If the drug is life saving to you and dangerous to the baby, you may want to feed the baby on formula and express and discard your milk until you are done. Sometimes it will be possible to tke alernive drug with fewer or less serious side effects.

Many drugs are known to be safe. Ask your doctor if you question the safety of any medication. He should know exactly what substances are in the medications he prescribes, and he can find out from the manufacturer if he doesn't.

DRUGS DANGEROUS FOR BREASTFEEDING

- Anticancer drugs—Do not breastfeed.
- Radioactive isotopes—Do not breastfeed.
- Antithyroid medications (thyroid pills)—Do not breastfeed.
- Cough medicines—Avoid those with iodine, for these can alter the baby's thyroid activity.
- Diuretics—Avoid, or do not breastfeed.
- Nicotine—Avoid cigarettes; nicotine can reduce the milk supply. If you are pregnant, remember that heavy smokers have smaller babies.
- Oral contraceptives (birth control pills)—Avoid these. They reduce the milk supply and may have far-reaching effects. Stay away from any drugs containing hormones.
- Steroids—Don't take these while breastfeeding.
- Anticoagulants—There have been one or two cases of near death in babies of mothers who took the anticoagulants given before heparin by injection was used. The anticoagulant, heparin, is controversial; some suggest that warfarin should be the drug of choice.
- Tetracyclines, sulfa drugs, (anti-infective drugs)—avoid while breastfeeding; they can cause jaundice in the baby. Tetracycline stains the teeth brown.
- Antibiotics (penicillin)—These can cause sensitivity reactions in some babies. If any are prescribed for you while you are breastfeeding, make sure your doctor is taking into account a possible reaction in the baby. Generally these are safe, although it's good to avoid long-term use, if possible.
- Ergot (for migraine)—Avoid these. Don't worry, though, if you are given ergometrine or ergotrate just after birth to contract the uterus. This won't hurt the baby.
- Atropine—Avoid this; it reduces milk production.
- Cortisone and derivatives—Avoid these.
- Bromides—Avoid these because they cause drowsiness in the baby.
- Laxatives containing senna, cascara—Avoid these.
- Flagyl—Avoid.

Some Common Drugs—How They Affect Babies

It is not harmful to take *aspirin* in moderation when needed. Aspirin is sometimes prescribed in large quantities for rheumatoid arthritis. In this case, you should consult with your doctor as to whether breastfeeding is a good idea. The amount of aspirin reaching your baby may interfere with the ability of his blood to clot well. Keep in mind that taking aspirin can sometimes mask the symptoms of an illness that should receive attention.

Tranquilizers and mood changing drugs (Valium is the most commonly prescribed) should be avoided, although many doctors will prescribe them even if the mother is breastfeeding. If you are depressed, try to find some other mothers who can give you friendship and emotional support.

Antihistamines seem to cause no great effects, although they may make the baby drowsy. They should be taken only in moderation.

Insulin, taken by diabetic mothers, is not harmful to the baby, as it is broken down in the baby's digestive tract.

Epinephrine, the bronchial dilator, does not reach the baby when taken by the breastfeeding mother.

Alcohol is not harmful if it is taken in very small amounts; in fact, a small glass of beer may be considered a good thing for a nursing mother. The trouble with alcohol is that excessive indulgence is harmful for both baby and mother. The baby of an alcoholic mother goes through alcohol withdrawal symptoms after birth and is a very sick baby.

Mothers who are addicted to drugs such as *heroin, cocaine,* or *morphine* give birth to babies who are also addicted. Since heroin is secreted into breastmilk, mothers who are addicts at the time of birth should not breastfeed immediately.

There may be situations in which it is necessary to weigh the risks to yourself and the baby when it comes to your taking various medications. The dosage and the length of time the drug must be taken are factors which should be taken into account. If you must take a medication which is harmful to your baby, you can give your baby formula during that time. Express your milk several times each day so that your supply will be plentiful when you resume breastfeeding.

REFERENCES

1. Reported in *The New York Times,* Sept. 20, 1977.
2. R.D. Kinbrough, R.A. Squire, et al., "Induction of liver tumors in Sherman Strain female rats by PCB Aroclor 1260," *Journal of the National Cancer Institute,* 55, 1453–59.
3. *Science,* 192 (16 April 1976) 240–43.
4. "Pollutants in breast milk of vegetarians," *The New England Journal of Medicine,* March 26, 1981.
5. William B. Weill, Jr., M.D., "The Hazards of Living: Breast Feeding and Environmental Contaminants," Statement prepared for the

U.S. Senate Subcommittee on Health and Scientific Research Hearings, June 9, 1977.
6. "FDA Publishes a Warning on Infant Formula," *Washington Post*, March 4, 1982.
7. Anita A. Jarvis, J.R. Brown, and Bella Tiefenbach, "Strontium 89 and strontium 90 levels in breast milk and in mineral supplement preparation," *Canad. Med. Assoc. J.*, 88 (1963), 136–39.
8. Barbara Wallace, Ph.D., and Kathy Cooper, *The Citizen's Guide to Lead* (Toronto: NC Press, 1986).
9. D. Jelliffe, and E.F.P. Jelliffe, *Human Milk in the Modern World* (Oxford: Oxford University Press, 1978), 107.

SUGGESTED SUPPLEMENTAL READING
Birth Defect Prevention News. Washington, D.C.: National Network to Prevent Birth Defects, NCAMP, 530 Seventh St., S.E., Washington, D.C. 20003
Birthright Denied: The Risks and Benefits of Breastfeeding. 2nd ed., rev. Ann Arbor, Mich.: Environmental Defense Fund, 1977.
Brown, Lester R. *The Twenty-Ninth Day*. New York: Norton, 1978.
Brown, Michael. *Laying Waste: The Poisoning of America by Toxic Chemicals*. New York: Washington Square Press, 1981.
Carson, Rachel. *Silent Spring*. Cambridge, Mass.: Riverside Press, 1962.
Jelliffe, D., and E.P.F. Jelliffe. *Human Milk in the Modern World*. Oxford: Oxford University Press, 1978.
Lawrence, Ruth A., M.D.: *Breast-Feeding: A Guide for the Medical Profession*. St. Louis: C.V. Mosby, 1980.

11

Shared Nursing

♦

During the pioneer period of The Farm, in the seventies, many of the women in the community became mothers. Since our community had almost no old people and few teenagers at the time, we had to rely totally on each other if we needed help in caring for our very young children during those early years. At the same time, we all had plenty of work to do besides taking care of our babies, whether it was food-getting, production or preparation, research, managerial or secretarial work in one of the businesses, teaching, working in the health care system, midwifery, creative work or housework, all carried out without the benefits of electricity, refrigeration, and, for part of the time, no running water.

The Farm Experience

We soon developed the custom of looking after each other's babies so all of our necessary jobs could get accomplished. Taking care of each other's babies often involved nursing each other's babies, because it seemed to most of us much simpler than having to express milk and find some way of keeping it from spoiling before it could be given to the babies. We each still maintained our primary relationship with our own children, but not to the point where we could not share our care, our love, or our milk, if that was needed by another baby in our care.

The first time I ever breastfed a baby other than my own was a day or two after the death of my second child, born quite prematurely while we were on our way to find land in Tennessee. A couple of my friends, whose birthings I had attended within the same month of my baby's birth, offered me their babies to nurse on a couple of occasions. I remember well how healing this was for me, and their babies certainly did not mind getting a different flavor of milk. I always felt a special closeness with those babies, and appreciated the willingness of their mothers to share the joy of their life, their healthy babies, with me at a time when I was in need of such intimacy.

Here are several mothers' recollections of shared nursing:

TIT BROTHERS

Sharon and I got pregnant within six weeks of each other, which was fun since we lived in the same house. We got pretty telepathic with each other and each other's belly. I was due in July and Sharon in August. If you have lived in Tennessee, you know these are the hottest and by far the worst months to be nine months pregnant. We sat around eating ice cubes together. I think our babies started knowing each other right then.

Marlon was born July Fourth and was a real fatty. He took to

Shared Nursing

nursing right away, and I had plenty of milk to meet his demands. John was born about six weeks later. Sharon had trouble with her nipples being hard to get hold of. John was having trouble getting them to work and was getting frustrated.

Since I had plenty of milk, I could nurse him and Marlon, too. We had Marlon try to nurse from Sharon. Being older, he had a stronger grip and didn't get frustrated as quickly. It felt real sisterly to share our babies this way and to be able to help Sharon and John. After a while John got stronger and more confident and was more successful.

We took care of each other's babies a lot that first year. It gave us a lot of freedom to have another mother to leave our baby with when we went out. The boys played together and nursed together every day. I think in a way they became like brothers.

Even though we moved to different houses, we still get the boys together every so often. They have a friendship that seems to be centered deeply. After weeks of not seeing each other, they would be really glad to get together and would talk about each other in between times together.

My Survey

When I conducted the breastfeeding survey among the members of my community, I asked for comments about the practice of nursing another woman's baby. (Does the idea of breastfeeding another woman's child bother you?) Here is a sampling of the replies I received.

> WOMAN FROM ALABAMA, BORN 1954: I've nursed a lot of babies besides my own and enjoyed it. It's interesting to see the different styles. Also, it really gives you a unique closeness. I nursed someone else's twins for nine months and, as a result, I love them like my own. I always had enough milk for one more. As a result, I could babysit for another mother while she got out and about. I see these kids at four to six years old now and still feel a special place in my heart for them.
>
> WOMAN, AIR FORCE, RAISED ALL OVER, BORN 1953: I was always overflowing with milk the first few months of nursing. The idea was foreign to me at first, but it made sense not to waste all the good food. So when I lived in a community that wouldn't be upset about it, I nursed several other babies. Some of my good friends had trouble keeping up enough milk, so I was glad to fix up their babies for them. It was fun to look at a different little face sucking my tit. Some babies, one in particular, would be so grateful to get a big slug of milk that she would touch me very lovingly the whole time.

The first time I offered her my tit, she was surprised and kept stopping and studying me. Once she realized who I was and that she was getting a good deal, she latched on and emptied me out real quick.

WOMAN (MIDWIFE), FROM CALIFORNIA, BORN 1949: The idea of a mother nursing another woman's baby seems perfectly natural to me. I've babysat many times and nursed the babies when their mothers were gone, and they've done the same for me.

One time a woman came from quite a distance to have her baby at our birth center. The same afternoon she arrived, her waterbag broke. She went into labor a few hours later and gave birth after a four-hour labor. Even though she had an easy labor, she was tired because of the traveling and fell fast asleep about an hour after the baby was born. Her baby girl was so beautiful and rosy. She was a very healthy, alert baby, but she definitely felt like she wasn't going to relax and settle down until she sucked. Her mother had put her to the breast for a little while before she fell asleep, but the baby hadn't really sucked very much. I was holding her, and I could feel very strongly how she wanted to nurse. I nursed her, and she sucked for about half an hour and got lots of milk and then felt so peaceful and happy, she fell right to sleep beside her mother. This was the only time I ever nursed a baby so newly born (except my own), because it never felt like there was any need—the baby nursed from its mother when it was ready. But this time there was no doubt in my mind. That was what the baby wanted, and it was lovely to provide such a newborn with something so gratefully received.

WOMAN, BORN 1943, IN LONDON: I wondered about this also, and, in the beginning, was shocked by the idea, thinking it was maybe too traumatizing for the baby. However, having lots of milk for my first, I nursed ten other babies for different reasons, to help their moms out, and I had a very good time doing it. Hungry babies would nurse voraciously, and then be astonished that you weren't Mum. All of them that I came into contact with enjoyed the 'joke' and were grateful.

WOMAN, FROM CHICAGO, BORN 1956: I'm single, having had no kids of my own, but I've watched a lot of infants for their moms. I once had a sneak preview to the experience of nursing when I was watching my close friend's seven month old. She couldn't get away to come be with him at the time, and she said, 'You nurse him. He wants to suck, and then he'll sleep.' My goodness, she wasn't kidding. He sucked so strong, it sent thrills and chills through me. I felt it was all I could do to keep from giggling with joy. He fell fast asleep quite contentedly.

MAN, FROM ITALY, BORN 1960: The main thing that counts is that a baby needs to get fed and if, for some reason, the mother can't do it, I don't see why it's not okay for some other mother to nurse that baby.

WOMAN, BORN BROOKLYN, 1950: It did bother me when I first heard of the idea of nursing someone else's baby. It felt like an irrational reaction, though, because when I really considered it, milk is milk and not essentially different from person to person. I think what bothered me was being that intimate with someone unrelated to me, i.e., not my own child or husband. This was in the first months of my first baby's life.

Later, when I was used to nursing and less personal about the act, I found it fun to see the difference among other babies, to see how hard or softly they sucked. It was fun to trade babysitting with a friend and know that if I didn't make it back for a nursing in time, my baby would still be fed and happy when I got there and vice versa. It made us all closer. I still feel a sisterly bond with those mothers and kids.

WOMAN, RAISED ALL OVER (NAVY), BORN 1949: I think nursing other mothers' babies helps you maintain that idea of being a mother to all children and to not think you're only supposed to care for your own children.

MAN, RAISED IN IOWA AND MINNESOTA, BORN 1944: It seems like a nice thing to do, quite clannish.

WOMAN, RAISED IN SOUTHERN ILLINOIS, BORN 1945: If we don't let our conditioned predispositions and preconceptions govern us, a lot of healthy changes like open breastfeeding can occur naturally and easily. Babies and mothers would be much better off.

MAN, RAISED IN SOUTHERN CALIFORNIA, BORN 1945: In my head, a revulsion button went off—how could you do that? Some kind of old thing about 'This is my family and that's your family.' I heard about it at first and had these thoughts. Wondered if it was perverted. Then my wife helped somebody out (she had no feelings like this), and I changed and was interested.

WOMAN, RAISED IN VIRGINIA, BORN 1954: Mothers nursing other babies is, in fact, revolutionary. A mother who is sick or on a strong medication can have another woman breastfeed for her and then resume it herself when that is over. Also, I have seen new mothers with a sick, small or premature baby that wouldn't suck enough at first. It really helps if she can nurse other babies a few times to help relieve the milk supply. Young babies rarely care whose tit they have, I've noticed.

WOMAN, FROM CONNECTICUT, BORN 1948: I have had friendships with women where we have looked after each other's babies and nursed them and put them to bed. It put me through changes the first time I nursed another baby but the baby was so nonconceptual. I soon got over it and got right down to getting acquainted with the hungry little baby and being its mom.

WOMAN, FROM WISCONSIN, BORN 1951: I babysat a friend's baby while she went out for a while. After a few hours, she started crying and wanted to nurse. A friend suggested that I nurse her, even though I didn't have any milk, just to get her to go to sleep. At the time, the idea didn't seem like a very good one. I felt myself getting uptight and strongly opposed to it, partly because my kid was older and I hadn't nursed for a few years and partly because, though I didn't recognize it then, of the inhibitions I had and the mainstream way of differentiating between my kids and other people's kids. I can't remember if I nursed her or not that time, but I can remember when I finally did nurse another kid, under similar circumstances. I remember looking into the baby's eyes and seeing that it certainly didn't matter to her whose tit it was. She was just grateful, and I felt those old inhibitions leave and was glad I could help her and then fell in love with her.

A few years later, I had another baby, and got to really nurse babies other than my own. I started looking forward to taking care of other babies. Cooperating with other women in this way meant that we could go out and do something without our kids, which I really appreciated, since with my first kid I had lived alone and, as a nursing mother, wasn't able to do many of the things I would have liked to have done. I felt like it was good, not only for me, but good for my kid (to share), and good for my relationships with other women; nursing each others' babies helped us to build strong, sisterly bonds between us.

Sometimes women who are babysitting have to improvise when it comes to caring for babies. Here are two babysitters' experiences:

WOMAN, FROM PENNSYLVANIA, BORN 1952: Many people may not know that when a baby nurses, there is satisfaction gained from more than just the milk. A good deal of time is spent sucking for the pure pleasure of it. I realized this for myself one night when I was babysitting for a nursing mother who had to leave the house for a brief period. She had nursed him and put him to bed, thinking he would nap for a while. But of course, soon after she left, he woke up ready for more. There I was, without even a bottle of water to help me out. Pacing the floor and changing his diaper did not seem to do the trick. There was only one thing I could think of to do—give him my breast. I had never nursed before but this baby was very satisfied with my equipment just as it was, milk or not.

WOMAN, CHICAGO, BORN 1956: I was babysitting for my niece for my sister, who was going out for the first time since she had the baby (who was breastfed). She was so excited about going out, she forgot to take me through the whole bottle routine. When the baby woke up, she was real hungry, so I got the bottle all warm and ready. But she did not accept the bottle. No way would she take the bottle. But she was getting hungrier and hungrier. Once I realized she wasn't going to take it, I had an idea: if I could get the baby to suck on me, then, after she had calmed down, maybe I could quickly slip the bottle into the baby's mouth. I had my boyfriend sit beside me and hold the bottle ready. I put her onto my tit, and she latched on right away. After she had sucked a little while and was more relaxed, I told him to hand me the bottle, and I quickly slipped it into her mouth. She drank almost the whole bottle.

When my sister called to check in for us, I told her about my trick, and how it had worked. The whole incident became a family joke for a while (in a nice way).

Just after this experience, my mother and I saw a television program about elephants. It showed how female elephants were either taught or encouraged to mind the baby elephants for their mother, and that they often nursed the babies while they were taking care of them. My mother was fascinated and said, 'Oh, that's why you nursed the baby!'

WOMAN, NEW JERSEY, BORN 1949: When I had problems getting my new babies to nurse on my flat nipples, mothers would bring their older babies who were nursing pros to me in hopes they would be able to get my nipples in shape. I thought it was real nice of them to try, but it would never work. The babies could tell I wasn't the one and they would just wriggle and fuss. I can remember how huge these lusty five and six month old ones would look with all their teeth, next to the tiny new ones.

Later, I did have successful experiences nursing other babies and enjoyed it very much. I helped nurse a little girl whose mom needed to take medicine which would have crossed into the breastmilk. I was glad that she accepted me, and I was fun to be with her. A few times, my breasts got very full, and I wanted to get them emptied out so I wouldn't be in danger of an infection; I called for a friend to bring her baby over to nurse. 'It's your first gig,' one mom said to her baby when she would hand her to me.

WOMAN, CALIFORNIA, BORN 1952: The first time I breastfed a baby other than my own was one evening at the clinic. I was in training there at the time. Dr. Williams, country doctor and good friend, would come weekly and give a class, as well as see some of the folks who were ailing. I helped bring people back into the room where the doctor and the midwives were.

On this night, there was a young woman visitor with a distressed little baby. One of the midwives had asked the woman to come in for the clinic because the baby was crying a lot, not nursing well or gaining weight. Dr. Williams observed the situation for a few minutes and recognized that the mother was not in a good mental state to care for the baby at the time. The baby could sense this and refused to nurse from her. I was asked to hold the baby for a bit while Dr. Williams and the midwives talked to the mother alone so they could calm her down.

I took the baby out. I wanted to help calm her, too. She was beautiful and obviously quite hungry. I took her into a room alone, and I talked to her for a bit. I had my own baby at the time (at home), so I had plenty of milk. I offered her my tit, and she latched on right away and sucked for a good, long while. Every now and then, she would stop sucking for a moment and take a deep sigh of relief.

After a while, one of the midwives came out with the mom. She was relieved to see her baby nursing. She thanked me. She went home with her baby to one of the midwives' homes.

I felt a bond with that baby. I never saw her again, but I was grateful for the opportunity to help her for those few moments.

Shared nursing may not appeal to every mother, nor is it practical for many women. Obviously, only women with no communicable diseases should do it. At the same time, in some situations and cultures, shared nursing makes sense and promotes a tender closeness between the women who share this aspect of their mothering.

SUGGESTED SUPPLEMENTAL READING
Jordan, Brigitte. *Birth in Four Cultures*. Montreal: Eden, 1983.
Rich, Adrienne. *Of Woman Born*. New York: Bantam, 1976.

12

Breastfeeding and the Nonindustrialized World

◆

Breastfeeding Becomes Political

The feeding of young babies became a political issue during the 1970s. Before then, opinions and advice about what and how mothers fed their babies were considered to be both too medical and too personal to be ventured forth by anyone but doctors, nurses, nutritionists, or ones parents. But during the 1970s, many minds changed, new information became available, and all sorts of people, including Catholic nuns, missionaries, ministers, ex-Peace Corps volunteers, political editorial writers, farmers, and corporation executives began caring and making known their opinions about the health, economic, and moral problems concerning what mothers from all over the world feed their babies.

The major development which caused the feeding of babies to become the subject of such intense public concern was the great switch in the world market from mother's milk to manufatured infant formula. The baby formula industry grew large and strong during the post-World War II baby boom, and when the birth rate in the industrialized countries dropped in the 1960s, the executives of the formula business took notice of the crisis faced by their companies. Articles appeared in business magazines with titles like "The Baby Bust" and "The Bad News in Babyland."[1]

Naturally, the boards of directors of the big companies considered it quite proper to begin marketing their products in countries in which there was little industry, little competition, little wealth, and plenty of young mouths to feed. This was considered sound business strategy at the time, the obvious way to protect the stockholders' investments. No one questioned the fairness or wisdom of the shift in corporate attention to the nonindustrialized countries.

Within a few years, companies such as Abbot Laboratories, American Home Products, Bristol-Meyers (through its Mead Johnson division), Nestlé, Borden's, and Carnation were opening plants and sales centers throughout the world. Nestlé, by 1977, had eighty-one plants in twenty-seven nonindustrialized countries and 728 sales centers in all parts of the world promoting its products.[2]

The nonindustrialized world offered easy pickings for the multinationals. The number of mothers breastfeeding their babies in these countries began to decline dramatically during the 1960s, partly because of the rapid and drastic social changes taking place in the developing urban areas and partly because of the high pressure and sophisticated advertising and promotional strategies of the infant formula companies. In 1951, out of 100 well-to-do Chinese mothers in Singapore, ninety began breastfeeding; by 1960, the number was down to fifty, and by the time the babies were three months old, fewer than ten out of every 100 mothers were breastfeeding.[3]

A study done in an Mexican village showed that while ninety-one babies out of every 100 were still being breastfed when they were six months old in 1960, by 1970 only nine out of 100 were still being breastfed at that age. In Uganda in 1950, fourteen out of every 100 babies were getting cows' milk in addition to breastmilk, and in 1955, thirty out of 100 were getting cows' milk supplements.

All over the world, in the very poorest of countries, large numbers of women were changing from the age-old practice of breastfeeding to the modern way—instant baby formula. This is not really a surprising change in lifestyle, when considered alongside all the other ways their lives were being transformed during that time. Contributing to this change, increasing numbers of mothers in the nonindustrialized countries were giving birth in urban hospitals, separated from their families and the traditional midwives who had once served them and who might have passed on to them a more time-proven way of feeding babies.

If living conditions in all these countries had been the same as those of the majority of the population of the U.S. and other industrial countries, the marketing of the baby formulas would probably never have become controversial. After all, Americans and many Europeans

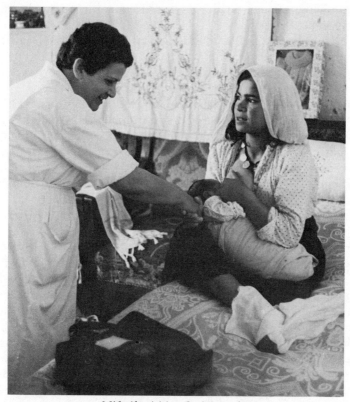
Midwife visiting Syrian mother

had already witnessed two generations raised on cows' milk, and they certainly seemed healthy enough. It would be quite easy to assume that the same would be true for babies in other parts of the world. But it isn't.

By the mid-1960s, we had the first signal that all was not going well with the introduction of this twentieth-century product into countries with eighteenth or nineteenth century conditions and lifestyles, even some with Stone Age lifestyles, such as the peoples of the Arctic Circle.

Reports of gastroenteritis and malnutrition, stemming from improper use of the formula and the apparatus that goes with it, came from all parts of the nonindustrialized world. Doctors and health workers started to point out that the mortality rate for bottlefed babies was about double that of breastfed babies in these countries. An interAmerican examination of mortality in childhood, investigating the causes of 35,000 infant deaths, found that "nutritional deficiency" as an underlying cause of death was "less frequent in infants breastfed for only limited periods."[4]

In 1974, a British public interest group, War on Want, began an international campaign claiming that the aggressive promotion of infant formula in poor countries was contributing to severe malnutrition and even to the death of the babies.[5]

When the group's pamphlet was translated into German as "Nestlé Kills Babies," Nestlé sued in a Swiss court for $5 million in damages. Lawyers for the corporation charged that the accusations in the pamphlet—that Nestlé's marketing techniques caused deaths, that its sales representatives were dressed similarly to medical personnel, and that its efforts were unethical and immoral—were all defamatory. The judge ruled in favor of Nestlé on this charge, but declared, "This verdict is no acquittal [of Nestlé]."

My Experiences in the Third World

I lived in Malaysia during the early sixties, and even though I was not a health worker and did not live at a standard of living anywhere near as poor as that of the majority of people in the country, I was aware of the nutritional problems caused by the feeding of infant formulas among working class people of the country. My neighbor, a well-educated teacher who lived at a standard almost comparable to that of an American teacher, pointed out to me the fat, pasty-white babies of many of the Chinese shopkeepers of the town where I lived. She told me that the Chinese mothers had recently given up breastfeeding and had begun feeding babies the canned, sweetened, condensed milk, which had previously been marketed just for grownups to add to their tea or coffee. Now the babies had also become consumers of imported food; in the process, they became unusually fat because of the extremely high sugar content of the canned milk. They were pale with anemia, because this particular form of milk had no iron added to it. Their unnaturally pale skin was valued in a country which had been dominated for a century by British colonial values. These babies, although fat, were malnourished, and they became sick easily, their health having been sacrificed to a look made fashionable and desirable by years of their parents' living with colonial and racist attitudes.

I was also aware that Nestlé and a couple of other formula companies were investing a tremendous amount of money in this small distant country. Canned and dried baby formula was, along with cigarettes, the most advertised product in all the media: advertisements in the movie theaters, billboards, radio, and magazines. Nestlé's advertising budget included producing commercials in the four major languages spoken by the people in that country: Malay, Cantonese, Tamil, and English, all aimed at convincing mothers that their babies would be healthier, more beautiful, and happier if they were bottlefed the modern way.

My next direct contact with the infant formula problem in nonindustrialized countries began in 1976, when I lived in Guatemala for six weeks, a few months after the great earthquake. This time I was a health worker, and I was living very close to the highland Mayan people whose average life expectancy was barely fifty years. I attended births and was called to visit sick and dying people of all ages. Most of the Mayans had kept their traditional ways, including breastfeeding, but in some of the towns, there had been more inroads made on their culture, especially in those towns which had been strongly influenced by the evangelical missionaries from the United States. These Mayans gave up their hand-woven *traje* and instead wore used, ill-fitting American suit jackets, trousers, and bargain basement dresses. Quite often the women, striving to be more "American," chose bottlefeeding over breastfeeding. Bottlefeeding was very widely accepted by the people of mixed European and Indian origin who lived in the towns.

The trouble was that few people lived at a standard that allowed for safety in feeding formula to the babies. Most people I saw did not have a source of running water near their homes and had to walk a kilometer or more to get water, which was then carried home by the women and girls. This water was used for drinking, cooking, cleaning, and bathing for the whole family and so had to be used very sparingly. Water was such a valuable substance that the people called it "that precious fluid" in the Cackchiquel language. Even so, it was quite polluted with micro-organisms, which cause serious and fatal diseases in humans—particularly in young babies, whose immune systems are not fully formed to protect them against such disease.

Many of the houses I visited were made of adobe and consisted of one or two rooms. Because of the destruction caused by the recent earthquake, many more people lived in one-room shanties made of cornstalks. The kitchen was the floor in one of the corners, the stove a ring of stones surrounding the cooking fire—not an easy set-up for sterilizing water used to prepare the formula or the bottle and the nipple.

Not only was water scarce; wood for cooking fires was just as hard to obtain. It could be bought for a high price in the market, but many people had to do backbreaking work just to get a little wood, because they could not afford the market price. The government put severe

fines on anyone who cut down a tree, even if the tree was on land owned by the individual wanting to cut the wood. As a result, few families could afford to do an adequte job of feeding artificial formula to their babies.

In the barrancas of Guatemala City, the hillsides covered with houses made of corrugated tin or cardboard, the situation was even worse. Here the mothers very often had to give birth in the city hospitals for the poor, instead of at home with midwives. This made them even more vulnerable to the promotional campaigns of the formula companies; many were given hormone shots to dry up their milk; nearly all were routinely separated from their babies; and many were sent home with a few days' supply of free infant formula, just enough to feed the baby until the mother's milk had dried up.

These mothers then had to fend for themselves. Since the illiteracy rate is very high among women in a country like Guatemala, there is no effective way for these mothers to find out the careful procedures required for the safe use of the formulas. They also had to find money to buy the expensive formula. Very often, mothers were unable to afford such an expensive food item that would cover only one member of the family, and they were forced to dilute the formula with water to make it go farther. This, of course, resulted in a large number of malnourished and dead babies.

The situation in Malaysia and Guatemala is multiplied many times over in countries all over the world, and the mortality rate is hard even to estimate. In rural Punjab, India, according to a 1974 report in the respected medical journal, *The Lancet,* "In the study population virtually all the infants died who did not receive breast milk in the first months of life."[6]

Before the 1960s, when breastfeeding was the usual way among the poor, severe malnutrition was usually held off beyond the crucial first year of the child's life. Now, according to World Bank nutritionist Alan Berg, the rapid change to bottlefeeding has caused the average age of the onset of malnutrition to drop from eighteen months, to a more critical eight months in several countries studied.[7]

Representatives of the formula companies usually argue that they are fulfilling, not creating, a need for their products. "Where there is no breast milk, the chances for survival are small if the baby who is not formula fed," said E. Steven Bauer, vice president of Wyeth International, a subsidiary of American Home Products, that makes an infant formula marketed world-wide (SMA and its international equivalent, S-26).[8]

The fact is that nearly every mother is physically able to breastfeed, especially poor women, whose breasts have not been rendered non-functional by various forms of breast surgery and who, until the past two decades, have not had psychological barriers preventing success in breastfeeding. I asked many village women in Guatemala if they had ever known of anyone who had wanted to breastfeed and couldn't, and none knew of any. Dr. David Morley surveyed a rural

Nigerian village and found less than one percent of mothers had serious breastfeeding problems.[9]

Besides this, representatives of the companies argue that their products are needed by women who work. Actually the percentage of women who work away from their families is very low. Most mothers in poor countries work very hard, but in almost all cases, their babies are constantly with them, tied to their backs.

The Struggle to Save Breastfeeding

Several countries are fighting back, among them New Guinea, Zambia, Tanzania, Brazil, and India. The public health officials in these countries recognize that human milk is one of the natural resources of the country. In the Philippines, $17 million was wasted on imported milk in 1958, and by 1968, the number of mothers breastfeeding had dropped by 30 percent and the dollar loss to the country had doubled.[10]

The countries which are trying to encourage breastfeeding have banned "milk nurses" — the women hired by the formula companies to promote their products to local women—and have enlisted all health workers to persuade storekeepers not to display formula company advertisements and to destroy the ads when they find them.

In 1976, groups from eight countries met in Bern, Switzerland to plan their efforts against the formula companies. The same year, The Sisters of the Precious Blood brought suit against Bristol-Meyers, charging that company with committing fraud in its statement to its stockholders (the Sisters themselves were stockholders, and had tried, unsuccessfully, to persuade the company to change its promotional policies). The suit was not successful, but the publicity it generated helped to launch another international campaign, The Infant Formula Action Coalition (INFACT, 310 E. 38th St., Minneapolis, Minn. 55409). This coalition's first action was to begin a boycott of Nestlé until the corporation agreed to stop all promotion of infant formula in the nonindustrialized countries.

In 1981, the World Health Organization (WHO) voted 118 to 1, with the United States casting the only negative vote, to adopt a nonbinding code restricting the promotion of infant formula products. Elliot Abrams, assistant secretary of state for international organization affairs (since appointed to be the assistant secretary of state for human rights), tried to explain the U.S. vote: "Despite our governmental interest in the encouragement of breastfeeding, the WHO recommendations for a complete ban on advertising to the general public of infant formula and the proposed restrictions on the flow of information between manufacturers and consumers run counter to our constitutional guarantees of free speech and freedom of information."[11]

This official stance brought the U.S. a flood of ridicule and criticism from abroad as well as from concerned people at home. Two high-ranking health officials resigned their positions in the U.S. Agency for International Development (AID) in protest of the Reagan administration's controversial decision on this issue.

The political debate became furious, and all sorts of people expressed opinions in the editorial pages of magazines and newspapers, in some cases, people whose ignorance on the subject seemed to be total. William F. Buckley, Jr., editor and publisher of the *National Review*, a political magazine with a right-wing bias, was one such novice to make uninformed editorial pronouncements on the care and feeding of infants.

The main substance of his editorial was how the poor mothers of the Third World would be in for really hard times (under the code passed by WHO) since "the services provided by the baby formula industry to teach mothers to prepare the formula correctly will be eliminated, and those unable to breastfeed would be forced to go back to the old native substitutes of cereal gruels of water and maize, rice or millet, flours, crackers, sugar, water, or mashed fruit."

According to Buckley, the United States was the only nation saintly enough among the 119 voting on the code to try to dissuade the governments of the member nations from voting against the interests and health of their babies. He concluded that "the real causes of starvation go unnoticed in all the hubbub of self-righteousness, and the infants of the Third World will have to wait a little longer before 'Western'-style nutrition will help to alleviate their suffering."

I don't mean to suggest that only medical types have a right to proclaim their opinions about infant care, but I do believe that we share the responsibility to study our subjects well before we do so. Mr. Buckley obviously did not reflect on how it was that so many millions of babies in the nonindustrialized countries survived prior to the time when "Western"-style nutrition became available.

In March 1982, largely in response to the growing strength of the boycott, the Nestlé company publicly released instructions to all its infant formula marketing personnel, suggesting a new company policy of compliance with the WHO Code. INFACT spokesmen welcomed the announcement with "cautious optimism" — since past violations of the Code by Nestlé had often been at odds with its stated public policy—and promised to continue monitoring the company's practices around the world.

Even if the formula companies totally comply with the WHO code, poor people in urban ghettos, barrios, rural areas, and Indian reservations in countries like the U.S. have the same problems with formula feeding as mothers of poor countries. Health officials say they see many babies who are sick or malnourished because their mothers do no know how to use infant formula. Dr. H. L. Kafka, chief of pediatrics for four Los Angeles health clinics, blames formula misuse for some of the severe diarrhea and dehydration he sees among children of low-income Hispanic families.[12]

Dr. Allan Cunningham, a pediatrician at the Mary Imogene Bassett Hospital in Cooperstown, N.Y., reported that bottlefed babies are hospitalized three times more often than breastfed babies before their first birthday. He also said that when only the first four months of life are taken into account, bottlefed babies are hospitalized fifteen times as often as breastfed babies.

The major formula companies in the U.S.—Ross Laboratories (Similac) and Mead Johnson (Enfamil)—control 90 percent of the domestic market. These companies feel threatened by the recent increase in the rate of breastfeeding, and consequently spend large amounts of money promoting their products.

Ross Laboratories gives doctors and hospitals free literature on breastfeeding, their own productions, which sometimes contain information more discouraging than helpful. The guide mentions not only the medical problems which may result from breastfeeding, but a few other items, such as leaking during intercourse and sagging breasts. Any doctor who reads one of these "college-outline series" booklets to review the current medical practice in breastfeeding has to wade through twenty-five pages of a forty-page booklet before he is told that breastmilk is the perfect food for babies. Not surprisingly, the inside cover of the booklet is a full-page ad for Similac.

Even during these relatively hard times for the infant formula companies in the United States, total sale were over $700 million in 1981. A program of aggressive marketing and public relations includes indirect advertising by giveaways of free notepads and pens to pediatricians, as well as the awarding of research and teaching grants. Ross Laboratories made one such grant in 1980—$1 million—to the American Academy of Pediatrics to help publish a journal. I think we can safely assume that this will not likely be a journal which will look for ways to promote breastfeeding.

A Similac sales manual emphasizes the importance of marketing formula to hospitals: "A hospital gained generates untold sales increases, while a hospital lost means watching helplessly as competition reaps all the benefits."

Such fatherly types these formula salesmen are! Of course, they argue that all this promotion is only done out of the goodness of their hearts and that it makes very little difference in their sales. If this were really the case, they would be quickly fired for squandering so much money.

Actually, the methods they choose are very effective, since they help to determine hospital policies which relate to breastfeeding, and they help to shape the attitudes of doctors, who have a lot of power in affecting the success of breastfeeding. Many hospitals are given all of the formula they use, free, as long as they promise to give each new mother a sample on leaving the hospital. Poor women are most likely to value these samples, and they may use them just because they have a money value. The amount given is just about the right amount to last a few days, long enough that the mother's milk supply will have decreased drastically.

Competition between the different companies involves an escalation in the value of gifts and perks offered that reminds me of the nuclear arms race. Ross and Mead Johnson not only give out free formula; they offer free architectural service for nursery design, cocktail parties, equipment, printing, fishing trips—anything that will stand off the competition.

Personnel in some hospitals have begun to fight back. Midwives, nurses, nurse-practitioners, and pediatricians try to provide help to mothers in breastfeeding. The Medical Center of the University of California at San Diego no longer gives discharge packs of formula to breastfeeding mothers. In that hospital, the breastfeeding rate increased from 60 percent to 80 percent. The Bronx Municipal Hospital stopped handing out all formula samples early in 1981, and the breastfeeding rate doubled.

Not all hospitals make such efforts to encourage breastfeeding. Some pro-breastfeeding staff members at the Los Angeles County General Hospital, University of Southern California Medical Center, tried to stop giving out samples to breastfeedng mothers in 1980. Kittie Frantz, a nurse-practitioner and director of the hospital's breastfeeding clinic, noted that fewer mothers were supplementing breastfeeding with a bottle after the staff members temporarily quit giving out samples. Top administrators intervened and ordered the staff to go back to giving out samples, citing the usual humanitarian reasons for their actions. Dr. Paul Wehrle, Los Angeles County Hospital's director of pediatrics, remarked at the time, "Some of these mothers have no money at all. I have a real concern about sending an infant out without some kind of safe and nutritious resource." One wonders if he will continue free deliveries of formula to these same poor women when they run out of the sample supply they are given. This may be no more than coincidence, but Wehrle, in 1981, was a member of the board of the American Academy of Pediatrics, the group which accepted a $1 million grant from Ross Laboratories.

We cannot afford to lose essential knowledge and skill on a global level any more than we can assume that elephants and whales will survive if the human species does not alter its behavior. When you breastfeed your baby, if you are female, or if you help make it possible, if you are a male, you make it less likely that babies in the Third World will die of malnutrition. Our own society will be much more peaceful and wise if we relearn and repopularize breastfeeding. To accomplish this goal, we need extensive cooperation among men as well as women. Women need to learn to cooperate more closely with each other: mothers and daughters, as well as mothers and women who have not chosen motherhood. If we are wise, we will learn to recognize what technologies contribute to survival and which do not.

REFERENCES
1. Roy J. Harris, Jr., "The Baby Bust," *The Wall Street Journal*, (January 4, 1972); "The Bad News in Babyland," *Dun's Review*, 100, (Dec. 1972), 104.
2. Mike Muller and Andy Chetley, *The Baby Killer*, (London: War on Want, 467 Caledonian Rd., 1975). Contains extensive references and bibliography.
3. D.B. Jelliffe and E.F. Jelliffe, *Human Milk in the Modern World*, (Oxford: Oxford University Press, 1978).
4. Ruth Rice Puffer and Carlos V. Serrano, *Patterns of Mortality in Childhood*, Scientific Publication No. 262, (Washington, D.C.: Pan American Health Organization, 1973), 161.
5. Muller and Chetley, *The Baby Killer*, passim.
6. J.B. Wyon and J.E. Gordon, *The Khanna Study* (Cambridge, Mass.: Harvard University, 1971), p. 187, in William A.M. Cutting, *The Lancet*, 7870 (June 24, 1974):1340.
7. D.S. McLaren, *The Lancet*, 7461 (August 27, 1966): 485, in Alan Berg, *The Nutrition Factor* (Washington, D.C.: Brookings Institute, 1973), 95.
8. *The New York Times Magazine*, December 6, 1981, 104.
9. Muller, *The Baby Killer*, 6.
10. Alan Berg, "The Economics of Breast-Feeding," *The Saturday Review of the Sciences*, (May 1973) 30.
11. Stephen Solomon, "The Controversy over Infant Formula." *The New York Times Magazine*.
12. Mary Ellen Schoonmaker, "Here's Looking at You, Kid," *The Progressive*, December 18, 1982, p. 4.

SUGGESTED SUPPLEMENTAL READING

Lappe, Frances Moore, and Joseph Collins. *Food First.* New York: Ballantine, 1978.

United Nations General Assembly. *The International Bill of Human Rights.* Glen Ellen, Cal.: Entwhistle Books, 1981.

Chetley, Andy, and Mike Muller. *The Baby Killer* (pamphlet). London: War on Want, 467 Caledonian Rd., 1975.

Stanway, Penny, M.D., and Andrew Stanway, M.D. *Breast is Best.* London: Pandora, 1980.

13
People's Attitudes Towards Breastfeeding

♦

> We old people of the Bloods are very disturbed about the behavior of the young people. There is very little respect today. A lot of us think the reason for this is that a lot of young people were bottlefed. The milk they were raised on came from cows, so the young people of today have taken on the nature of cows. You know that cows only think of themselves, even though they like to run in bunches. Many of the young people are just the same.
>
> PAULA WEASEL HEAD,
> *Blood elder of the Blackfoot tribe*

The Attitudes of Babies

Babies love breasts. No matter how wide the variation in adult attitudes, all newborn babies share the same attitude toward breasts: they love them with absolutely no reservations, no guilt, no shame. Any baby, breastfed or not, enjoys being held close to her mother's or any woman's breasts who love her. She adores her unperfumed smell, loves the warmth, the softness, and the energy which radiates from her breasts. For the baby, the deliciousness of the milk is equated with the deliciousness of mother. She is the Goddess of Food and All Good Things.

People's Attitudes Towards Breastfeeding

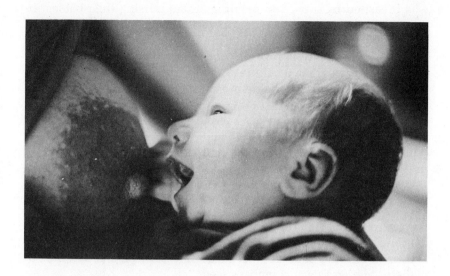

It should be mentioned here that babies do recognize differences in the breastmilk of their mother and that of another. As discussed earlier, the baby who is allowed to lick her mother's nipple during the few minutes after birth will be able to reliably distinguish her own mother's breastpad by smell from the breastpads of other mothers.

Even with this ability to distinguish his own mother's milk, a hungry baby will nurse from "strange breasts." Some older babies or toddlers are adventurous in their tastes, too. I remember one little boy whose full-breasted mother had nursed him for a year and a half. He had just turned two and was cuddled in his babysitter's lap, his face just even with the small breasts under her T-shirt.

"Is there any tits in that shirt?" he asked.

"Yes," she laughed, never having been asked such a thing before.

"Can I eat them?" he asked politely.

I remember another instance, when my friend, Margaret, and I were lying next to each other. My daughter, who was two at the time, was sprawled on top of us, her bottom and legs on me and her torso on Margaret. At one point, my daughter raised her head and looked long and deep into Margaret's eyes. Her face was very pure and angelic as she asked, "Margaret, can I suck your nose?"

The Attitudes of Children

Children's attitudes towards breasts and breastfeeding vary somewhat, according to the age of the child, and whether or not the child was breastfed or is used to seeing mothers nursing their babies. In general, young children, being innocent, do not get hung up about the sexual aspects of breastfeeding. Instead, they tend to be fascinated by your ability to provide food from your body. Of course, a child who grows up in a culture which primarily breastfeeds, watching a baby being given a bottle is a novelty which provides an equal curiosity.

One of the questions in my survey of people in my community who had been born between 1940 and 1964 was, Can you remember your thoughts and reactions the first time you ever saw someone breastfeeding? It was very striking to see how many of the respondents had very clear memories of the occasion, even when they had been very young at the time. Here is a sampling of their responses:

WOMAN: I remember it distinctly. I must have been four or five. A friend of my mother's came over and was breastfeeding. I went over to her and squeezed her breast and asked if she had milk in them. She was terribly embarrassed.

MAN: I was nine years old, and it was the sister of one of my friends. She pulled her breast out and started nursing her kid. I thought, 'She's doing that and I'm in the room!' Another reaction was, 'So that's what they look like!'

MAN: It was a hippie woman in San Francisco in the late 60's. I thought, 'There it is—breastfeeding'. I took her picture because she looked so good. When I was a kid, I shared a bedroom with my grandmother after my grandfather died. I saw her breasts a lot while she was undressing, and that removed any funny edge I had had before about seeing breasts.

WOMAN: I was twelve, and the woman was a friend of my aunt's. I remember being very interested. It felt very nice between her and her baby. She was very uninhibited about nursing in our home, and I remember how her nipples looked. When I had my own children, I never had any problems with nursing. Her example may have helped.

MAN: I think my first reaction (I was in grade school) was, So that's what those things are for.

WOMAN: I saw someone breastfeeding when I was about fourteen. It was my friend's mother, and I distinctly remember not knowing whether I should look. I didn't look and left the room shortly thereafter to avoid what I thought was an embarrassing situation.

MAN: I was about nine years old. I was embarrassed. Then I couldn't get that picture off my mind. I dreamed about that baby nursing, and I enjoyed the dream.

WOMAN: I was five or six, and it was in Iowa, at a neighbor's house. I thought, The baby is sucking on her tit! It was neat to realize that was what tits were for. After that, seeing puppies nurse, too, made me realize we were animals.

WOMAN: I was twenty and had just arrived on The Farm. At first, I just had to look; I couldn't keep my attention away. I enjoyed watching the mother and the baby.

WOMAN: The first idea I had that people did breastfeed was from looking at Catholic missionary magazines of African women nursing. I would just stare at the pictures and feel real good about seeing what grownup women looked like. My dad did not get Playboy magazines, and my family never saw each other naked, so this was my first experience of knowing what a breast even looked like. I thought it looked very important to be feeding a baby like that. The mothers looked really content in the pictures. I didn't see a white person's breasts until I saw a Playboy magazine at the age of twelve.

WOMAN: I was five years old, and it was a neighbor woman who was nursing her fifth child. I don't remember thinking it was strange. It felt very natural. I do remember asking the woman if there was milk in one breast and orange juice in the other one.

WOMAN: I was born in 1945 to Italian-Catholic parents. All the babies were bottlefed. The first I remember knowing that there was such a thing as breastfeeding was after an uncle of mine had gone back to Italy and brought back a wife. She still had the old country ways about her. One day, we were riding in a car, and she pulled out her tit and started nursing her baby. My aunts and mother were highly embarrassed that she would do such an old-fashioned thing in public. I don't recall having any feelings about this at the time, except that breastfeeding was a thing of the past and bottlefeeding was the modern way.

WOMAN: I don't remember the first time I actually saw someone nursing, but I do remember how I found out that's what breasts were for, when I was about eleven. I learned from a Playtex nursing bottle commercial, where they say, 'most like mother herself.' What an amazing realization that was!

WOMAN (FROM AMSTERDAM): It was an aunt nursing her baby. I must have been five or six years old. I was very excited and remember envying her because it seemed such a nice thing to do. I used to go and lean against her when she was nursing. She was very warm.

WOMAN (RAISED AT VARIOUS U.S. AIR FORCE BASES WITH SIX YEARS IN GERMANY): The first time I saw someone nursing was on a bus in Germany when I was about seven. I didn't think much about it because I was in a foreign country with lots of unusual traditions. I just thought it was one more thing that Europeans did, like peeing on the side of the road. Since then, I saw films about African people and other traditional tribal ways. Always I saw nursing mothers. I felt like it was natural and obviously passed down as the way to feed a new baby. I was convinced of this when I nursed my four babies myself.

WOMAN: I was five. My mom asked me if I wanted to go in the next room and see a baby being fed. I think this was the first time I remember seeing a baby. The mother was a friend of my mom's. It felt all pink and yellow glowing. I was utterly surprised. So this is what they're for, how they are used, I thought. Now, the more I see it, the more I like it. It feels when I'm there, very open and loving, it calms me just to be around it.

MAN: I am the second of nine kids, and we were all breastfed. I always thought it was nice. I remember being amazed about how the milk would just stream out of my mom's tits as she was about to begin nursing.

MAN: I don't remember the first time I saw breastfeeding. It's like asking when was the first time I saw a dog or cat or a tree. How old was I? I guess I was a few hours old. All I remember is that I was hungry and that my mom would feed me.

My own children have developed a very practical attitude about breasts. My son, five years old at the time, seeing me at my desk, asked me what I was doing. I said I was writing a book to help mothers so they could feed their babies from their breasts. He looked puzzled, so I told him that some people don't know how to breastfeed their babies and that some mothers do not want to feed their babies this way. Looking troubled, he asked, "What do they think their breasts are for—to look fat?"

Attitudes about Breasts During Puberty

In many ways, young women in North America have a much rougher time going through puberty than the young women in more traditional cultures where I have lived and visited. Puberty in North America is ignored or hidden, for the most part, by everyone except the advertising and marketing industries.

More traditional societies usually mark the passage of a child into adult status by some sort of ceremony or ritual. Among some Native Americans, the first menstruation would be a ritual day, far more important than a wedding would be in mainstream U.S. As one woman put it, "Everyone gathers to celebrate all night with their campfires and their food. Then at sunrise the next morning, the whole Nation gathers together to watch her race into the light of a new day and to glory in the fact that she is now Woman.[1]

I spent a little while in Lesotho, the small, very poor country which is surrounded by the Republic of South Africa. I got to be present on the day when the young men and women performed the dances which have been part of the puberty rituals of the Basuto people for centuries. Despite pressure from Western missionaries, many of the girls still danced the traditional way, with their breasts uncovered. The girls' dance involved some lovely moves, with rhythmic ways of shaking their breasts. Like the Native American way I have just described, this dance was a very public function. Everyone was there, and the onlookers, men, women, and children would present gifts of coins and cookies to the young women as they danced.

It seemed to me that the young women's breasts were revealed to show that they were indeed becoming women and that this even was something joyful and worthy of celebration and respect by the whole village. No one cared whose breasts were biggest, most shapely, best; it was obvious that all were being celebrated for their loveliness. The girls' dignity and lack of either coquettishness or embarrassment was

quite noticeable to my North American eye, used to the steamy looks and heavy makeup of the models on magazine covers and television commercials. Instead of setting out one young woman to be Miss America or Miss Teenage America, these people considered all of their young women to fill the ideal of beauty manifested in girls becoming women.

I would have appreciated such a send-off. My growing up in central Iowa during the 1950s was a relatively painful experience. I was one of those who slumped, because my closest peers noticed that I was the last among us to show any breast development, and our culture seemed to take it for granted that competition in this department was inevitable and perhaps even desirable.

A friend of mine, a woman who was born in Guatemala about 1915, told me about her problem with self-consciousness when her breasts began growing. She said,

> I started growing my breasts at the age of fifteen. I was so bashful, and I didn't want it to happen. I was just ashamed of it, and I started walking around with my shoulders bent over to hide it. My brother noticed this and said, 'Why are you walking that way?'
>
> 'What way?' I said.
>
> 'Oh, you are not walking the proper way. It's because you are embarrassed about developing.'
>
> I blushed, and he said, 'That's what it is. You shouldn't be ashamed of that. That's what makes women beautiful. Try to walk straight because you have a very nice way of walking, and that way, you are ruining your figure.'

Because he was so direct and understanding, she took his advice to heart and quit slumping her shoulders as she walked. I was too hung up about my small breasts to listen to my father when he told me to stand up straight. I waited for another ten years and had a baby before I ever tried to stand up tall.

Many Afro-American women have been raised to think that breastfeeding is for poor people. Sondra Abdullah-Zaiman, an Afro-American midwife, remembers a grandmother interfering with her daughter's first attempts to nurse her newborn son:

"That baby don't want that dry old bag in its mouth."

Sondra and I disagreed; we knew that baby did, too, want his mother's breast.

Breastfeeding and Rape

If I had been asked a few years ago to make a connection between breastfeeding and rape, I would have been totally at a loss. The two activities would have seemed to have so little to do with one another that I could not have found any sensible way to relate them. As I researched attitudes in North America and the history that created these attitudes, I began to see that my own attitude was more old-fashioned and quite a bit more innocent than some I was beginning to notice among other people.

My father gave me a lot of encouragement when I first sat down to nurse his first grandchild in his presence. I remember him laughing and telling me how much milk my mother had when my older brother was a baby, so much that she had to pour the extra "down the kitchen sink." His attitude was like that of most people who grew up on farms and learned to appreciate the workings of the bodies of all the creatures who were part of the farm. Having been raised this way, I was shocked to hear that all fathers weren't like him and that some women's fathers had made them feel so ashamed about breastfeeding that they could not nurse their babies in their fathers' presence. I nursed each of my babies and had never been treated badly for it.

The first time I ever heard any connection made between breastfeeding and rape was in the newspaper and radio reports that followed the First Canadian Suck-In, a planned action in 1981 in which fifty Toronto nursing mothers brought their babies to a shopping mall and nursed them in protest because a nursing mother had been expelled from that same mall the week before. One of the men interviewed at the occasion remarked that breastfeeding was the cause of "all the rape."

My Survey

I was amazed and shocked by the man's comment, and at the same time, I wanted to understand what kind of environment and treatment had created such a perverse attitude. My intrigue with this sentiment led me to include a question relating to attitudes about breastfeeding in a survey I conducted among people who had given birth on The Farm during the 1970s. The question was, "How would you explain one Canadian man's reaction to seeing a number of women breastfeeding in public, that this was the cause of 'all the rape' Do you understand this?" I knew that this man's reaction was an extreme one, yet it was indicative of the attitudes that existed then in that part of Canada. I felt that it might be a good indicator of the degree of shock experienced by many people when they see breastfeeding for the first time.

> A WOMAN, RAISED IN CANADA AND SCOTLAND, BORN 1948, replied to this question: Ignorance! It makes me wonder what kind of mind does he have. He must be kinky!

WOMAN, FROM W. GERMANY, BORN 1950: If a man can't stand seeing a naked tit without having uncontrolled sexual desires, he has to grow up more. It is quite dangerous for a woman to have to live among this kind of macho-ness.

WOMAN: It has to do with lumping all that private stuff together.

MAN, FROM ALASKA, BORN 1945: He must not like women very much. I seriously doubt any rapes have occurred because of breastfeeding. If he's looking for someone to blame, I could suggest television and movie producers.

WOMAN: If you think that a breast's main or only function is as a sex object, then you would think that if you see one in public that it is just too much.

WOMAN: For a man to be so hung-up and self-centered as not to see that there is something else going on there—the feeding of the baby! There are no antisocial aspects to breastfeeding. Everything about breastfeeding is good for the individual and good for the society.

MAN, FROM NEW JERSEY, BORN 1945: Only a very deprived person would feel and think this way, someone who was probably not handled very lovingly by his mother when he was a baby, was not in touch with his own feelings of nurturing, and was not used to receiving much love in the present.

For one thing, rape is not really so much a crime of sexual turn-on as it is a crime of violence, power, and dominance, forcing someone to submit to something against her or his will. If sexual stimulation is what is desired, there are plenty of easier, safer ways to get it than rape.

For another thing, the vibrations put out by a nursing mother and baby are vibrations of satisfaction, not of frustration. Rape would be caused more by a tease—a sexy commercial, perhaps, with subliminals.

The person who says the sight of a nursing mother could cause rape is obviously afraid that he won't be able to handle it himself.

MAN, FROM MASSACHUSETTS, BORN 1941: I think it works the other way around. In our, let's say, Western techno-society, there's an obsession with breasts in the media and advertising. My eye has been attracted in this direction since I was ten or twelve. Having had a wife who breastfed our babies has put my attitude toward breasts in proportion more, made breasts less of a big deal in that sense, and has emphasized the practical aspect of breasts more than their sexual aspect. I think that if more breastfeeding went on in the greater society, people (or men) would get cooler with it. When I think about this, I think that rapes might in part be caused by having breasts on the brain so much through media and not having a respect for the female principle, not knowing women who are breastfeeding and being friends with them, not having it be a normal thing to see breastfeeding.

WOMAN, FROM IOWA, BORN 1947: No, I don't understand this.

MAN (DOCTOR), FROM CHICAGO, BORN 1941: Watching women nurse could 'cause rapes' only if the watcher were truly perverted . . . rather, I believe that for little children to watch breastfeeding is the only normal means of 'sex education' and probably prevents rapes and sexual perversions.

MAN, FROM NEW JERSEY, BORN 1950: I understand that there is such a repressed sexual vibration that our forerunners grew up with that in a court of law a man is considered not capable of controlling himself. Many rape trials are thrown out of court if the woman was not wearing a bra. A bill to prosecute men who rape their wives just lost and one legislator who cast a crucial vote against it said, 'When you get married you expect a little sex.' I could go on and talk about Wilhelm Reich getting his books burned in the U.S., but I think you get the picture about what I think.

WOMAN FROM NEW JERSEY, BORN 1950: I would explain it this way: He is a man who 1. probably was not breastfed himself, 2. is sexually inhibited, 3. is conditioned by mainstream societal practices, one of which is a taboo on breastfeeding, 4. is easily shocked, and 5. is misinformed to such an extent that he would dare to cause havoc in a peaceful situation. It makes me wonder if the man was sexually aroused and secretly wanted to rape, or if he was just being sarcastic. In any event, I wonder how his mother and father treated him as a boy. I doubt that the facts of life were presented to him in a free fashion.

We, who live in the industrialized countries, need to find ways to help our young people, boys and girls making the passage into adulthood with a sense of dignity, responsibility and grace. In my opinion, we have much to learn from the traditional cultures of the world about rites of passage.

A friend of mine learned about the sense of humor that some traditional people have about breasts when she spent a few weeks on the Akwesasne reservation in New York State. She tells it like this:

I hung out with this really old, wise Indian woman, super-wrinkly, no teeth, and feisty as she could be. We got into talking about nursing. She was very glad to see me nursing my baby and said she couldn't understand why folks bottlefeed.

'It makes their shit smell so bad,' she said. She had about fifty grandkids and great grandkids. One of her six year old great-grandkids was having a terrible tantrum, yelling and screaming. The old woman grabbed her up on her lap, pulled up her shirt, and asked,

'Want to nurse?' That blew the kid's mind, and she straightened right up.

People who live in industrialized societies need to realize that some technologies cause more problems than they solve. Too often our love affair with technology short circuits the love we should have for ourselves by twisting our attitudes toward our own bodies. First, we need to be aware of what a healthy attitude toward the body is. Then we should pass such attitudes on to future generations. A good way to start would be to allow breastfeeding mothers to be seen on television, both in dramas and on public interest programs. What is seen on television soon becomes the norm in the country.

Breastfeeding cannot become really widespread in the industrialized countries without the active support of men. Men must allow and help breastfeeding to happen in individual and community situations, as grandfathers, fathers, husbands, brothers, and friends. Women need to know, in ways that do not make them feel self-conscious, that it is good for the world that they are breastfeeding. The women who are courageous enough to try breastfeeding in a society in which there are social penalties for nursing babies appreciate any peace and comfort they are provided to make their job easier, more valued, and more comfortable. Of course, the babies appreciate this care, too.

One of the greatest obstacles to breastfeeding is the anxiety and alienation that develops in some men because of the graceless and sometimes brutal way families can be treated in hospitals in industrialized countries. I know there are exceptions (mostly because of the pressure of consumer groups and supporters of alternatives in childbirth practices), but it is still comparatively rare that either a laboring woman or her mate is allowed to truly relax during the powerful flow of energy that is part of labor and giving birth. It is no wonder that many women emphatically believe that every childbirth must be torturous pain and that anyone who says it can be pleasurable is either a fool or a liar. Quite obviously, if many women are terrified of childbirth, their men will also have some fear of the process. While more and more men are choosing to be with their wives during labor and childbirth, there is still a large percentage of men who love their spouses but who have no wish to participate in the process of giving birth. Some are afraid that they will not be able to alleviate any of their mate's pain and that they could not stand to witness this without being able to help it.

A man does not have to be physically excluded from the birth of his child to miss out on the experience of childbirth as all that it can and should be. In many cases, insensitivity or lack of attention paid to making the father an integral part of the process can be enough to shut him out of the real experience. This is one reason why it is as important for men to prepare themselves for fatherhood as it is for women to prepare themselves for motherhood. The passage into parenthood is one of the most profound experiences of one's life; the changes people go through at this powerful time usually affect them in some way for the rest of their lives.

Men and Childbirth

Hippies were some of the first people to rebel against the idea that fathers should have nothing to do with the process of childbirth. So much has been made of the hippie culture being primarily a drug culture that many of the most powerful motivating ideas that came out of the late 1960s have been forgotten or were never known by the mainstream culture. The large increase in the number of natural childbirths in California in the late 1960s was characterized by young women who gave birth without anesthesia and were able to do so because they had the help of the fathers of their babies during the time of birth. Tens of thousands of young men lost their fear of certain natural phenomena and gave a renewed value to such intrinsically female functions as giving birth and breastfeeding babies.

Since that time, childbirth education classes have been organized in cities and small towns all over North America, and more fathers participate in the births of their babies, becoming close and attentive to their children in ways our mothers' generation would never have expected of our fathers.

Fathers who participate in the birth process rarely mention some of the feelings that were supposed to be so common among new fathers: jealousy and resentment of the newborn baby. Most men I see at births have tears in their eyes as the baby emerges, and there is an increased tenderness in them after having seen what is involved in bringing a new person into life. I believe that fathers who experience the births of their children are more apt to have their paternal instincts and feelings awakened than those who are somehow separated from the process, and are kept from spending the quiet hours after the birth adoring their newborn babies. Fathers who intimately experience birth seem to have an increased tenderness in them after having seen what is involved in bringing a new person into life.

One father expressed his feelings this way:

> The day my first child was born, I was lying beside her and just grooving on it all. Then it was like a glow started inside me and her, too, that just grew until it filled our whole universe together, just one glow of energy together. She was me; we were completely one. Who could be jealous of himself?

The Attitudes of Men

Another man commented about his wife's breastfeeding their child:

> You could tell our baby enjoyed it immensely. I don't feel jealous or left out. If I hold her just the right way, she knows I'm taking her to the tit. She starts grinning at me, telepathic with me, when we're on the way.

Here, one father expresses his coming to a better sexual relationship with his wife after their passage through the ceremony of birth together:

> My mother breastfed me, but I don't remember it. I remember the obstetrician, though, who coached her through four babies before me and one after, and he was a kind, old man who loved children. My mother breastfed all of us, so I grew up with the idea that breasts and breastfeeding were a normal part of family life.
>
> We lived on a small dairy farm where we did all our milking by hand, and I learned how to milk when I was in fifth or sixth grade. . . . I had to learn how to be gentle while squeezing hard, and later on, as an amorous teenager, I became convinced that I had some talent in this department and was (insufferably) proud of it. (I hope no one is offended by the juxtaposition of breastfeeding and dairy farming, but I do feel that, although the emotional involvement and the motivation are different, the tactile sensations are quite similar.)
>
> A few years later, I met a woman, and we became undeniably clear-headed and cleanly telepathic, while we were meditating together one morning. So, without having really gotten to know each other very well, we decided to get engaged, in recognition of the rare and beautiful telepathic experience we had.
>
> Our early attempts at lovemaking were diminished greatly, I

thought, by her consistent rejection of my efforts to touch, squeeze, rub, or fondle her breasts. This was complicated by the fact that I thought that by conscientiously massaging her left breast, which was smaller than the other one, I could encourage it to grow larger until they matched. She dismissed this idea as superstitious hogwash and showed less than no interest in having me work to improve her symmetry.

In spite of all this, we stayed together, and, after a somewhat short engagement, we were married. After a few months, we decided to have a child, although our relationship continued to be rocky at times, and soon after that, our child was conceived. Still I felt rejected sometimes, inadequate, paranoid, horny, and uptight. Was there something wrong with me or was it her? Lovemaking was sometimes fun but not always. There was a feeling that something was missing.

The midwives who attended our child's birth exclaimed at one point during labor, "What nice breasts she has!" They encouraged me to squeeze her breasts, saying it would help her through transition. I felt awkward doing this with other women present, but it seemed like a helpful and positive thing to do, so I made a rather self-conscious attempt.

After the birth, we had to pay attention to her breasts for what they really were: a life-sustaining source of nourishment for the baby. Sometimes, when they would get sore or swollen, she would ask me to massage them, instructing me as to how to do it the way that felt good to her. This changed the whole perspective between us. Eventually we both lost our self-conscious attitudes and grew to love each other more. The old hang-ups seem so far away now, it's as if they never existed.

Men and Breastfeeding

Another father described some of his changes this way:

I was a breast man in my teens and twenties. I love breasts. They're soft, always soft, even in old age. I remember the first time my young girl friend let me touch her breasts. Such a wild, whirling ecstasy. Breastfeeding was far from my experience, and I had no idea what they are really for, until my first kid. . . . that I was in on a feeding long enough to feel what was going on. I didn't recognize it, but the same warm, sexy glow built up and then just hung in there. My previous sexual experiences were so directed and driven towards a climax, I hardly even noticed the warm feeling, and I certainly never felt it start in my crotch and tingle up my body. It's really our sexual birthright as humans to feel this. Knowing how to feel sexy and feel love at the same time and have them be the same feeling is our new discovery.

There's still a place for showing someone who's not cool the door, but I am so thankful to be anywhere close to a mother breastfeeding her baby. The baby is so uncomplicated, he's hungry, he needs love, and he cries for momma. And then the baby relaxes, satisfied and drinking. It's so easy to forget what it feels like, how to feel.

Another man who participated in my survey had this to say:

I think women's tits are beautiful, as it seems that most men do. And I wonder if having been breastfed helps a man to be better able to innately understand some aspects of women more easily than other men, to be more compassionate with them. I don't know; there will always be differences between men and women that may never seem understandable, and I am not the greatest husband myself. But it is too bad that in this culture the men have so dominated it that women feel they have to hide their tits so as not to provoke an attack by a man.

Another man remarked:

The trouble is that most American men weren't around any breastfeeding until they were in their twenties. My mother fed me bottles by schedule. She regretted it later and told me she wished she had breastfed us. She said, "We mothers listened to the doctors. We thought we were being avant-garde.'"

The men I surveyed about whether they had been breastfed as babies fell into roughly three categories. The first and by far the smallest number was the group who had been breastfed for several months. Invariably these men indicated that they were pretty good friends with their mothers. The second category were the guys who had been bottlefed, but whose mothers later regretted not having breastfed. Some of this group had been nursed for a few days or weeks but their mothers had given up for one reason or another. The third and largest category (60 percent of the men surveyed) were either sure they had been totally bottlefed or were afraid to ask. For many, the entire subject was taboo, as far as talking with their mothers was concerned.

One man said,

I don't think my mother was the type.

Another answered,

I don't know whether I was bottle or breastfed. I couldn't ask my mother that. Maybe my wife could.

One man reported that he had to ask his mother if he had been breastfed when he and his twin brother were being studied as part of a university experiment. She answered that they had been bottlefed, and when they asked why, she exclaimed, "There were two of you. What do you think I was, a cow or something?"

Contrast this response with another man's experience talking with his mother:

She said she had really looked forward to nursing her baby. Her breasts had been big and full of milk. The doctors shot her up with hormones and dried up her milk. I had been born prematurely. It was a long seven weeks until I was home. She said she really felt up and down during those two months. I never asked my father, but I'm sure he thought that breastfeeding was the way to go, over bottles.

In a balanced situation, men and women are at peace about breastfeeding. Men all around the world in all sorts of societies with all kinds of taboos and customs protect the functions of breastfeeding and sustaining the young. One respondent to my survey described his surprise in finding out that different cultures have different attitudes about what parts of women's bodies ought to be hidden:

The first time I ever experienced culture shock was watching a woman breastfeeding. I was in the Sinai Desert living with a group of Bedouins. These are the last remaining indigenous tribe living in that part of the Middle East. They are a proud people who show a lot of love and respect for each other. They have a strong set of values and traditions. One tradition says that women must keep their faces veiled. Now this was different from anything I had ever lived around before, but what really had an effect on me was the first time that one of these Bedouin women raised her robes exposing her tits to me as she breastfed her baby. I'm not exactly sure of all the reasons behind the veiled face, but she acted as if everything was perfectly all right. It was only I who was taken by surprise. I realized that in cultures where women breastfeed their babies, that everyone in the culture grows up seeing tits being used for that which they were meant. They have a natural attitude towards them. It's only in cultures like ours, where you almost never see a woman breastfeeding, that tits become the object for something else, usually something to lust after.

There have been many works of art from the earliest of archeological periods, depicting the sacred process of nursing babies. Traditionally, in most societies, an attitude of respect and reverence has been taught. In our society, in which a sacred function has been confused with something profane, it is especially important that fathers and grandfathers learn to put the value back in breastfeeding. Mothers care what their fathers and husbands feel about their breastfeeding.

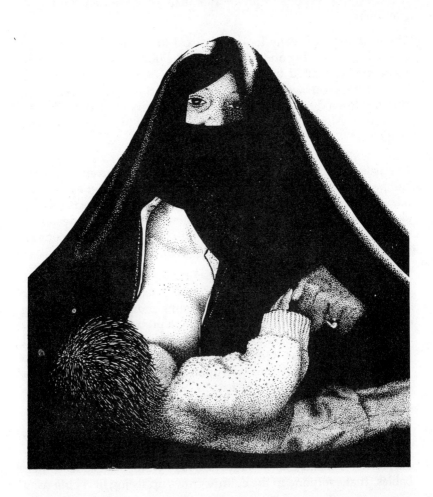

As one man said,

Some of the problems that our society has with getting back to breastfeeding exist because we've been separated; we've gotten away from oneness on the most primal levels. I think it has probably made the whole sexual area rougher to deal with. Breastfeeding is one of those oneness things. Getting back to it does feel really good. It's fulfilling. It seems that, originally, fluids from the body shouldn't be repulsive. We get separated from natural behaviors and then don't know how to behave naturally. And there's the mammal thing, the warm and cuddly thing. I want to say that there's at least a body of men who think it's real sexy to get it on with a nursing mother and to let the fluids flow.

REFERENCES
1. Daphna Ayalah and Isaac J. Weinstock, *Breasts* (New York: Simon and Schuster, 1979), p. 270.

SUGGESTED SUPPLEMENTAL READING
Jones, Carl. *Sharing Birth*. New York: Quill, 1985.

14

Fear of Fluids

♦

> I recall the feeling, puzzled, baffled, when I found out some words were dirty and the rest clean. The bad ones in French are the religious ones, the worst ones in any language were what they were most afraid of and in English it was the body, that was even scarier than God.
>
> MARGARET ATWOOD, Surfacing

One of the legacies of Victorian times has been a pronounced revulsion to the secretions of the body. If you watch network television for a couple of days, you could easily get the idea that tears are the only socially acceptable secretion of the human body, provided that they are shed only by women and very young children.

It is strange indeed that countries which so pride themselves on their fastidiousness should make social rules which often force their most vulnerable members to eat in places designed for the excretory needs of the other members of the society. Anyone else would be criticized for using the public restroom as a dining room. Yet, a sociological study by Martha E. Thompson of Northeastern Illinois University, entitled "Breastfeeding in Public," involving a survey of a random sample of Chicago area restaurants in 1985–86 showed that it was not uncommon for restaurateurs to prohibit breastfeeding anywhere in their restaurants except the restroom. Although a majority of the restaurants sampled do permit breastfeeding (59 percent), smoking, on the other hand, is more often permitted (87 percent).

The more conservative restaurant managers have the support of none other than "Miss Manners" (Judith Martin), the arbiter of etiquette to the "baby boom" generation. Her popular book, *Miss Manners' Guide to Excruciatingly Correct Behavior,* touches on the subject of public breastfeeding in this way:

> I find public breastfeeding highly offensive. The argument that it is a natural function carries no weight whatsoever. Would you change the baby's diaper on the dining-room table while people are eating? That's also a natural function. When other people are present, the proper thing is for a woman to withdraw to another room and nurse in private—even in her own room.[1]

"Excruciating" is right. It seems to me that Miss Manners has got the ends of the baby mixed up, not to mention the difference between food and feces. One is eaten; one is not. Please give us a revision, Miss Manners. You are usually much clearer and more sensible than this. Holding such positions, however cutely ("Exposing the female breast for any purpose other than getting a suntan on southern French beaches is considered an exhibition, which is not to say it should not be done when that is the intent.") puts you in the category of the Toronto man, whose response to one reporter who covered the Toronto Suck-In was,

"To me, it's just like urinating or defecating in public," or the other man who remarked, "If I exhibited my testicles in public, I would be arrested."

To which the reporter replied, "No one asked you to."

Obviously, this issue of public breastfeeding involves deep-seated attitudes, which people are often reluctant to look at. Humor is one way of dealing with shame or embarrassment about the body which leads to discomfort with natural functions and events. If any of the words I have used so far in this book have been upsetting or embarrassing to you, please remember that they are only words and that many people use them with total comfort and respect. I have not felt free to alter people's language in their written or spoken statements to me, even though I have been aware that some of their language may be upsetting to other people.

Attitudes about any of the body's secretions can go deep because we usually form them when we are very young, imprinting them off the people who cared for us during the most leaky and vulnerable time of life, babyhood. Because these attitudes can so profoundly affect the ability to breastfeed, it is worthwhile trying to come to an understanding of them, and of how they affect us as individuals and as a society.

Some of the most feared words in the English language are the monosyllabic vernacular versions of several of these words: spit, snot, booger, sweat, pee, piss, and shit. You may find that you feel a strong physical sensation just upon seeing them in print, yet hundreds of millions of people in several countries use these words daily, not as "cuss" words, but because these are the words with which they are the most familiar.

Any child can immediately sense the inherent power in a sound which causes lots of grownups to make the great fuss that these words sometimes cause. The British swear word "bloody" and the North American "Oh, shit!" reflect the same cultural revulsion towards the body and its secretions. The underlying assumption seems to be that the dreaded substances are dirty, and if you get any of them on you, it may not be possible to ever get clean again. It is as if the people who are affected by Victorian attitudes feel that the prohibited secretions are filthy in thought, word, and deed. One must avoid becoming unclean in thought and word by using Latinate words such as "sputum," "perspiration," or "fecal matter" when these secretions are mentioned. The "polite" words, which came into the language from the ruling sector of English society in the Middle Ages, function as sterile gloves for people's minds. These are the Latinate words in our culture because the Normans spoke French and the language of the peasants was Anglo-Saxon.

Revulsion towards the secretions of the body affects people's touch just as it affects how they react to reading or hearing the sound of the secretion power words. The best feeling touch, the kind that carries with it the most energy, is when the person who is touching is doing so with complete awareness of what she is touching and what is in her mind, with total acceptance of how this feels in terms of heat, moisture, softness, and feelings in her own body. When people are revolted by what they are touching, they withdraw their attention or awareness from what they are touching, and that attention is transferred into thinking, "Yuck, I'm soiled!"

Being touched this way makes vulnerable people (all children) feel unworthy and untouchable in a very real sense. This is why attitudes related to human secretions and the ways these attitudes are translated into touch have such relevance in transmitting parenting skills and encouraging the phenomenon of bonding.

Bare-breasted goddess

We could begin to think of breastmilk not only as food but as medicine. I quote from the [Manchester] *Guardian*, December 1, 1982:

A Zimbabwe man owes his eyesight to a quick-thinking African woman who washed his eyes with breast milk after he had been attacked by a spitting cobra.

Known locally as Mhungu, the four-feet-long snake spat at Mr. Kenneth Hampson when he tried to remove it from beneath his car bonnet while on a trip through the bush north of Bulawayo to pay his employees.

The spitting cobra directs a jet of venom into the eyes of its victims at a range of up to six feet. The venom is deadly for some creatures and can cause blindness in human beings. But Mr. Hampson was saved by a passing African woman carrying a baby on her back. She squirted breast milk into his eyes, neutralising the venom.

Welsh postcard

Later, in Bulawayo General Hospital, Mr. Hampson said he was still partially blind in one eye, but had been told he would soon regain full sight.

'I am really very grateful to this woman and I would like to give her some reward,' he said. 'But I was in too much pain to find out her name or where she lives.' A Bulawayo reptile expert said that milk was an effective first aid for cobra venom in the eyes because it neutralises the neurotoxins in the venom and soothes pain.

One woman summed up my feelings quite well when she said, "Nursing my baby connected me with the animal kingdom in a way I didn't relate to before. Middle-class America is geared more to the supermarket than to normal bodily secretions and seems to try to clog and stop up all the leaks. I was so glad to nurse and find out the equipment worked, that it had a function that was vital and not just ornamental. Nursing was a completion of the pregnancy, giving birth process, being able to take care of this little helpless critter with your God-given animal stuff. It helps you relate to the universe."

15

Reviving the Mother Instinct

♦

> We are the curators of life on earth; we hold it in the palms of our hands. Can we evolve spiritually and emotionally in time to control the overwhelming evil that our advanced and rational intellect has created? We will know the answer to this question in our lifetime. This generation will die having discovered the answer.
>
> DR. HELEN CALDICOTT, Missile Envy

We have all heard how fiercely protective mammalian mothers can be in defense of their young. Biologists and others who have observed the behavior of animals all seem to concur that animal mothers will show extraordinary courage when it comes to protecting their young, that they will attack larger animals than themselves, including the male of their own species. As Rudyard Kipling wrote in his poem, "The Female of the Species":

> ... every fibre of her frame,
> Proves her launched for one sole issue, armed and engined for the same;
> And to serve that single issue, lest the generations fail,
> The female of the species must be deadlier than the male.

With the planet in the incredibly dangerous predicament it is now in, it seems worthwhile to ask whether humans possess any of the instincts that are operative in animal species which live in the wild. Now and then we do read in the newspapers about a courageous mother who acts selflessly and heroically in saving her child. One such instance took place when Anna Harrop, of Prince George, Canada, chased and frightened a grizzly bear who was carrying away Harrop's three-year-old son in its teeth.

"I never thought, 'That's a brown bear or a black one or a grizzly,' " She said, "I just thought, 'That's my baby.' The only rational thought I had was, 'I've got to make a lot of noise because bears are scared of noise.' "

Screaming as she ran, Mrs. Harrop reached the bear, the bear dropped the Harrop boy from its jaws, and Mrs. Harrop scooped her son into her arms virtually uninjured.

There have been lots of instances of individual mothers who have faced similar dangers to their offspring with this type of extraordinary bravery. Collectively, though, there has been a lot of evidence in the last hundred years to suggest that we women have lost the ability to respond courageously to danger facing our offspring. Women got into the habit of accepting whatever the doctor, the chemical industry, or the Pentagon offered, whether it was good for the kids or not. Women accepted chloroform for childbirth during the first two decades of this century, despite its dangers, which were documented but not widely publicized at the time. Some of the leading feminists of that era championed the use of this drug, unaware of the dangers it posed for mothers and babies. During the 1950s and 1960s, American women unquestioningly took a drug called DES when it was prescribed by their doctors during pregnancy. It was a decade or two before most of them learned that the drug caused cancers in the reproductive organs of many of their daughters and genital abnormalities in many of their sons. On the other side of the Atlantic during the same period, pregnant women took a new sleeping pill called Thalidomide; many of their sons and daughters were born without limbs.

Women in most of the industrialized countries have been able to vote and to participate in politics since the early part of this century. Even so, it has been obvious that women, as a group, have had almost nothing to do with the course of international and military events since the time we have been able to vote. It was not a group of mothers who discovered and shared with each other the secrets which made possible the building of the atomic bombs. We could ask if those bombs would have been dropped on Hiroshima and Nagasaki if an equal number of women had sat in on the male councils of war who decided to carry out the destruction, but we can never answer this hypothetical question.

When we stop to consider the safety of our offspring, things have gotten much worse since the mid-1940s. Not only do most Americans fear the power of the Soviet Union; they now find that they have good cause to fear our own people. It is not the Soviets who have polluted our air, our drinking water, or our food, causing an unmistakable rise in the numbers of cancers and other life-threatening diseases afflicting all ages, but particularly our children.

The scary thing is that we tend to see the protective mother-rage only after the damage has already been done to the child. The women of Three Mile Island, Love Canal, and Niagara Falls have spoken up. I can never forget the woman I saw on television, a former resident of Love Canal, who attended the public hearing held by the representatives of Hooker Chemical, the company responsible for poisoning the area where the suburban housing project of Love Canal was later built. This conservatively-dressed woman spoke with such force and fury as she addressed the Hooker executives and spokesmen that her statement went out on the network all over the country, uncensored.

"You guys aren't even human!" she screamed.

"You're just a pile of assholes!"

Her monumental rage was aroused when she realized, too late, that she had trusted men with no sense of morality with the welfare and the health of her children.

Anyone who has studied history knows that it took a long time for the human race to get itself (and everybody else) in the fix we are now facing. It appears, too, that there is an unfortunate tendency for the human race to ignore the lessons to be learned from the study of history. As my grandmother always used to tell me, though, "Can't never did anything." If we are going to bother to have children, to write books, fix dinner, wash the clothes, earn our livings, and all the rest of it, we might as well try to save the world.

Perhaps because my work as a midwife puts me so closely in touch with the feelings of parents and babies, I have come to the opinion that a large part of the reason why women collectively have had so little to do with monitoring the safety of the enterprises of men is because we let control of our reproductive processes get out of our hands. When women stopped being the main decision makers about how they, their daughters and granddaughters would go through childbirth, they did not turn the reins over to their husbands, fathers, or brothers, but rather to men who were largely strangers to them.

Once men gained control of the reproductive processes, they were able to affect women during a time in their lives when they were most vulnerable to external conditioning—pregnancy, childbirth, and lactation. I believe that women do have powerful instincts to protect their young, but that it is possible to condition women and females of some other species, as well, to suppress their instincts so that they tend to behave in ways which run counter to their more basic promptings. I believe that one of the reasons why feminists of the late 1960s and 1970s were so quick to see in motherhood only a trap or an option for weak women was the cultural perception that we North Americans had grown used to, that mothers were generally passive and submissive people.

That is why an event that happened in our neck of the woods made the top of the news for a day.

It is good to be polite when we can, but we may find times when we must act in ways that would not seem polite in the most conventional sense. I think of the Romany Gypsy woman who passed through middle Tennessee during the spring of 1976 with about forty other relatives and friends of her clan. The Gypsies were suspected of having stolen money from at least three area grocery stores, and the entire group, including women and children, were jailed in one town.

The whole affair turned out to be a trying one for the police, who were unable to determine what language they were speaking, let alone even a word they were saying. Police officers, at the jail where the Gypsies were to be kept overnight, attempted to take a young baby away from one of the mothers. The mother began talking loudly and excitedly, but the officers couldn't understand her and continued trying to take her baby into their custody. At that point, the young mother bared her breast and aimed a fine spray of milk into the approaching officer's face. At last the police understood, and she was allowed to keep her baby with her until she and her friends were released from jail.

I recently attended Helen Caldicott's last speech given in the U.S. before her return to her native Australia. Her main message to American women is that we have the responsibility of saving the world. She doesn't expect that a sufficient number of men, by themselves, will ever show the motivation to change the deadly course we are now under. She is not very optimistic that we are going to get out from under the psychic numbing that is characteristic from living all or most of our lives under the nuclear sword in time to save the world; in fact, at one point in her speech, she referred to us as "wimps."

In my travels, I have come across one political system which seemed to make a good deal of sense to me. Interestingly enough, this system had been in operation on the North American continent for about four hundred years before the first European settlers came to North America. The people of the Six Nations (more commonly known by the name the French called them: the Iroquois) had a system of government which was admired and studied by some of our founding fathers, most notably, Thomas Jefferson and Benjamin Franklin. Jefferson and Franklin sat in council with the chiefs of the Six Nations, and they tried to incorporate some of the basic principles of the system which they observed to work so well. Unfortunately, they left out one of the most important elements of the Six Nations' form of government: the part played by the women. Only men sat as chiefs among the Haudenosaunee, but it was the women who chose the chiefs—only the women. In their clans, there were Clan Mothers, women who were highly respected and who spoke for the other women. They sat as silent observers in the councils. They picked the chiefs. They had been watching the men from the time they were born and they knew them: how long they sucked their thumbs, whether they were bullies as kids or greedy at mealtime. They could spot those with natural leadership qualities pretty early, as well as those who had compassion and those who were too impetuous to be given a lot of responsibility over other people. An additional safety factor was also built in, since the people of the Six Nations obviously knew that power could corrupt even a good man. The Clan Mothers also had the power to dismiss a chief if they felt that he was no longer to be trusted. This power has been exercised within recent years, in fact. The chief in question, I'm told, told the Clan Mothers that he would not step down, since that custom was an old one which was not being followed anymore. At that point, Clan Mothers spoke to members of the Warrior Society who then escorted him from the meeting.

One other power resided with the women of the Six Nations. That was the power to decide if a war would be fought by their men. Because women live a little closer to birth and death than men, it was thought that women should have the say-so over whether the blood of their husbands, their brothers, their sons and grandsons would be spilled. I think that we women could take this power today so that we could have a check on the power of our political leaders who, we have seen, are fallible. Would 59,000 young American men have had to die in Vietnam if their grandmothers, mothers, wives, girlfriends, and sisters had collectively said "No, they're not going"? We'll never know the answer to that one, but my hope is that we will learn from some of the people who lived in peace in this land for centuries before our own ancestors came here.

Like them we need to start considering how our actions and those of the multinational corporations we support and the politicians we elect will impact on our children, our grandchildren, their children, on down to the seventh generation from us.

SUGGESTED SUPPLEMENTAL READING

A Basic Call to Consciousness: The Hau de no sau nee Address to the Western World. Mohawk Nation, via Rooseveltown, N.Y.: Akwesasne Notes, 1978.

Caldicott, Helen. *Missile Envy.* New York: Bantam, 1985.

Bertell, Rosalie. *No Immediate Danger.* Summertown, Tenn.: The Book Publishing Co., 1985.

Huddle, Norie. *Surviving: The Best Game in Town.* New York: Schocken, 1984.

Appendix A: Resources

♦

Breastfeeding Support and Information
La Leche League International
9616 Minneapolis Ave.
Franklin Park, Ill. 60131
312-455-7730

    Send a self-addressed, stamped envelope to locate a La Leche leader and discussion group in your area.

Boston Association for Childbirth Education
Nursing Mothers' Council
184 Savin Hill Ave.
Dorchester, Mass. 02125
617-244-5102

Childbirth Education Association of Greater Philadelphia
Nursing Mothers' Support Groups
5 East Second Ave.
Conshohocken, Pa. 19428
215-727-0131

Nursing Mothers Council, Inc.
P.O. Box 50063
Palo Alto, Cal. 94303
408-272-1448

Nursing Supplementation Devices

A nursing supplementation device consists of a plastic pouch which holds formula or expressed milk and a thin plastic tube leading from inside the pouch. It lies along the mother's breast, ending at her nipple. The baby draws milk into his mouth as he sucks at his mother's nipple.

Nursing supplementation devices may be ordered from:

Lact-Aid
$29.50 plus shipping
Lact-Aid International
P.O. Box 1066
Athens, Tenn. 37303
615–744–9090

Supplemental Nutrition System
$23.95
Medela
P.O. Box 386
Crystal Lake, Ill. 60014
800–435–8316 (From Illinois, Alaska, or Hawaii, call collect 815–455–6920)

Breast Pumps

Hand-operated Pumps. These pumps are desirable to many mothers because they are not expensive, and they are portable.

Bicycle-horn pumps. These pumps are easy to find in most pharmacies, and they sell for under $10. Their disadvantages are that they can be uncomfortable and can even damage the nipple or breast, and they are hard to clean. It is possible for a culture of bacteria to grow in these pumps, so if you use one, you will want to wash it very carefully after each use and discard it after using it for a few weeks. An additional disadvantage is that they don't hold much milk, so they must be removed and emptied frequently.

Medela Manualectric Breast Pump. This pump works by suction when the plunger is pulled outward. It sells for about $25 from Medela, Inc., Crystal Lake, Ill. 60014. There are Medela pump rental stations as well. You can phone toll-free 1-800-435-8316, or from Illinois, Alaska or Hawaii collect 0-815-455-6920.

Evenflo Breast Pump. These pumps are widely available and advertised, and they are inexpensive. One model sells for $10; the other for $15. Some mothers can get along with them, but many others have complained about their difficulty of use and discomfort in using them.

Le Pump Breast Pump. This pump is one of the best bulb pumps, and is reasonably comfortable. It can be found in some surgical supply stores for about $20. For more information, call toll-free 1-800-832-1400.

Nurture Pump. This pump has a softer funnel that supposedly massages the areola when the bulb is squeezed. It can be ordered for $40.00 plus $1.25 for shipping from Lact Assist, Inc., 4026 Woodmont Boulevard, Nashville, Tenn. 37205. If you want to order by phone, call 615-383-7179.

Ora'lac Pump. This pump works by the mother's sucking on the tube to create the suction and release. You may be able to find it in a pharmacy. If not, you can send $30 (includes shipping and tax) to Ora'lac Pump, Inc., Box 2400, Sitka, Alaska 99835. Phone 907-747-8270.

Lloyd-B Pump. Squeezing a trigger creates the suction for this pump. There is a valve near the trigger to release suction. To order, send $40 (shipping and tax included) to Lupco, Ltd., 1615 Old Annapolis Road, Woodbine, Md. 21979. Phone 301-489-4949.

Egnell Hand Breast Pump. This pump is widely available and easy to use. Its angled head makes it possible to use without the mother having to lean forward. You slide the outer cylinder away from the breast in order to create suction. The pump is priced in the $15–$20 range. Available also from Egnell, Inc., Carey, Ill. 60013, or call toll-free 1–800–323–8750. From Illinois, Alaska and Hawaii, call collect 0–312–639–2900.

Marshall-Kaneson Breast Pump. This straight head pump is available in many pharmacies and discount stores for $10–$15. You can order from Marshall Electronics, Inc., Lincolnshire, Ill. 60069. Phone toll-free 1–800–323–1482. Within Illinois the number is 1–312–634–6300.

Battery-Operated Pumps. The battery-operated pump costs only a little more than hand-operated pumps and require only one hand to use. The main drawback with these pumps is that you need to replace batteries rather often.

Egnell Lact-B. This pump, made in Switzerland, uses two AA batteries to create suction. The pump is available from Egnell, Inc., Carey, Ill. 60013 and from Egnell breast pump rental stations. Call toll free 1–800–323–8750. From Alaska, Illinois and Hawaii call collect 0–312–639–2900.

Natural Choice. This pump uses two AA batteries but has the advantage of coming with a recharger. You can order it from Crystal Medical Products, 118 Barrington Commons Plaza, Barrington, Ill. 60010. Call toll free 1–800–248–9235; from Illinois call 1–312–382–4414. The price is $49.95 including shipping.

Electric pumps. These pumps, which plug into the wall socket, have some advantages over any type of hand-held pump. They can be used while you do something else requiring the use of your hands. Most are gentle and efficient and may be somewhat faster in emptying the breast than hand-operated pumps. A few kinds have a suction pattern that varies in order to simulate the sucking of a baby. Plug-in pumps are less portable and more expensive than the pumps mentioned so far.

Medela Electric. This automatic pump can be rented for about $2 per day from rental stations. The rate is reduced to $.99 if you agree to rent the pump for at least five months and pay in advance. Contact Medela, Inc., Crystal Lake, Ill. 60014. Call toll-free 1–800–435–8316. From Illinois, Alaska or Hawaii, call collect 1–815–455–6920.

Egnell Electric. To buy this pump, you'll need to spend a thousand dollars. It rents for about $2 per day through rental stations. If the pump is used for four months or more, the rental rate drops to $1 per day. Contact Egnell, Inc., Carey, Illinois 60013 to locate a rental station near you. The toll-free number is 1-800-323-8750. From Illinois, Alaska and Hawaii, call collect 0-312-639-2900.

AXicare CM-6. This pump is semiautomatic and is relatively small and portable. The price is a little over two hundred dollars and includes carrying case. Suction is generated by placing your finger over a vacuum release hole. Contact D. A. Kadan, Inc., toll-free at 1-800-DA-KADAN. From New York, call 1-914-614-6030.

Precious Care. An even more inexpensive semiautomatic pump from Gerber, this one can be ordered from Sears for $34.95. A finger must be placed over the vacuum release hole to create suction.

Breast Shields

Breast shields are available by mail or phone order.

Medela Breast Shields
$11.95
Medela
P.O. Box 386
Crystal Lake, Ill. 60014
800-435-8316 (From Illinois, Alaska, or Hawaii, call collect 815-455-6920)

INTERESTING HISTORICAL TIDBIT
Over a century ago, the French obstetrician, P. Cazeaux, in his book, *A Theoretical and Practical Treatise on Midwifery including the Disease of Pregnancy and Parturition,* gave this advice to mothers who wished to prepare inverted nipples for breastfeeding: "Direct and repeated suction is, doubtless, the best means that can be employed. This may be performed by the husband or an intelligent servant-maid. In the want of a sufficiently accommodating individual, a large puppy may be used, first taking care to wrap its paws." A Native American grandmother from the Onondaga Nation told me that the same remedy was once used among her people.

Appendix B: Additional Reading

♦

You should be able to find most of the books cited in your local bookstore. If you can't find them or order them locally, contact the following mail order bookstores.

Birth and Life Bookstore
P.O. Box 70625
Seattle, Wash. 98107
206-789-4444

ICEA Bookcenter
P.O. Box 20048
Minneapolis, Minn. 55420
612-854-8660

Morning Star
3708 Essex Rd.
Dept. PMW85
Baltimore, Md. 21207
301-3775

NAPSAC Mail Order Bookstore
P.O. Box 267
Marble Hill, Mo. 63764

Appendix B: Additional Reading

La Leche League pamphlets may be obtained from:
La Leche League International, Inc.
9616 Minneapolis Ave.
Franklin Park, Ill. 60131
312-455-7730

Anderson, Kathryn. *Nursing Your Adopted Baby*. Franklin Park, Ill.: La Leche League International, 1983.

Danner, Sarah Coulter and Edward R. Cerutti. *Nursing Your Neurologically Impaired Baby*. Rochester, N.Y.: Childbirth Graphics, 1984. ($.50, from Childbirth Graphics, P.O. Box 17025, Irondequoit Post Office, Rochester, N.Y. 14617-0325.)

Appendix C: Composition of Mature Breast Milk, Cow's Milk, and a Routine Infant Formula*

♦

COMPOSITION/DL	MATURE BREAST MILK	COW'S MILK	ROUTINE FORMULA WITH IRON†
Calories	75.0	69.0	67.0
Protein, g	1.1	3.5	1.5
Lactalbumin, %	80	18	
Casein, %	20	82	
Water, ml	87.1	87.3	
Fat, g	4.0	3.5	3.7
CHO, g	9.5	4.9	7.0
Ash, g	0.21	0.72	0.34
Minerals			
Na, mg	16.0	50.0	25.0
K, mg	51.0	144.0	74.0
Ca, mg	33.0	118.0	55.0
P, mg	14.0	93.0	43.0
Mg, mg	4.0	12.0	9.0
Fe, mg	0.1	Tr.	1.2
Zn, mg	0.15	0.1	0.42

Appendix C

COMPOSITION/DL	MATURE BREAST MILK	COW'S MILK	ROUTINE FORMULA WITH IRON†
Vitamins			
A, IU	240.0	140.0	158.6
C, mg	5.0	1.0	5.3
D, IU	2.2	1.4	42.3
E, IU	0.18	0.04	0.83
Thiamin, mg	0.01	0.03	0.04
Riboflavin, mg	0.04	0.17	0.06
Niacin, mg	0.2	0.1	0.7
Curd size	Soft Flocculent	Firm Large	Mod. firm Mod. large
pH	Alkaline	Acid	Acid
Anti-infective properties	+	±	−
Bacterial content	Sterile	Nonsterile	Sterile
Emptying time	More rapid		

*Composite of a number of sources
†Enfamil
From: Avery, G. B., ed. *Neonatology: Pathophysiology and Management of the Newborn*, 2nd Ed., Philadelphia: J. B. Lippincott, 1981, p. 1020.

Index

♦

Abdullah-Zaimah, Sondra, 188
Abrams, Elliot, 176
Abscesses, breast, 117
Acetaminophen, 56, 143
Adoption, nursing after, 96–98
Afterpains, 56
AID (U.S. Agency for International Development), 177
Allergies: to cow's milk, 9; to foods in mother's diet, 107, 110, 123, 126; to solid foods, 144
Anemia, 116
Antibiotics, 101, 116, 142, 158
Appetite: fluctuations, 109; spurts, 142
Areola (area around nipple), 33, 50
Attitudes: about bodily fluids, 201–2; about breasts, 2, 39, 186, 188; about breastfeeding, 182–99; about public breastfeeding, 131–32
Audebert, M. (19th century physician), 98

Babies: myths about, 20; normal behavior, 111; premature, 81–94; sleepy, 76; tem-

Babies *(continued)*
    perament of, 45–47, 65. *See also* Newborns
"Baby blues," 19. *See also* Depression, postpartum
Bauer, E. Steven, 175
Beans, 147
Bilirubin, 77–78
Birth centers, 65
Birth control, 141
Birth control pill, 141
Birth defects, nursing baby with, 94–96
Biting, 143
Blood incompatibility jaundice, 77
Bonding, maternal-infant, 13–24, 46–48; failure of, 14
Borage tea, 97
Bottlefeeding: guilt about, 2; introducing, 137; supplemental, 90. *See also* Formula, infant
Bras, 10, 72, 114; during pregnancy, 32; nursing, 34–35
Breast infections. *See* Mastitis
Breast milk, appearance of, 58; blood in, 69; collecting, 82–83, 134, 137–38; compared with formula, 7–8; composition of, 218; expressing, 12, 67–68, 82–83, 95, 136–38; freezing, 133–34, 137–38; immunological properties of, 8–9; lack of, 112–13; medicinal properties of, 203; as natural resource, 11; nutritional components of, 10; overabundance, 117; pollutants in, 157; for premies, 82–83; producing, 29–32, 98–99, 109, 113–14, 127; size of, 108–9; storing, 134, 137–38; testing for chemicals in, 155
Breast pads, 74
Breast pumps, 71, 74, 92, 95, 134
Breast shields, 71–74
Breastfeeding: benefits of, 7–13; compared with bottlefeeding, 47; disadvantage of, 12; discreet, 130; duration of, 30, 54–55; during pregnancy, 147; ecological consequences of, 10–11; establishing, 43–60, 65–66; first, 48–51; first for premies, 90; frequency of, 30, 57–58, 60–61, 66–67, 72, 80, 108, 127; hospital policy,

Index

36–37, 55–56, 60; learning about, 26–32; loss of knowledge, 4–5; popularity of, 3; preparing for, 26–42; in public, 4–5, 130–33, 200–2; and rape, 188–91; revival of, in North America, 3–5; shame about, 2; shared, 161–68; as survival skill, 1; and television, 192

Breastfeeding demonstrations: in Oxford, England, 133; in Toronto, 133

"Breastfeeding kit," from hospital, 55–56

Breasts: big, 32–34, 58; care of, 32; during pregnancy, 27–29, 32–34, 39; engorged, 114–15; lopsided, 119, 145; lumps, 99, 114–15, 117–18; massaging while pregnant, 29; myths about, 31–32; pain in, 68–72, 115–18

Breckinridge, Mary, 149

Buckley, William F., Jr., 177

Burping, 62, 79, 127

Cabbage, in mother's diet, 107, 123

Caffeine, 127; in mother's diet, 107

Calcium needs, maternal, 106

Caldicott, Helen, M.D., 205, 208

Caloric needs, maternal, 105

Caregivers, maternity, 35–36

Cereals, 147; baby, 144

Cerebral palsy, nursing baby with, 95–96

Cesarean birth, 35–36; nursing after, 52

Chauffaille, Angeline, 98

Chemicals, in breast milk, 153–58

Childbirth, and men, 193–97

Childbirth Without Fear (Grantly Dick-Read), 16

Chocolate, in mother's diet, 107, 123

Cleft lip, nursing baby with, 94–95

Cleft palate, nursing baby with, 94–95

Colds, baby's, 125

Colic, 123

Colostrum, 57, 81–82, 97; appearance of, 29

Crying, 65, 111; causes of, 142; intense, 121–24, 126

Cunningham, Allan, M.D., 178

DDT, in breast milk, 153–55

Dehydration, 127–28

Depression, postpartum, 112, 119–21

DES (diethylstilbestrol), 206
Diabetic mothers, 99–101
Diaper rash, 70; thrush (yeast), 116
Diaper service, 38
Diapers: as sign of adequate milk intake, 75, 80, 110; when to change, 62
Dick-Read, Grantly, M.D., 16
Diet: of diabetic mother, 100; of mother, 104–7; of mother, while nursing twins, 90; of mother, postpartum, 120, 141; of mother, while relactating, 97
Dietary supplements: for baby, 110; for mother, 107, 120
Down's syndrome, nursing baby with, 95
Drugs, 153
Ducts, blocked milk, 75, 100, 114–16, 118

Ear infections, 95, 126
Eggs, 147
Emotions: during pregnancy, 39–42; postpartum, 112
Engorgement, 74, 114–15; treatment for, 67
Environmental Defense Fund, 154
Epilepsy, nursing mothers with, 101
Estrogen, 30
Experience of Childbirth (Sheila Kitzinger), 60–61

Failure to thrive, 128–29
The Farm (community): breast milk study, 154–55; breastfeeding, 161; breastfeeding survey, 163–68, 184–86, 189–92
Fathers, 39, 44, 140, 192–97
Fatigue, postpartum, 112, 116, 119–20
Fish, 147
Fluoride supplements, in baby's diet, 110
Foods to avoid, 107
Foods, solid. *See* Solid foods
Foremilk, 58
Formula (infant), 114; cost, 10–11; nutritional components of, 10; promotion in non-industrialized world, 173–75; supplementary, 98, 108, 128
Frantz, Kittie, 179
Frontier Nursing Service, 149
Fruits, 146

Fussiness, 111, 142, 146. *See also* Colic; Crying

Garlic, in mother's diet, 107
Gentian violet, 70
Grandmothers, 98
Green peppers, in mother's diet, 123
Growth spurts. *See* Appetite spurts
Guardian (British newspaper), 203

Herpes Type 1, 99
Herpes (genital), and breastfeeding, 99
Hindmilk, 58, 127
Hippies, 193
Home birth, 65
Hormones, 96, 98, 140; during nursing, 30, 41–42; postpartum 112; during pregnancy, 41–42
Hospitalization, of mother, 134
Huggins, Kathleen, 128
Hydrocephalus, nursing baby with, 95–96
Hydrocortisone preparation, 71
Hyperthyroidism, nursing mothers with, 101

INFACT, 176
Instincts, maternal, 44–45
Iron, in baby's diet, 110
Iroquois, 208

Jarvis, Anita, 156
Jaundice: breast milk, 77–78; newborn, 76–79, 93
Juice, 146

Kafka, H.L., M.D., 178
Kennell, John, M.D., 13–16
Kitzinger, Sheila, 60–61, 133
Klaus, Marshall, M.D., 13–16

LaLeche League, 27, 83, 85
Lancet, 175
Language, and breastfeeding, 202
Lanolin, 34, 71
Latch-on, 50–54, 72–74; difficult, 52–54, 67, 79
Lead, in breast milk, 156

Leaking milk, 74–75; during lovemaking, 140
Leonard, Carol (midwife), 66, 125
Let-down reflex, 58–60, 75, 127; failures in, 116; slowness of, 113
Love Canal, 207
Lovemaking, 140.
Lubricant, for making love, 140

Mastitis, 100–1, 115–18, 142.
Maternal-Infant Bonding (Marshall Klaus and John Kennell), 13
Maternal protectiveness, 206
Meconium, 57, 80
Medications, 134, 157–58
Miss Manners' Guide to Excrutiatingly Correct Behavior (Judith Martin), 201
Missile Envy (Helen Caldicott, M.D.), 205
Mortality (infant), in nonindustrialized world, 171
Multinational formula companies, 170

National Review, 177
Natural childbirth, relation to breastfeeding, 4
Nestlé boycott, 170–72
Netherlands, maternity policy, 38
Newborns, nursing, 50–51; weight loss, 57
Night waking, 79–80, 142, 151
Nipple creams, 32, 55, 71–72
Nipple shields, 33; to improve nipple shape, 73–74
Nipples: blistered, 69; care of, 32, 55; cracked, 50, 68–72, 116; flat, 33–34, 73–74; gummed, 69–70; inverted, 33–34, 73–74; irritated, 71–72; preparation for nursing, 33–34; rubber, 84; sore, 50, 59, 68; thrush, 70–71; treatment for sore, 70, 71, 72
Nursing manners, 147–49
Nursing Mother's Companion (Kathleen Huggins), 128
Nursing pads, 34–35, 70. *See also* Breast pads
Nursing patterns, 142
Nursing positions, 50–52, 125; belly-to-belly, 51–52; football hold, 52; side position, 52, 74; twins, 90–93
Nursing styles, baby's, 108

Nursing supplementation devices, 97, 99, 128
Nystatin suspension (Mycostatin), 70

Onions, in mother's diet, 107, 123
Osteoporosis, 106
Oxytocin, 30, 56, 75

Pacifiers, 71, 127, 145
Parent-Infant Bonding (Marshall Klaus and John Kennell), 13
PBB (polybrominated biphenyl), in breast milk, 154
PCB (polychlorinated biphenyl), in breast milk, 154–55
Poop (baby's), appearance of, 111
Postpartum period, depression in, 19
Poultry, 147
Pregnancy: breasts during, 27–29; hormones during, 27–30
Premature baby, 81–94, 119
Progesterone, 29–30
Prolactin, 29–30
Protein, 144–46
Pyloric stenosis, 124–25

Refusal to nurse, 125–26, 145
Relactation, 98–99
Resources, 211

Schedule, nursing, 60–61
Sexual intercourse. *See* Lovemaking.
Six Nations, 209
Sleep, lack of, 65, 120, 148
Solid foods, 110, 114, 143–47, 149; first, 144; introducing early, 145
Sore nipples, 59; avoiding, 53–54, 68–69; causes of, 70; treatment of, 70–72
Spina bifida, nursing baby with, 95–96
Spiritual Midwifery (Ina May Gaskin), 27
Spitting up, 124
Strontium 90, in breast milk, 156
Sucking problems, 79
Supplemental feeding, 109
Support, 84; importance, 37–38
Surgery, breast, 99

Technology, dependence upon, 26
Teething, 142
Thalidomide, 206
Third World, 187–88, 197–98, 203
Thompson, Martha E., 200
Three Mile Island, 207
Thrush, 70–71, 100, 116, 126; diaper rash and, 70; nipples, 70–71
Tofu, 106
Toilet training, 202
Tongue sucking, 79
Tongue-tied baby, 79
Travel, with nursing baby, 130, 142
Truby-King method of infant raising, 60
Twins, 90–94; nursing, 90–94; premature, 92–94

Vegetables, 146
Vegetarian diet, 76, 147; pollution in breast milk, 155
Vitamin A, 106
Vitamin B, 97
Vitamin B_6, 107, 156
Vitamin B_{12}, 76, 147
Vitamin C, 106, 117, 142
Vitamin E, preparations, 71
Vitamin supplements, in baby's diet, 110
Vomiting, 124

War on Want, 172
Weaning, 117, 119, 149; to bottle or cup, 150–51; diabetic mothers and, 100
Wehrle, Paul, M.D., 179
Weighing the baby, 108
Weight gain, 61; in baby, 108; slow, 61, 145, 126–28
Weight loss, newborn, 57, 80
Wide Neighborhoods (Mary Breckinridge), 149
Williams, J.O., Jr., M.D., 128
Work options, 135–36
Working mothers: benefits for, 139; choosing a caregiver, 136; options for, 134–36, 161; in Cuba, 135; in Scandinavia, 135; in United States, 135; rest and, 138
World Health Organization (WHO), 176–77

Yeast (monilia) infection, 101. *See also* Thrush

Related Books

The Vaginal Birth After Cesarean (VBAC) Experience
Birth Stories by Parents & Professionals
LYNN BAPTISTI RICHARDS & CONTRIBUTORS
304 pages   Illustrations

The Laughing Baby
Remembering Nursery Rhymes & Reasons
ANNE SCOTT
160 pages   Illustrations
Musical Scores   Rhymes

Silent Knife
Cesarean Prevention & Vaginal Birth After Cesarean
NANCY WAINER COHEN & LOIS J. ESTNER
464 pages   Illustrations

Transformation Through Birth
A Women's Guide
CLAUDIA PANUTHOS
208 pages   Illustrations

Immaculate Deception
A New Look at Women and Childbirth
SUZANNE ARMS
416 pages   Illustrations

Ended Beginnings
Healing Childbearing Losses
CLAUDIA PANUTHOS & CATHERINE ROMEO
224 pages   Photographs

Other Books of Interest

Academic Women
Working Towards Equality
ANGELA SIMEONE
176 pages

The Trials & Tribulations of Little Red Riding Hood
Versions of the Tale in Sociocultural Context
JACK ZIPES
320 pages   Photographs

Women Teaching For Change
Gender, Class & Power
KATHLEEN WEILER
240 pages

Unequal Access
Women Lawyers in a Changing America
RONALD CHESTER
160 pages

Women's Work
Development & the Division of Labor by Gender
ELEANOR LEACOCK,
HELEN I. SAFA
& CONTRIBUTORS
320 pages   Photographs

The Psychology of Spiritual Growth
Channelled from the Brotherhood by
MARY ELIZABETH CARREIRO
160 pages
A Gentle Wind Book, Volume I

Women & Change in Latin America
New Directions in Sex & Class
JUNE NASH, HELEN I. SAFA
& CONTRIBUTORS
384 pages   Photographs

Modern Religion & The Destruction of Spritual Capacity
Channelled from the Brotherhood by
MARY ELIZABETH CARREIRO
160 pages
A Gentle Wind Book, Volume II